The edible garden

THE AUSTRALIAN
Women's Weekly

The edible
garden

acp
books

CONTENTS

Planning for production 6 Cultivation for success 12

the spring garden 18

Garden Peas 22
Potatoes 26
Onions 34
Asparagus 40
Broad Beans 44
Beetroot 48
Spring Herbs 52

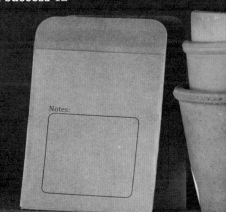

the summer garden 58

Tomatoes 62
Beans 68
Cucumber 72
Salad Greens & Edible Flowers 76
Capsicum 84
Eggplant 88
Zucchini & Squash 94
Rhubarb 98
Sweet Corn 102
Summer Fruit 106
Summer Herbs 118

the autumn garden 122

Globe Artichokes 126
Avocado 132
Pumpkin 138
Carrots 144
Olives 150
Autumn Fruit 156
Autumn Herbs 172

the winter garden 180

Brassicas 184
Broccoli 186
Cauliflower 190
Cabbage & Brussels Sprouts 196
Asian Greens 202
Mushrooms 210
Silver Beet & Spinach 218
Citrus Fruit 224
Winter Herbs 234

Preserving the crop 240
Essential gardening
equipment 244
Conversion chart 246
World climate zones 247
Glossary 248
Index 250

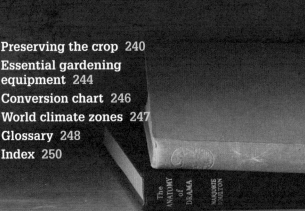

Planning for production

An edible garden supplies all the special plants cooks love to use. To have on hand those special textures and tastes, fresh and lush from the garden, grown as you like them, harvested at the peak of perfection and in just the quantity you need – that's what an ideal edible garden provides.

A gardener's garden contains fine and carefully cultivated specimens of seasonal fruit and vegetables, planted in neat rows, as dictated by time-honoured books, and usually cooked by equally time-honoured methods – they're rewarding, productive and an economic boon to the family. But the edible garden has more subtle supplies: a bit of this, a trial of that, a few seasonal stars, a little something happy in a pot or among the flowers. The edible garden helps you add a bit of magic to a meal. It's that happy mix that lets you turn cooking into creation.

Your edible garden will no doubt include many collected treasures from other cooks' gardens: some saved seeds, a piece broken off to strike or a snippet of something shared after a successful trial. Most likely there'll be seed trays, cuttings of 'new' varieties in pots ready to plant into the garden proper, an assembly of herbs at the ready and various experiments with unusual shapes and colours. There's always the chance that some of these new varieties will become kitchen standards and you'll wonder how you ever lived without them.

But, of course, the dictates of climate and available space are the controllers of what becomes reality in your garden. Being able to get your hands on just the right plants can sometimes be a bit of a struggle. You'll see glorious pictures in gardening books and strange varieties in shops, and wonder where to buy seeds or seedlings to grow your own. Then there's time, alas, so often in very short supply. *The Edible Garden* is for those ready to bridge the divide between the great kitchen indoors and the great garden outdoors, and wanting to create their own unique kitchen garden. Let's look at suggestions to help you down the garden path with your arms loaded or your fist proudly wrapped round something garden-fresh for your table.

The possibilities of small spaces

First rule Forget the segregation of vegetables into beds. Herbs, vegetables and flowers can all be grown together for stunning visual displays.

Get rid of the lawn Dig it up; remove all the roots or they'll reach up through your garden and steal valuable water and nutrients. A sea of herbs and vegetables looks twice as good as a featureless sward.

Take advantage of height Grow climbers like cucumbers, peas and beans on tripods among floral displays. Let unstaked mini tomatoes wander among tall shrubs or between stakes. Nasturtiums can clamber among them too.

Mix colours Chillies look stunning among flowers, and the red and yellow stems of ruby chard are also striking. Grey-leafed vegetables like artichokes, broccoli and sage extend the colour palette, so do purple-leafed beauties like beetroot, basil and beans.

Mix leaf shapes and forms Lemon grass provides a wonderful grassy profile, while the solid and textural greenness of silver beet, curly-leafed kale or carrots offers a good contrast to floral colour.

Use vegetables and herbs as borders Mignonette lettuce, chives, oregano and radish make good edging plants and team happily with violas, dwarf nasturtium and alyssum.

Don't forget vertical surfaces Cover fences with wire, twine or lattice for beans, peas, chokos, passionfruit, cucumber or grapes.

Don't let concrete deter you Tiny pockets of soil can be created by building up garden beds using rocks, wood or bricks to create well-drained spots beside steps or even straight onto concrete. Such raised beds will happily accommodate herbs, and with frequent watering and nourishment, small lettuce, rocket or asian greens.

dictates of climate

Choosing the wrong plants for your climate will make gardening much more difficult than it actually is. Of course we all want to grow a lemon or lime, quinces or nuts, asparagus or raspberries, mangoes or passionfruit, things that tempt us but in reality are climatically impossible. Some of us will take up the challenge, attempt to create the right microclimate with wind, shade or sun barriers, even moving large pots about: sometimes we succeed, but more often it's a huge struggle for, most likely, a meagre result. It's much wiser to accept the limitations of your garden conditions and choose those herbs and vegetables that grow well. You'll find that, in any climate range, you will still have considerable choice of fruits, herbs, flowers and vegetables. Seek out those plants that provide flavour, texture or colour contrasts.

Study successful gardens in your area to see what works well. Talk to local gardeners. This way, you'll find your garden will be much more successful, and seasonal variation, rather than a limitation, will become a welcome delight.

dictates of space

Some lucky gardeners have large vegetable plots with space for everything. Make no mistake though, such gardens are a lot of work, both in preparation and maintenance. Other gardeners take advantage of tiny spaces – a patch of concrete, a balcony, a collection of pots – and still grow delicious vegetables and herbs, things that a cook needs to add a special flavour, a decorative flourish and that home-grown touch.

An edible garden can be as large or as small as you have space, time and the inclination for working in it. Also, when time is short, a small garden can be infinitely more rewarding and successful than a large, ambitious garden that takes up so much time and energy that it is often abandoned. Make the most of your space.

year-round harvest

Undoubtedly, one of the genuine joys of home gardening is the thrill of enjoying fruit and vegetables in season at their best. Supermarket shopping has dulled and denied our appreciation of such gastronomic thrills as new-season pears and peaches, fresh baby potatoes, oranges in winter and freshly picked ears of corn.

A carefully designed edible garden, however small, can yield favourite fruits and vegetables for a varied and colourful seasonal table. The enthusiastic cook with a kitchen garden at the ready will rise to the cooking challenge and explore the wonderful world of fresh herbs and home-grown produce.

plant supplies

The easiest way to acquire seeds and plants is, of course, to buy them from local nurseries. This way you'll always buy what's in season. Choose the healthiest looking plants; green, not lanky or leaning, still growing robustly and not in flower.

It's also easy to raise seeds from packets, which, in most areas, can be sown directly where you want them to grow in spring. In cold, frosty climates, use a special seed-raising mix and sow seeds early indoors or under glass. Plant out the seedlings that come up when all danger of frost has passed.

Many mail-order companies supply seeds, and the variety of choice is exciting. Some specialise in unusual or heirloom varieties, and so in your edible garden you can experiment with, amongst others, unusual and rare tomatoes, swiss chard, beans and pumpkins. Seeds are inexpensive and much delight is gained from raising and nurturing little-known vegetables and experimenting with colours and striking leaf shapes.

The other means of acquiring seeds is to save your own from the last year's harvest (provided of course they are not hybrid forms) and the seeds will germinate next year. In doing this, you will be partaking in an age-old horticultural practice, keeping alive rare varieties, and your favourite tomatoes, pumpkins and beans will be yours forever. Gardening is also a great way of sharing. Gardeners love to swap stories, wisdom, experiences, old wives' tales, seeds and seedlings. Don't worry if you raise too many seedlings or have leftovers from punnets, as there's always someone nearby who will share in your enthusiasm for gardening.

potted plants

Choose pots big enough to easily hold the mass of roots that are to fill them, or they'll be forever thirsty and weak. Small pots dry out too quickly and if plants wilt, quality is reduced. They need to be 10cm (4") wider and deeper than the root ball. Terracotta is impressive but is expensive. Plastic pots are cheap, however, they don't dry out as quickly, but will blow over and deteriorate with exposure to the sun. A metal or wooden container like a bucket, wheel-barrow or half-barrel will do a perfect job as a pot, but must have holes for drainage. Wooden crates and polystyrene boxes have been successfully used for vegie plots, the latter being especially good as they are an appropriate shape and depth, and the polystyrene is an insulator, stabilising the temperature of the potting mix.

Most trees will grow in pots but not to full size because their roots are restricted. Citrus trees are often potted. Olives are content to grow in pots, so too are guavas and bay. Miniature varieties of apples, peach, nectarine and cherries are also ideal. Herbs make excellent potted plants as most love good drainage. Choose pots that suit their shape: tall herbs like dill, rosemary or tarragon look good in tall, wide pots; weeping types like thyme or savory are better suited to cascading on their own over pots 15-20cm (6-8") high, or as borders to the mound-shaped sage, parsley, basil or marjoram. Mint is best confined to a pot because it's so invasive, and potted chervil can be moved into semi-shade during the hottest part of the year.

Mini-tomatoes make excellent pot specimens, but demand large pots to accommodate their roots. Tall, staking tomatoes are not well suited to pots but capsicums, cucumbers, chillies, leafy green crops and bush beans will do well in pots, as will the winter vegetables like broccoli or mini cauliflower and peas.

Cultivation for success

fertilisers

Vegetables fall into three groups: leafy types, flowering/fruiting varieties and root crops. They all have their own preferences for essential elements.

Leafy vegetables and herbs (for example, spinach, basil, lettuce, cabbage) need large amounts of nitrogen (N) for vigorous growth and abundant foliage.

Flowering/fruiting varieties are those that grow a container of seeds (for example, pumpkin, cucumbers, peas and tomatoes). Their special requirement is potassium (K) to boost flowering.

Root vegetables require good supplies of phosphorus (P) for vigorous root development.

To supply these needs we have two choices of fertiliser: chemical or organic.

Chemical fertilisers are constructed artificially by combining elements to correct specific problems like magnesium, phosphorus or potassium deficiencies, or mixed to suit specific plant varieties. There are also complete plant foods, with a mix of all the elements for healthy plant growth. These are the most suitable for vegetable growth. They are mixed into the soil before planting time to avoid chemical burning of seedling roots. Soluble fertilisers are dissolved in water and, when applied, are taken up immediately by both the leaves and roots. Slow-release pelleted formulas are a more gentle method of providing nutrients, and less likely to shock plants.

For all chemical fertilisers, use only the quantities recommended on the package as overload will kill plants. The only additional need is nitrogen boosts in liquid dressings for leafy vegetables.

Organic fertilisers provide required elements in natural form and will not build up deposits of unused chemical salts in the soil. They are available as slow-release pelleted poultry manure (with a nutrient composition similar to the complete plant foods) or blood and bone, bone dust, linseed, cottonseed and castor meal. All organic fertilisers are slow-release formulas as they must decompose before the nutrients are available.

Seaweed and fish emulsions are foliar organic sprays. Their nutrients are available immediately.

Manures are not fertilisers but soil improvers. They help provide the light, airy composition required but their nutrient benefits are low. Manures must be well decomposed before seedlings are put in as the process of breaking down can kill the plants. Spread it on the garden a month before planting or spread out in sunlight until it loses its strong aroma. It is then safe to use. There are other soil conditions, like acidity or alkalinity (its pH), that influence how plants grow. In most gardens the soil pH is not a problem but by varying the sources of organic matter used, you'll prevent any imbalances developing. Should problems arise, take a soil sample to your nursery.

worm farms

Worm farms are a form of kitchen and garden waste recycling. They put to good use the incredible ability of earth worms to digest and decompose organic matter. You will need a three-layered stack of plastic trays (available as a kit from garden centres and hardware stores) and a large supply of worms. It's an odour-free and efficient way to recycle kitchen waste. The upper layer houses the worms in moist peat beds and here you add kitchen refuse, vegetable peelings, leftovers, shredded paper, coffee grains, tea leaves, leaf debris from the garden, etc. (Worms don't like onion and citrus skins or meat waste.) The second layer collects the worm castings, or vermipost, the nutrient-rich by-product of their digestive processes. This can be spread over the garden as mulch or used to raise seedlings. The bottom layer collects an equally valuable liquid, which can be used as a liquid fertiliser, neat for established plants or diluted to half strength for seedlings. Recycling at its best.

soil types

Yes, alas, you have to cultivate. There's no denying the major requirement for success with producing crops is the condition of your soil. There are two major soil types: clay and sand, and your soil will be at one end or the other of the scale, or somewhere in between, where the quantities of sand, clay and organic material are mixed.

Clay is fine-particled, hard when dry and sticky when wet. It will clump onto your shoes and your garden fork and stay there, moulded into shape. Clay soils have good supplies of the minerals and essential elements necessary for plant growth, but have little space for air, water and the roots to move through. To break up these heavy soils, spread on gypsum (available from your nursery or agricultural supply store), leave for a month, then dig in large quantities of organic matter, like compost and manure. A short-cut technique is to spread gypsum, add a layer of pelleted poultry manure and then build a garden bed on top of this, raised enough to allow room for root growth. Use garden soil mix, well-aged manure and compost mixed together. This is all you need to grow the first crop. The following season it can be dug in and combined with the underlying clay. Add more organic supplies each season. But don't dig clay soils when they're wet (they'll stick into clods) or when too dry (you'll become exhausted and the fine soil particles will blow away in the wind). Soil that is just moist is easiest and best to dig.

Sand has large particles visible to the naked eye. The soil will not compact, even when squeezed. Air (essential for the roots) fills the gaps, but water (essential for the whole plant) drains away too rapidly. To slow down the rate of water loss and to increase the nutrient- and mineral-holding capacity of the sand, add large quantities of manure and well-rotted compost.

Loams are the middle group; they are sand or clay mixed with enough organic material to make them workable, and are the ideal garden soil. But even they need regular applications of the organic duo if they are to remain productive.

potted plants

PLANTING OUT POTS

Good soil and constant watering are essential, no matter what pot you use. Normal garden soil can't be used. Well-matured compost is okay, but reduces in volume and requires topping up. Commercial potting mixes are the other alternative, but they vary in quality. As your plants have to live in it, it's worth spending money on a top-quality potting mix.

Gravel or pottery shards in the base of a pot are said to improve drainage, but there's no evidence that this is true. Modern potting mixes are blended to be used without need for added drainage material. To pot up, almost fill the container with potting mix. Level it out, dig a hole for the plant and place the plant in the hole making sure that it is no deeper or higher in the potting mix than it was in its original pot. Firm potting mix around the plant, sprinkle a ration of controlled-release fertiliser around it and then lightly cover the fertiliser with more potting mix. Finish by watering in. If the potting mix slumps when wetted, add a little more. A fortnight or so after planting start to water over the plant with soluble fertiliser and repeat once a fortnight to keep plants robust.

RE-POTTING

For small pots, replace the mix for each new planting. For large pots, dig the soil well and add fertiliser and top-ups of compost to keep the mix light.

Re-pot your plants when they become root-bound. If small enough to handle, pull the dampened plant from the pot and carve away some of the roots. Replace in new potting mix and prune to keep the top and bottom in proportion. Water well and start the fertiliser regime 2 weeks later.

WATERING POTS

It's so easy to forget. They dry out very quickly and you'll come home to dead treasures on the doorstep. If you're busy, a watering system is a great boon, and friendly neighbours are essential when you go away. Don't stand pots permanently in water-filled saucers as their roots rot. It can be an emergency measure for weekends away, but take them out as soon as you return.

no-dig gardens

These can be used for problems like weed-ridden, severely compacted or rocky soils, and even over concrete. Wood, bricks, garden walling and sleepers can be used to frame a garden bed. The bed must be strong enough to bear the weight of wet fillings, and up to 1.2m (4') high if you want to grow fruit trees in it, or just 30-40cm (12-16") tall if it's for vegies or herbs.

SOIL-BASED SITES

Build up the following layers:
1 light cover of pelleted poultry manure
2 5cm (2") layer of damp newspaper
3 complete layer of lucerne hay 'biscuits', 5cm (2") thick and flaked off the bale
4 10cm (4") layer of chicken manure
5 20cm (8") thick layer of straw
6 another layer of pelleted poultry manure
7 10cm (4") layer of straw.
Water well and plant into pockets of compost placed into hollows made in the top layer of straw.

CONCRETE OR PAVED SITES

Start with a 5cm (2") layer of lucerne hay 'biscuits' then add layers 4, 5 and 6. Add another layer of lucerne biscuits topped with layers 4-6. Repeat layers until the garden is

2-3cm (2") below the top of the bed. Do not dig and disturb the layers. Place plants into compost pockets in the top layer of straw and keep the bed well watered. After each harvest, add compost to top-up, but eventually replace the whole structure when the level falls low enough to fit in layers 3-7.

crop rotation

Rotating crops makes the nutrients added by one plant available to subsequent plants. For example, legumes trap nitrogen in nodules on their roots. Leafy vegetables, which need large quantities of nitrogen, will benefit from the added nitrogen if planted after legumes. Likewise, root vegetables planted after leafy vegetables will utilise the phosphorus not needed by the leafy vegetables. Fruiting plants such as tomatoes, peas, cucumbers and the like will make use of spare potassium.

Crop rotation ensures soil-living pests and diseases favouring one plant group cannot build up in the one spot. Gardening in this manner, though requiring planning and knowledge, means all the nutrients in the soil are used and the garden is worked to maximum effect.

companion planting

Some plants grow better if you plant them alongside each other. United they support, shelter and provide root space and nutrients for each other. Some herbs deter insect pests. In edible gardens this is great news. A careful selection of plants and companions means that you can grow much variety within a small space, while at the same time you help control pests. Nor are insect infestations likely to reach plague proportions as they can easily do in larger, single-crop garden beds. Here are some well-known plant combinations:

Beans grow more strongly with summer savory and when planted alternately with corn.

Cabbage, cauliflower and broccoli get protection from cabbage moth when near celery, sage or rosemary. Calendula attract hover flies, which eat aphids on peas or broad beans. Nasturtiums repel aphids among the peas and beetles among pumpkins and cucumbers.

Potatoes are more disease-resistant when planted among horseradish and, when planted with beans, are less likely to suffer beetle damage.

compost

Compost is a very effective way to recycle and reduce garden waste; it reproduces in the garden what happens in nature where vegetable matter decomposes and returns to the soil.

There's no mystery about composting. You can, if you want, simply pile waste on open ground and wait. However, the whole process is sped up if you build a wooden- or wire-sided container 1m (3') high. Make sure your compost pile is in the sun, there is earth beneath, air and water can penetrate and there is easy access. Add non-diseased garden waste, kitchen waste and shredded paper. The rule is that, if it was once alive, it's suitable to compost. Avoid bones and meat waste as they encourage scavengers and flies. Between each addition, add layers of lawn clippings or leaves. Herbs (comfrey, yarrow and tansy) and blood and bone will speed up the process. When full, the pile can be turned and left. It's ready to spread onto the garden or dig into the soil when its dark, earthy-smelling and there's little or no trace of the original ingredients.

pests and diseases

Alas, they turn up. The first step in managing garden pests is to accurately diagnose them. Infestations of leaf-eating insects are easy to identify. Caterpillars can be found on or under leaves making inroads into them. Some beetles chew leaves as well.

Chemical sprays will kill insects and unwanted pests, but can be harmful to humans and beneficial insects. It's wiser to kill them by hand (possible in an edible garden) or treat them with safe sprays like garlic spray (see instructions, page 17), or use pyrethrum-based alternatives or any of the new generation ultra-low toxicity chemicals such as Max Guard or Confidor. For caterpillars, try either Dipel or Success, two bio-insecticides with no toxicity to humans, animals or birds.

Chemical baits are available for slugs and snails, as are safer, organic alternatives. Gather them by hand at night and tread on them or drown them in a mix of water and detergent, kill them as they drink from saucers of alcohol or milk, or make barriers of sawdust or grit. Sap-sucking insects range from

minute dots (thrips), to moving masses (aphids), static hard pinheads (scales), small flies (white fly) to beetles (stink bugs). There are commercial chemical treatments for all of these, but if you wish to remain organic, crush by hand where possible, blast off with water or try garlic spray or chilli spray (see home-made sprays, right). Other leaf problems include fungus, mildew and rust. They cover and eventually kill leaves. Commercial sprays will save the plant if used early enough and stop the spread of spores. Alternative treatments include bicarbonate of soda spray or milk spray (see home-made sprays, right).

Soil fungus can be reduced in small areas by pouring on boiling water prior to planting. Check that the soil is not full of active worms. Collect stem-eating grubs in the soil during the day and at night when active on the surface. Marigolds repel grubs and nematodes for several metres.

Fruit-fly needs special attention in areas where they occur. Once they were only able to be controlled with regular applications of toxic chemicals, but now there are bio-insecticides that turn their natural enemies against them. Look for sprays containing the bacteria Spinosad, which kills the female fly before she can lay her damaging eggs but which leaves nothing in or on the crops you eat. If you live in a fruit fly area, hanging a Dak Pot in or near susceptible plants will warn you that the fly is about. Dak Pots are not a control measure. Their purpose is to let you know when spraying against fruit fly should begin. Home-made remedies are also effective against fruit fly, one of the best being a plastic drink bottle with a 200ml solution of Vegemite and water in it. A funnel, made from the cut off top of another drink bottle, is pushed into the side of the first bottle. Fruit flies are attracted by the smell of the rotting Vegemite solution, enter via the funnel but cannot get out again. Empty and refill regularly.

Don't leave dropped fruit on the ground where the fruit fly larvae pupate. Collect and seal tightly in plastic bags then 'cook' the damaged fruit in the sun for two weeks.

home-made sprays

GARLIC SPRAY Controls aphids and caterpillars.
Soak 100g (3oz) chopped garlic in 2 tablespoons mineral oil or liquid paraffin for 48 hours. Add 2 cups hot water and 30g (1oz) pure soap flakes. Cool and strain finely (lumps will clog the spray nozzle). Store in glass or plastic, clearly labelled. To use, dilute 3 teaspoons in 4 cups water for spraying.

CHILLI SPRAY Use against leaf eating beetles and caterpillars.
Blend a large handful of fresh chillies in 2 cups hot water. Add ½ cup pure soap flakes. Cool and strain finely. Store clearly labelled. To use, dilute 4 teaspoons in 4 cups water. Spray on leaves or dribble neat on ant trails and around infested pots.

BICARBONATE OF SODA SPRAY Use routinely to control powdery mildew.
Mix together 2g (¼oz) bicarbonate of soda and 2 teaspoons pure soap flakes in 4 cups hot water. Cool and spray weekly on leaves.

MILK SPRAY Controls powdery mildew if used at the first sign of disease and reapplied daily.
Combine 2 cups milk in 4 cups water. Spray regularly.

spring

Spring garden diary

spring is the season of anticipation

Even though the calendar may announce its arrival, often the weather does not. We usually get the odd hot spring day, a foretaste of languid summer making us anticipate its delights, and then the next day there's a sharp, cold reminder to bring us back to reality. However, it's the lengthening daylight hours that summer-growing plants respond to, so don't despair if chilly winds blow.

PLANTS START TO GROW BECAUSE THEY HAVE TO; THEY'VE BEEN BECKONED. THE LEAVES AND BUDS UNFURL WITH SPLASHES OF SUBTLE COLOUR, AND THE FULL DISPLAY OF SPRING FLOWERS STRENGTHENS AS THE SEASON TAKES HOLD. IN A CORNER OF THE VEGETABLE GARDEN, ASPARAGUS RESPONDS TO THE DIRECTIVE, BEES ARE HEARD AMONG THE PEAS, AND THE BROAD BEANS FLOWER. TARRAGON AND CHIVES OBEY THE COMMAND AND WAVE THEIR LEAVES IN THE BREEZE LIKE BANNERS.

If you live in the tropics, it's time to plant okra.

Early-bird gardeners will have already raised tomato, basil, capsicum and zucchini seedlings under cover during late winter, or will have been down to the local nursery for seedlings. Gardeners in frost-prone areas must time their planting out carefully so that they can avoid tricky, late frosts.

TOMATO

Date Collected:

Collected From:

Collected By:

IF SPACE IS NOT A PROBLEM, LEAVE GARDEN BEDS FALLOW OVER WINTER, COVERED IN MANURE AND MULCH. THEY WILL BE READY FOR PLANTING IN SPRING. AREAS SHADED IN WINTER ARE BEST REVITALISED IN THIS WAY.

MOST CITY GARDENS DON'T HAVE THE LUXURY OF SPACE. TO MAKE ROOM FOR SPRING, CLEAR EXISTING BEDS, REMOVE RAGGED, TIRED-LOOKING PLANTS THAT ARE NO LONGER PRODUCTIVE AND, ABOVE ALL, BE INVENTIVE WITH YOUR PLANT COMBINATIONS AND SPACE-SAVING IDEAS. COMPOST ALL DEBRIS; CHOP UP TOUGH STEMS TO SPEED UP DECOMPOSITION.

Now, your most difficult gardening decision is whether to plant favourites or new varieties. All are worth a try. Remember, good soil preparation, combination planting and crop rotation will ensure an abundant and wonderfully diverse kitchen garden.

pick now	*plant now*
most gardens beetroot, broccoli, broad beans, cabbage, cauliflower, endive, leeks, lettuce, onions, peas, radicchio, rhubarb, silver beet, spinach	**subtropical and Mediterranean gardens** beans, capsicum, carrot, chilli, choko, cucumber, eggplant, lettuce, melons, potatoes, radish, sweet corn, tomatoes, zucchini
temperate and cool gardens asparagus	**temperate gardens** asparagus, broad beans, cabbage, leeks, peas, and any of the above as frosts cease

Save wizened bean or pea pods and store for the next sowing. Dig up clods and break up roots in the soil. Add well-rotted compost.

Garden Peas

You might consider it useless growing peas at home when the frozen alternative is so convenient, but the flavour of a just-picked pea makes it all worthwhile. Like sweet corn, peas have a high sugar content, which slowly converts to starch after picking. If you gather peas young and eat them straight off the bush, you can really taste the difference.

Today's gardener can grow many kinds of peas. Common varieties include green or 'garden' peas, whose pods are not eaten; sugar snap and snow peas, which are both eaten pod and all; snow pea sprouts or shoots, which are the small-leafed, growing tips of the plant; and pea tendrils (usually snow pea tendrils), which are the thin, curly bits with a few leaves that peas use for climbing, although the name is often given to shoots.

Less common in the greengrocer, but gorgeous from your garden, are petit-pois or baby peas, which are simply ordinary green peas picked very young and small; they are necessarily expensive when bought but an exquisite luxury, especially eaten raw.

Green peas deteriorate rapidly after picking as their sugars immediately begin to turn to starch, to the detriment of both their flavour and tenderness. They are often tough when cooked; the chances of avoiding this is in selecting carefully and using promptly. Green peas can be boiled with or without mint and served with any meat or fish dish, pureed with potato and cream, mixed with other vegetables such as mushrooms or artichokes, braised with shallots and lettuce if they are reasonably young, or used for soups or in pie or pasty fillings, risottos and creamy pasta sauces. Peas in the pod will yield just under half their weight of shelled peas; 1kg (2lb) will serve 4.

Pea pods are lined with a tough membrane that makes them too fibrous to eat, but they can be cooked with green peas to sweeten them, or cooked in a dried- or fresh-pea soup to add a fresh, sweet flavour; remove before serving.

Sugar snap peas look like small green peas but their pods do not have the tough membrane of ordinary peas, so are eaten whole. They can be briefly boiled, used raw in salads, added raw to stir-fries and noodle dishes or added at the last minute to clear soups. Small ones can be used in risottos or pasta sauces.

Snow peas have flat, edible pods enclosing tiny peas that do not mature. They are eaten whole or sliced. They can be very briefly boiled and served alone or with other vegetables such as mushrooms to accompany meats or fish, or can be used in a vegetable tart filling. They can be used raw in salads or added to stir-fries, noodle dishes and spring-roll fillings, and can be added at the last minute to clear soups or used in risottos or pasta sauces.

Pea shoots and pea tendrils can be used as a garnish or in salads, stir-fries, noodle dishes and spring-roll fillings or added at the last minute to a clear soup.

Baby peas are best boiled and served plainly with a little butter or cream so their delicate flavour and tenderness can be appreciated. The classic French dish 'petits-pois à la Française' (a mix of braised lettuce, peas, shallots and bacon or prosciutto) can be prepared using ordinary green peas, but is better made with fresh baby peas.

Frozen peas vary from full-size to 'baby peas'. They are the answer to the 'tough pea' problem as they are marketed as being picked at their optimum point of development and frozen within hours. They are indeed tender, brightly coloured and quite good-tasting, but don't match truly young, fresh peas for the finer shades of flavour and texture. They are, however, a great convenience and a good product provided they have been correctly handled between the freezing plant and the frozen-food cabinet in the supermarket. Freeze your own from any over-abundance in the garden.

preserving the crop

STORING	All peas should be eaten as soon as possible after picking. If they must be stored, rinse and dry thoroughly on absorbent paper and store in the refrigerator. Enclose all pea types in paper bags enclosed in plastic bags. Don't pod peas until you are ready to cook them.
FREEZING	An oversupply of green peas can be blanched and frozen (see Freezing, page 240). Sugar snap peas and snow peas do not freeze well, but a pea puree will, so cook the peas, puree, then freeze.

green peas

snow pea tendrils

snow peas

Try unusual varieties, like wrinkled peas, said to have superior flavour and winged, or asparagus, peas for something completely different. In a small kitchen garden, you'll be able to grow enough for a small harvest once or twice a week; in a large garden you'll have supplies to freeze or give away.

In the garden

In cool temperate gardens peas grow almost all year round. They need some shade when the sun is hot. The plants are frost-tolerant, but the flowers and young pods are not, so plant to avoid frosts at flowering time. In warmer gardens, peas make a useful winter crop; in tropical gardens, plant after the wet to avoid mildew. Prepare a well-drained and sunny site by digging over well. As weed removal is difficult between seedlings, a mulch mat on either side of the rows or in the centre and around the outside of a tripod should help. Leave a 2cm (1") gap for the seeds. Put down controlled-release fertiliser or blood and bone and cover it with a 3cm (1¼") thick layer of damp newspaper, spreading 10cm (4") beyond the seed position. Gravel or lucerne will hide it and stop it blowing away. The weeds can't break through until the paper disintegrates, and the pea roots can reach the fertiliser right through their growth. Put in stakes and wire or twine for row planting, and tripod supports and connecting twine if growing in teepee shapes. Peas grow 2m (6') high.

Wet the soil and plant the seeds 5cm (2") deep so birds and mice won't find them, spacing them about 10cm (4") apart if they are to grow up frames, closer if they are to be self-supporting on the ground. The seedlings will break through in about a week, taking longer if the soil is cool.

Water regularly after the seedlings emerge. Flowers will start in a couple of months and pods a week later. Don't let the pods grow too big as the peas will be mealy and the plants will stop producing. The more you pick, the more the plants produce. Peas for shelling should have space between each pea and the pod shouldn't be tight. Peas eaten in the pod (snow peas and sugar snap peas) should be pliable, about 8cm (3-4") long with small pea formations visible.

At the end of the season, cut off the stems at ground level and compost undiseased stems and leaves. Leave the roots and their nitrogen nodules in the ground for a crop of lettuce or silver beet to use.

PESTS AND DISEASES

Problems include aphids. Hose off, crush between your fingers or spray with pyrethrum sprays. Another problem is mildew which can kill pea plants. Use a commercial spray or try the bicarbonate of soda spray (see page 17) which won't harm bees, peas or predators.

For the table

TO PREPARE

• Green peas should only be podded just before using. Sugar snap and snow peas need to be stringed: pinch off the stem end and, with a thumbnail, pull down the strings on both sides. Pea shoots and tendrils need picking over to remove any tough stems or ends.

• Sugar snap peas and snow peas need very little cooking. Add to boiling water and cook until they just change colour. If they are for salads, remove and cool in iced water.

snow pea sprouts

sugar snap peas

• Green peas require slightly more cooking and the older the peas, the longer time required, generally about 2-4 minutes. Don't overcook as this toughens peas. Never add bicarbonate of soda to the water – the peas stay green, but you destroy their nutritional value.

TO SERVE

• Fresh pea soup is fantastic. Cook peas in chicken stock and blend with the pulp from a roasted bulb of garlic. Stir in cream or more chicken stock, if necessary. Add snipped chives, salt and pepper. Serve chilled or hot.

• Secure blanched snow peas around cooked prawns with toothpicks and serve with a soy-chilli dipping sauce.

• Serve green peas, sugar snap peas and snow peas tossed through a little gremolata (a mixture of garlic, lemon rind and parsley).

• Fry some fine bacon strips until crisp, add a little balsamic vinegar and some blanched sugar snap peas.

• Sugar snap peas and snow peas, when lightly blanched, can be used as crudités, and is particularly good with bagna cauda, the Italian anchovy sauce.

• For a spring salad, toss blanched peas with lettuce, asparagus tips, spring onions, chervil and parsley leaves; dress with a vinaigrette and add crumbled blue cheese.

• Dinner becomes something more than grilled fish or chicken with this simple pea sauce (particularly good with Atlantic salmon). Cook some peas in a light chicken stock until very soft; sieve and thin with more chicken stock, if necessary. Season with salt and pepper.

peas with mint butter

2¼ cups (350g) fresh shelled peas
40g (1½ ounces) butter, softened
1 tablespoon finely chopped fresh mint
1 teaspoon finely grated lemon rind

1 Boil, steam or microwave peas until tender; drain.
2 Meanwhile, combine remaining ingredients in small bowl.
3 Serve peas topped with butter mixture.

prep & cook time 10 minutes **serves** 4
note You need approximately 1kg fresh pea pods to get the required amount of shelled peas needed for this recipe.

Potatoes

Rare is the person who doesn't eat potatoes, whether as the ubiquitous chip, comforting mashed spuds or via more sophisticated cooking methods. Nor is a potato merely a potato these days. A shopping trip means negotiating the unfamiliar names of pontiac, desiree, coliban, kipfler and many more – all with their different textures, tastes and colours.

Few gardeners ever grow potatoes; they are well worth the effort, though, as each kind has its own distinctive flavour and texture.

A potato that is low in moisture, low in sugar and high in starch will bake to floury perfection with a crisp outside, and make golden, rather than dark, chips. It will also perform well when cooked in fat around a roast, though its low sugar content means it will take longer to brown than some others. However, these types of potatoes will tend to fall apart if boiled, so stick to roasting and frying.

A **waxy potato**, lower in starch and higher in moisture, will boil beautifully and cut into clean slices for salad, but will not have that lovely mealy texture and crisp outside when baked or fried. Experts classify potatoes as floury or waxy by their specific gravity (weight for size compared to a given standard); the higher the specific gravity, the higher the starch level and the more floury the potato. The sugar/starch/moisture balance changes as the potato matures – sugar is gradually changed to starch as the tuber grows, and the final levels reached vary considerably from one variety to another.

The way a potato is grown also makes a difference: one grown to full maturity on the plant, in the right soil, will taste better and keep better than one that was harvested earlier or grown in sandy soil, which doesn't suit potatoes so well but makes machine harvesting easier.

Baking and frying varieties include russet burbank, idaho, coliban, king edward, spunta and kennebec.

Mashing varieties include the all-rounders desiree, dutch cream, which is particularly smooth and creamy, nicola and pontiac, both which give a firm-bodied mash, and the floury types king edward and spunta, which give a fluffy mash – you may prefer to steam, rather than boil these before mashing, in case they break down in the boiling water.

Boiling varieties include new potatoes of any variety, pinkeye, bintje, pink fir apple, nadine, jersey royal, red lasoda, petrone and purple congo, which has a purple skin and flesh.

All-rounder varieties, which will perform satisfactorily with any cooking method, include nicola, dutch cream and kipfler, which have particularly good flavour, desiree, pontiac, sebago and royal blue, a blue/purple-skinned, yellow-fleshed potato with a buttery flavour.

preserving the crop

STORING	Potatoes should be stored in a cool, dark, airy place. Remove 'eyes' as they appear, and the life of your potatoes will be extended. Refrigerating potatoes converts the starches to sugar, causing them to become sweet. Direct sunlight produces a green skin – these potatoes should not be eaten. Dirty potatoes store better than washed ones, so don't wash until ready to prepare.
FREEZING	Fresh potatoes are not suitable for freezing.

baby, new or chat potatoes

kipfler potatoes

pontiac potatoes

In the garden

Potatoes are easy to propagate. You simply keep a few of your favourite varieties, let them sprout and grow your own. All you need is a sunny, well-drained site and enough room.

Potatoes must be grown in frost-free conditions, so wait until there's no risk of late frosts. They can be planted all year where winter conditions are mild. In tropical areas, don't plant them in the 'wet' as they'll rot. Select a sunny, well-drained position. If the soil was not manured for the previous crop, add compost so the soil is light. Break up heavy clods. Don't add lime, but do add a complete or slow-release organic fertiliser.

Potatoes grow from whole potatoes or small pieces (golf-ball size) that have started to sprout. You can sprout your own (just keep until shoots form) or buy seed potatoes from nurseries (guaranteed virus-free, which is important if you've had dieback problems with potatoes or related crops such as tomatoes, capsicum and eggplant).

Make a furrow about 15cm (6") deep and position the potato pieces about 40cm (16") apart, with their 'eyes' or sprouts facing up. Backfill with fine soil and mulch to reduce weeds and late-frost damage.

When the leafy stems are about 20cm (8") tall, hill up the soil to about 5cm (2") below the top of the stem on each plant, creating furrows between them. Hilling encourages more stems to develop and hence more potatoes. It also prevents light reaching the potato tubers – when exposed to light they turn green and are poisonous.

Potatoes need regular watering to keep the tubers well-shaped and smooth-skinned. Use the furrow to irrigate your crop and make harvesting easier. If space is limited, you can also plant potatoes in tyres or log beds. Add new tyres or extra logs with a further dressing of soil each time the stems elongate.

New potatoes are ready to harvest when the flowers are fully open, about 12 weeks after planting, and the tubers are about the size of hen eggs. Investigate under the plants for tubers, without destroying the root connections, and leave undersized tubers to fatten up later.

If you leave potatoes longer, they develop their familiar hard skins and so can be stored. Harvest when the foliage has browned. Lift gently with a fork or with your hands to avoid damage. Shake off the soil and dry for a few hours out of the sunlight. Give them a rumble to remove excess soil, then store in an airy basket, hessian bag or box in the dark, away from pests.

sebago potatoes

desiree potatoes

king edward potatoes

For the table

TO PREPARE

• A common mistake is to boil potatoes covered. This results in a messy stove-top. Instead, just cover potato pieces with water, bring to the boil and cook, uncovered, for 10-15 minutes or until soft.

• Potatoes cook perfectly in the microwave. When cooking whole, pierce the skins all over with a fork, dampen the potatoes, cover with microwave-safe plastic wrap and cook in 5-minute intervals until soft when tested with a skewer. Potato pieces need a shorter cooking time.

TO SERVE

• Wedges don't have to mean high fat. Place peeled potatoes in a pan of cold water and bring to the boil; remove from the heat and let stand for 5 minutes. Drain and cool until they can be handled. Cut each potato into 6-8 wedges. Place 2-3 tablespoons of vegetable oil in a bowl, add the wedges and rub all over with oil. Place the wedges on a large baking tray, sprinkle with sea salt and chopped herbs, if you like. Bake in a 200°C/400°F oven for about 30 minutes or until the wedges are starting to crisp. Turn only once.

• The secret to the perfect chip is frying them twice and sprinkling with salt as soon as they leave the oil – not 5 minutes later. Dry potatoes on a clean tea-towel or paper towel before frying and always use hot, clean oil.

• For delicious, creamy mashed potatoes, peel and cut potatoes into small pieces. Cover with cold milk. Bring to the boil and cook until soft but not falling apart. Drain, reserving any milk, then mash in the same pan, adding the reserved milk and a little butter.

• The creamy texture of boiled baby new potatoes, with just a sprinkle of sea salt, is loved by all.

• Try grated potato cakes with smoked salmon, sour cream and dill accompanied with a glass of chilled champagne for a delicious indulgent brunch.

• The Irish love their potatoes and colcannon is a Halloween favourite. Boil potatoes until tender and mash with hot cream and soft butter. Melt extra butter in a large frying pan and cook finely chopped onions and a crushed garlic clove until soft. Add finely sliced savoy cabbage and cook, stirring, until cabbage just wilts. Fold potato mixture into cabbage mixture.

• Potatoes carry the flavourings of the ingredients they're cooked with: try adding some roasted garlic, creamed corn, sun-dried tomato pesto or basil pesto to plain mashed potato.

vichyssoise

vichyssoise

50g (1½ ounces) butter
2 medium leeks (700g), trimmed, sliced thinly
750g (1½ pounds) coliban potatoes, peeled,
   chopped coarsely
2 cups (500ml) chicken stock
2 cups (500ml) water
1¼ cups (300ml) pouring cream
2 tablespoons coarsely chopped fresh chives

1 Melt butter in large saucepan; cook leek, covered,
stirring occasionally, about 20 minutes or until softened
(do not allow leek to brown).
2 Add potato, stock and the water to pan; bring to the
boil. Simmer, covered, until potato is tender.
3 Cool 10 minutes, then blend or process soup, in batches,
until smooth; place soup in large bowl. Stir in cream;
cover, refrigerate 3 hours or overnight.
4 Divide soup into serving bowls; sprinkle with chives
just before serving.

prep & cook time 50 minutes (+ refrigeration) **serves** 6
notes Vichyssoise is the classic French creamy potato
and leek soup that is generally served cold. You can also
use desiree or pink fir apple potatoes for this recipe.

herbed baby potatoes

1kg (2 pounds) baby new potatoes, unpeeled
1 tablespoon olive oil
60g (2 ounces) butter
2 cloves garlic, crushed
2 tablespoons fresh herbs, such as rosemary,
   tarragon, thyme or sage, chopped finely (see notes)

1 Place potatoes in large saucepan, cover with cold
water; bring to the boil. Remove from heat and stand in
hot water 5 minutes; drain. When cool enough to handle,
cut each potato in half.
2 Heat oil and butter in large frying pan; add potato,
cut-side down. Cover; cook over medium-high heat
10 minutes or until the surface is golden and crisp.
3 Add garlic to potatoes in pan; cook a further 5 minutes.
Sprinkle herbs over potato; toss gently. Season with
cracked black pepper and sea salt.

prep & cook time 35 minutes **serves** 4-6
notes Choose the herb to suit the meal, e.g. sage with
pork, rosemary with lamb, etc.
Serve hot as a side dish or at room temperature as a salad.
The potatoes will be more crisp if served hot.

herbed baby potatoes

portuguese potatoes

portuguese potatoes

600g (1¼ pounds) sebago potatoes, peeled,
  chopped coarsely
2 tablespoons olive oil
2 cloves garlic, crushed
1 large brown onion (200g), chopped coarsely
4 medium tomatoes (760g), chopped coarsely
2 teaspoons sweet paprika
2 teaspoons finely chopped fresh thyme
½ cup (125ml) chicken stock
1 tablespoon peri peri sauce
1 tablespoon coarsely chopped fresh flat-leaf parsley

1 Preheat oven to 220°C/425°F.
2 Toss potato and half the oil in medium shallow
baking dish. Roast, uncovered, about 30 minutes or
until browned lightly.
3 Meanwhile, heat remaining oil in large frying pan; cook
garlic and onion, stirring, until onion softens. Add tomato,
paprika and thyme to pan; cook, stirring, about 1 minute
or until tomato just softens. Add stock and sauce to pan;
bring to the boil. Reduce heat; simmer, uncovered, stirring
occasionally, about 10 minutes or until tomato mixture
thickens slightly.
4 Remove potato from oven; reduce oven temperature
to 180°C/350°F.
5 Pour tomato mixture over potato; bake, uncovered,
about 20 minutes or until potato is tender. Serve
sprinkled with parsley.

prep & cook time 1 hour 10 minutes **serves** 6
notes You can also use pontiac potatoes for this recipe.
Peri peri (piri piri) is a hot Portuguese sauce made
with chilli, garlic, ginger, oil and herbs, and is available
from supermarkets.

sour cream and chive potato pancakes

sour cream and chive potato pancakes

900g (1¾ pounds) sebago potatoes, peeled
1 medium brown onion (150g), chopped finely
¼ cup finely chopped fresh chives
2 eggs, separated
2 tablespoons plain (all-purpose) flour
½ cup (120g) sour cream
⅔ cup (160ml) vegetable oil
80g (2½ ounces) butter

1 Grate potatoes coarsely; squeeze excess moisture from
potato with hands. Combine potato in large bowl with
onion, chives, egg yolks, flour and sour cream.
2 Beat egg whites in small bowl with electric mixer until
firm peaks form; gently fold into potato mixture.
3 Heat 2 tablespoons of the oil with 20g of the butter in
large frying pan; cook heaped tablespoons of the potato
mixture, uncovered, until browned both sides. Drain on
absorbent paper; cover to keep warm.
4 Repeat to make a total of 20 pancakes.

prep & cook time 35 minutes **makes** 20
note It is important to squeeze as much excess moisture
as possible from the potato so that the pancakes hold
their shape while cooking.

Onions

Onions are one of the most widely used vegetables of all – they feature in every cuisine. It may seem an impossible task to be self-sufficient in onions, as you'd need a small farm, however, unusual and special-purpose onions are well worth the effort and the little space they require in a kitchen garden. They are easy to grow and you'll have some bunching varieties for life. Onions store well in dry conditions, and tiny onions are easily pickled.

Brown onions are the workhorses of the family, used for everything from a well-charred slice for a hamburger to a softly gold and luscious mass as the start of french onion soup. If a recipe calls for onion without further description, brown onion is the one intended, though white onion will do. They vary in size and in degree of pungency and sweetness. Brown onions store well and develop more pungency as they age. Some varieties, usually large and light-skinned, are mild, sweet and softer than others; they are usually sold separately.

White onions are thinner-skinned than brown and are often believed to be milder, but they are, on average, more pungent. They come in sizes from large to tiny, which are often sold separately as pickling onions. The very tiny pickled pearl onions sold in bottles, often dyed a violent green or red, are not sold fresh in Australia. White onion is preferred to brown if used raw, for example as fine rings in a salad, simply on the grounds of its colour. In cooking, it can be used the same as brown.

Green onions, spring onions or shallots are, confusingly, the names usually given to bulbless onions (white onions picked before they develop bulbs, or bunching onions which grow in clumps and never develop bulbs). The term 'scallion', which dates back in English to at least 1500 as a name for a long-necked, bulbless onion, remains in general use only in America.

These onions are usually sliced and eaten raw or only lightly cooked. They are mild in flavour and pungency; the white stems and the first few centimetres of the green tops are eaten.

Spring onions or salad onions are the names usually given to young white onions whose bulbs have only developed into a size somewhere between that of a cherry tomato and ping-pong ball. They are sold with their green tops still on and are used for salads or for cooking whole.

Red onions and purple onions are often called spanish or bermuda onions. They are usually used raw in salads and for garnishes. They are milder and sweeter than white or brown onions; to reduce their mild pungency even further, pour boiling water over onion slices then drop into ice water, then drain and dry.

Shallots or eschalots grow in clusters in the same way as garlic. European shallots may be golden-brown or pinky grey, Asian shallots are pink/purple. They are mild, sweet and intense in flavour. Chopped, they can be used in a delicate sauce or savoury butter, but are usually cooked whole – roasted or caramelised. Asian shallots are eaten raw, or sliced and deep-fried then tossed in a stir-fry or used as a condiment; these are available in packets in Asian food shops.

preserving the crop

STORING	Brown and white onions should be stored in a cool, dark, airy place. Red onions and the sweeter yellow onions store for longer in the refrigerator. Spring onions and green onions should be trimmed as little as possible and stored, wrapped in a damp tea towel, in a plastic bag in the refrigerator. Ideally, use straight from the garden. Bought green onions can be planted in the garden, or even a pot, until they are needed; they last for months and there is no waste.
FREEZING	Onions from the garden can be peeled, chopped and frozen for up to 3 months (see Freezing, page 240) in well-sealed plastic bags. Small onions can be frozen whole if peeled and blanched; seal well so they don't spoil other food in the freezer. Onions can be gently fried, with or without garlic, and frozen for up to a month to give you a head start for busy, mid-week dinners.
PICKLING	To pickle small onions or shallots, salt peeled onions overnight, rinse and pack into sterilised glass jars (see Bottling, pages 240-242), adding a few spices such as cloves, peppercorns and dried chillies as you go. Pour over warmed vinegar (malt, white or cider) to cover. For sweeter pickled onions, dissolve ½ cup white sugar in 4 cups of vinegar. Seal the jars and store in a cool, dark place for 3-4 weeks before opening.

In the garden

The soil for all bulb crops needs to be light and well dug so the roots can penetrate. It must also be well drained to prevent rot. If there are any hard clay clods, dig in coarse sand and fine organic material to open it up. Mix it in well.

Should you have a hard clay base near the surface, raise the bed by mounding it over with garden mix or very fine compost. Sprinkle blood and bone or a complete fertiliser over the surface and rake in. Make shallow furrows only 0.5cm (¼") deep and sprinkle in the selected seeds. Cover with compost or seed-raising mixture and water well. If planting seedlings, place 10cm (4") apart.

GREEN ONIONS

Green onions (scallions or bunching onions) can be planted all year round in subtropical and tropical climates, and all but mid-winter in temperate and cold gardens. Buy seed specific to this crop. They can be harvested in 8-12 weeks. For continuous supplies, repeat the planting every 4-6 weeks.

Here is a labour-saving (cheat's) technique for cultivating green onions. When a recipe calls for green onions and you've bought a bunch, you'll probably have some left over. Trim their stems by half and plant as a bunch, just covering the roots. They'll continue to grow and be waiting the next time you need some. They certainly won't turn into those soggy disappointments you find in the bottom of the refrigerator.

BULB ONIONS

To grow onions that will develop into bulbs, you need to select the appropriate seed. 'Early' or winter-growing onions are sown at the start of autumn to give you white spring onion shapes in, surprisingly, spring. These can be also pickled and used in dishes requiring whole small onions. 'Mid' and 'late' season onions are planted in mid-autumn or late autumn and are harvested in summer after their leaves have dried out. Varieties include white, red and brown onions. These slow-maturers, after drying in the sun, are the best for storage.

UNUSUAL VARIETIES

There are a few unusual onion varieties home gardeners might like to try as they are both versatile and productive and take up little space. They are all multiplier onions; that is, they develop clusters of bulbs.

Golden (or french) shallots are expensive and often difficult to buy. Small bulbs can be grown at home, either from seeds but more often from bulbs bought at the greengrocer's shop. The bulbs are separated and pushed 5-7cm (2-3") deep into the soil, 15cm (6") apart, in autumn or early winter. They'll multiply rapidly and you'll be able to lift them in 3-4 months. Store in a dry place and keep enough for next season's planting. They don't appreciate very wet or humid conditions.

Potato onions, like golden shallots, expand their clusters of bulblets underground after planting in autumn. The bulbs expand as well as multiply. Harvest in spring or summer before the humidity rots them.

Tree or egyptian onions grow from bulbs planted in autumn and multiply underground. They also produce many small onions at the top of the flower stalks. If not gathered, these weigh down the stem until it touches the ground where they root and start a new cluster.

Welsh (or japanese) bunching onions are also called 'ever-ready onions' and are perhaps the most useful small onions of all. In a well-drained sunny spot they will remain evergreen throughout the year and the leaves and stems can be cut and used like chives or green onions. To harvest, break off what you require and push the soil back around the clump. If the clump is too tightly packed, lift it with a fork, break off the excess and replant. The cluster will continually expand and will need dividing every couple of years to provide new space and soil to grow into.

For the table

TO PREPARE

• Remove the skin (or, in the case of green onions, the coarse outside layers) and trim the root end without cutting it off. In green and spring onions, trim the green tops to a few centimetres or remove altogether, according to the recipe.

• Shallots are tedious to peel but are easier if separate cloves are first dropped into boiling water for about 10 seconds to loosen the skins.

• If a large quantity of brown or white onions is to be chopped, large ones are the best to choose because there are fewer to peel.

• The biggest problem with onions, as we all know, is that they make our eyes water. Various remedies have been proposed: wearing goggles, holding a spoon in your mouth, only chopping onions on the full moon after midnight... The best way is to use a razor-sharp knife that minimises squashing the onion tissues that release the fumes; the best of the rest seems to be to chill them well before chopping or even semi-freeze them after peeling. The food processor chops onion quickly and easily and is good for chopping coarsely, but not for finely chopped as it releases too much liquid and they will steam in the pan rather than frying.

• When cooking onions with a roast dinner, cut in half and thread them through the un-cut sides onto skewers. They will be easy to turn and the centres won't pop out.

• The first step in many recipes is to fry chopped onion slowly to a soft, golden mass; this takes about 20 minutes and requires frequent checking and stirring. A quicker way is to warm the butter or oil, add the onion and stir until the pieces are well coated, then barely cover with warm water and cook over high heat until the water has evaporated. Stir the now softened onion on medium to low heat for a few minutes until it is golden, adding a little more butter or oil if needed.

TO SERVE

• The smell of onions on a barbecue can incite the neighbourhood. For perfect onions, slice them thickly, put them in a heatproof bowl and pour over enough boiling water to cover. Let stand for about 15 minutes, drain and pat dry. Toss in some vegetable oil and cook as usual. They can be prepared several hours ahead, covered and stored at room temperature.

• Sliced onion and tomato salad, drizzled with cider vinegar and olive oil, sprinkled with sugar and left to stand for about 30 minutes is also an old favourite. Try adding watermelon with a few olives and a sprinkle of shredded fresh parsley.

• This delicious onion sauce is easy, can be prepared ahead and goes well with grilled, roast or pan-fried pork. Heat some olive oil in a heavy-based pan; add some sliced onions, cover and reduce the heat to low, cook for about 20 minutes, stirring occasionally. When very soft and golden add some peeled, sliced apples, several crushed juniper berries, apple juice and a splash of gin. Cook, uncovered, for about 15 minutes or until the apples are soft and most of the liquid has evaporated. This sauce keeps well, covered, in the refrigerator for several days, or can be frozen for up to a month.

• Glazed golden shallots are beautiful to look at as well as to eat. Cook peeled shallots in a little oil and garlic over low heat, covered, for about 20 minutes or until very soft. Remove the lid and add some stock; bring to the boil and boil, uncovered, until the stock has almost evaporated. Add a little sugar to the stock for sweeter glazed onions, if you prefer. Serve as an accompaniment.

• Make a quick Thai salad using finely shredded red onions, whole mint leaves and wedges of roma tomatoes. Dress with a mixture of fish sauce, lime juice and a touch of palm sugar. Add some shredded cooked chicken, rare roast beef or flaked poached fish to make a main course. For those who like it hot, add some shredded chillies or a touch of sweet chilli sauce.

green onions

red, spanish, or bermuda onions

spring onions

onion tart

This pastry is very easy and good for any savoury tart, but you can also use thawed ready-rolled pastry sheets, joined with a little egg yolk.

1 tablespoon olive oil
30g (1 ounce) butter
5 large brown onions (1kg), halved, sliced thinly
3 teaspoons fresh thyme leaves
4 cloves garlic, crushed
¼ cup (40g) finely chopped seeded black olives
150g (4½ ounces) goat's cheese
pastry
1½ cups (225g) plain (all-purpose) flour
60g (2 ounces) butter, extra
2 tablespoons grated parmesan cheese
125g (4 ounces) cream cheese
1 egg
1-2 tablespoons lemon juice, approximately

1 Make pastry.
2 Meanwhile, heat oil and butter in large heavy-based frying pan. Add onions; cook, covered, over medium heat, about 5 minutes or until onions are softened. Uncover; cook, stirring occasionally, about 20 minutes or until onions are golden brown. Stir in thyme, garlic and olives; cook a further 10 minutes. Cool to room temperature.
3 Spread combined goat's cheese and remaining cream cheese over pastry shell. Top with onion mixture; bake in oven about 30 minutes or until filling is firm.
pastry Process flour, butter, parmesan and half the cream cheese until combined. Add egg and enough juice to make ingredients cling together. Wrap pastry in plastic wrap; refrigerate 30 minutes. Preheat oven to 200°C/400°F. Lightly oil 23cm (9") loose-based flan tin. Roll pastry on floured surface until large enough to cover base and side of tin; lift pastry into tin, gently ease into side, trim edge. Place tin on oven tray; line pastry with baking paper, fill with dried beans or rice. Bake 10 minutes. Remove paper and beans; bake a further 10 minutes or until pastry is browned lightly, cool. Reduce oven temperature to 180°C/350°F.

prep & cook time 1 hour 35 minutes (+ cooling) **serves** 6
note This tart will keep well, removed from the tin and covered, in the refrigerator for several days. Serve tart at room temperature.

Asparagus

Golden daffodils or sweetly perfumed freesias announce spring is here, but keen cooks are watching for the first spears of asparagus to break through their richly manured beds.

Asparagus has been called both the King and Queen of vegetables. The versatility of this regal vegetable is hard to beat. It has a flavour all its own yet easily accompanies other distinctive flavours – especially fish. Asparagus can be served with melted butter and lemon, or a sauce such as hollandaise, as a first course or as an accompaniment to meats or seafood. It can go into salads, soups and sauces, or can be used in a quiche filling, savoury custard, frittata, gratin, mousse, stir-fry or many other dishes.

It comes in green, white and purple varieties – white asparagus is produced by earthing up the asparagus bed to cover the growing shoots to prevent them from greening. Purple spears are sometimes available at greengrocers. They are similar in flavour to the white and green spears and turn green when cooked. Green asparagus comes in various thicknesses, purple is fatter and white fatter again. All have a juicy texture and delicate, earthy/woody/grassy aroma and flavour, though purple is the sweetest and white the mildest.

In the garden

What do you need for a harvestable stand of asparagus? Deep, fertile, free-draining soil that contains plenty of rotted organic matter and a cold winter. The plants need to experience a period of dormancy over winter and, to induce dormancy, frosts starting in autumn are desirable. Regular frosts or snow in winter are what the plants expect, but as long as its quite normal for your winter day-time temperatures to max out at 10°C (50°F) or less you'll have no trouble growing asparagus. It's on the coast where the nights are chilly but the days are mild to warm that asparagus isn't worth the effort. Asparagus also requires space in order to yield a worthwhile harvest. The minimum area is 1 square metre (1 square yard) or a 2m (6') row.

You can start asparagus from seed but this adds an extra 2 years to its establishment. Most gardeners buy 2-year-old crowns, the term for the root stock. Plant in winter 10-15cm (4-6") deep in trenches with added manure and a little lime if the soil is acid. Place at least 30cm (12") apart. Fill the trench, add controlled-release fertiliser and water well. As asparagus can crop for at least 20 years, it's worth taking the time to prepare the planting site well. Of course, it must be in full sun.

Don't harvest any of the first year's spears, which will appear in spring. Instead, let them grow naturally so as to build up the plants' roots. In the second spring, you can pick spears for a month but, after that you must let the spears develop into leafy stems. In the third spring, the plants will be well established and so vigorous you can safely pick spears from the time they first appear until early summer.

To help the plants establish themselves and develop the necessary root system, in the first spring and summer after planting feed and water generously. Apply 2-3 watering cans of water to every square metre of planting once every 7-10 days if it doesn't rain, and water over with liquid or soluble fertiliser once a month. Reapply controlled-release fertiliser in early summer.

In autumn, the leaves will turn golden and in winter asparagus plants are pruned back to ground level. For white (blanched) asparagus, hill up old manure or compost 25-30cm (10-12") over the plants in late winter. For green spears, add a light covering of manure or compost and let the stems develop in sunlight.

To harvest, cut green spears when they are 15-20cm (6-8") long (or, if longer, where they snap) and before the tips open. To cut white spears, wait until the hilled spears break through the surface, push the knife into the soil about 15cm (6") and cut the stems off below the ground. Harvest every day for the periods mentioned above.

preserving the crop

| STORING | Ideally, eat asparagus the day you pick it. Otherwise, stand it upright in about 2cm of water in a glass or mug, cover with a plastic bag and store in the refrigerator. Use within a day or two. |
| FREEZING | Asparagus can be frozen after blanching (see Freezing, page 240). Do not thaw before using; drop in boiling water for about 2 minutes or until heated through. |

purple asparagus

green asparagus

white asparagus

For the table

TO PREPARE

• Like most vegetables, asparagus spears taste better if eaten the day they are harvested. Remove the woody ends of each stalk by bending the stalk near the bottom so it snaps at its natural breaking point – where the woodiness turns to crispness. If the skin towards the broken end still seems tough, it should be trimmed off with a vegetable peeler; white asparagus usually requires peeling almost to the tip.

• Asparagus can be boiled, steamed, stir-fried, cooked in the microwave or char-grilled. Whatever the method, cook for only a few minutes (or for seconds in the microwave), just until crisp/tender, still firm and bright-coloured. Because the pigment that gives purple asparagus its colour is soluble, the stalks turn green as they cook – brief cooking will minimise this.

• The traditional way of boiling asparagus was in a special tall pot with only the stems in water so that the tender tips would not overcook, but brief steaming or boiling in a wide pan such as a frying pan will give a good result.

• Cooking it in the microwave is particularly successful: arrange the stems around a plate like the spokes of a wheel, tips to the centre; flick with a few drops of water, cover with plastic wrap and cook on HIGH (100%) for 30-45 seconds, depending on quantity and the wattage of the oven. The microwave cooks fastest near the oven walls, so this method works perfectly to cook the tips less than the stems. It won't matter if they overlap.

• To char-grill, steam thicker stems for 2 minutes or microwave for 20-25 seconds, then coat lightly with cooking-oil spray and grill briefly; thin stems are oiled and grilled without pre-steaming.

TO SERVE

• For salads, use asparagus fresh or blanched. The addition of lemon juice or vinegar will change the colour of asparagus to a murky green so don't add any dressing until the last minute.

• It's traditional to serve fresh asparagus spears with rich, buttery sauces. You may like to add brown butter together with a scattering of roasted chopped hazelnuts or a strong mustard hollandaise.

• Asparagus makes ideal finger food. Wrap strips of sliced smoked salmon around single blanched spears and serve with a lemon, tarragon cream dipping sauce.

• Pour a very garlicky vinaigrette over still-warm asparagus and serve with grilled fish and baby potatoes. All you need is a little crusty bread to mop up the sauce.

• Creamed asparagus soup can be made from pureed cooked asparagus. Serve either warm or cold and topped with crisp fried prosciutto and thin slices of garlic bread.

• A softly poached egg balanced on top of several warm asparagus spears and finished with shavings of parmesan cheese makes an easy entree or light lunch.

asparagus with poached egg and hollandaise

asparagus with poached egg and hollandaise

500g (1 pound) asparagus, trimmed
2 tablespoons white vinegar
4 eggs
¼ cup (20g) shaved parmesan cheese
1 tablespoon coarsely chopped fresh dill
hollandaise
1 tablespoon white wine vinegar
2 egg yolks
200g (6½ ounces) unsalted butter, melted

1 Make hollandaise.
2 Boil, steam or microwave asparagus until tender; drain.
3 Meanwhile, half-fill a medium deep frying pan with water; bring to a simmer. Stir in vinegar. Break one egg into a cup, then slide into the pan; repeat with remaining eggs. Cook eggs, uncovered, about 2 minutes or until egg white is set and the yolk is still runny. Remove with a slotted spoon; drain on absorbent paper.
4 Serve asparagus topped with eggs, hollandaise, cheese and dill.
hollandaise Blend or process vinegar and egg yolks until smooth. With motor operating, gradually add butter in a thin, steady stream, processing until hollandaise thickens.

prep & cook time 35 minutes **serves** 4

asparagus and brie bruschetta

340g (11 ounces) trimmed asparagus spears
3 garlic cloves, sliced thinly
2 tablespoons olive oil
430g loaf turkish bread
200g (6½ ounces) brie cheese, sliced thinly
bunch fresh thyme sprigs

1 Preheat oven to 200°C/400°F.
2 Combine asparagus, garlic and half the oil in large baking dish. Roast, uncovered, 10 minutes.
3 Cut bread crossways into 6 pieces, place on oven tray; heat in oven 5 minutes.
4 Top bread with asparagus mixture, cheese and thyme. Bake about 10 minutes or until cheese melts. Drizzle with remaining oil.

prep & cook time 30 minutes **serves** 4

asparagus and brie bruschetta

Broad Beans

Today, broad beans enjoy enormous culinary popularity. They're the first beans of the season and have a delightful shape, colour and flavour. Their brilliant green colour, revealed by peeling, is irresistible and their robust and earthy flavour makes them a treat to serve. A springtime crop of broad beans requires pre-winter planning, but the sound of bees in their flowers and their elegant grey-green foliage makes broad beans one of the chief delights of the spring kitchen garden.

In the garden

Broad beans are at their most productive in spring after surviving the cold of winter. Plant in autumn to winter in most climates, but not when the soil is very cold in frost-prone areas. The plants themselves do not mind frost, but the seeds won't germinate in these conditions.

There are two varieties of broad beans: one grows 2m (6') tall and a dwarf form reaches 1m (3'). Choose a site that enjoys winter sun, dig it over, distribute blood and bone, and water well. Press the seeds 5cm (2") into pre-moistened soil 15-20cm (6-8") apart. Sow in rows running north-south for maximum exposure to the sun, or in circular clusters. Shoots will appear in about 2 weeks. Water once, then, without too much bother except weekly watering if the rain stays away, the bean plants will start to grow, but ever so slowly compared with summer crops. The plants will need support as the stems grow tall and soft and become top-heavy with beans in spring. Place a strong stake at each corner of your patch or at intervals around the cluster and attach rounds of twine. Make the first round at 30cm (12") high and another at 80cm (30") when needed. Tuck lanky stems into the enclosure. White and black flowers appear fairly soon but beans don't develop until the weather warms up towards the end of winter and bees start to visit. Tiny black beans with a flag of withered blossoms means your crop is under way, about 18-20 weeks after planting.

The bean pods can be harvested while still pliable before the beans have hardened. At this stage they can be cooked and eaten whole. Otherwise, let the beans swell in the pods before picking; carefully press the pods with your fingers to assess how large they are.

For the table

TO PREPARE

• If picked very young, broad beans can be eaten pods and all. Generally, pods are harvested later and only the podded beans are eaten. Cook in plenty of boiling water.

• Broad beans are usually popped from their leathery greyish-skins after cooking to emerge as tender, bright green kernels that are among the most delicate of vegetables. If they are to be pureed, the leathery skins are usually left on for texture and a stronger beany taste.

• Broad beans can be cooked in the microwave. Place podded beans in a microwave-safe dish with a little water, cover and cook until tender.

TO SERVE

• Broad beans are traditional partners with Mediterranean flavours, particularly tomato-based lamb dishes.

• Add cooked and peeled broad beans to casseroles at the last minute; they add flavour and great colour.

• For an easy spring salad, combine cooked, peeled broad beans and asparagus in a herbed vinaigrette.

• Gently fry onions and garlic with tarragon. Add cooked and peeled broad beans and toss gently until heated through. Serve as a side dish.

• For a broad bean dip, puree cooked, peeled broad beans with a little lemon juice, sour cream, ground cumin and lots of fresh herbs. Press plastic wrap to the surface of the dip to prevent discolouring.

Note: some people of Mediterranean origin are allergic to broad beans.

preserving the crop

STORING	Do not remove the beans from their pods until you are ready to cook them. Store broad beans in the refrigerator for up to a week. Any beans that escape your spring harvesting will be found later, dried on the plants. Store for use next season or, if not mouldy, store as dried beans.
FREEZING	If blanched, without their pods, broad beans can be frozen for up to 6 months (see Freezing, page 240).

broad bean and ricotta pasta

375g (12 ounces) orecchiette pasta
1 tablespoon olive oil
2 cups (300g) fresh shelled broad beans
1 clove garlic, crushed
½ cup (125ml) pouring cream
1 teaspoon finely grated lemon rind
2 tablespoons lemon juice
200g (6½ ounces) ricotta cheese, crumbled
½ cup coarsely chopped fresh mint

1 Cook pasta in large saucepan of boiling water until tender; drain.
2 Meanwhile, heat oil in large frying pan; cook beans and garlic until beans are just tender. Add cream, rind and juice; simmer, uncovered, until sauce thickens slightly.
3 Combine pasta, sauce, cheese and mint in large bowl.

prep & cook time 45 minutes **serves** 4
note Orecchiette is a small disc-shaped pasta, it translates literally as 'little ears'.

broad bean and ricotta pasta

char-grilled chicken with broad beans and chive butter

The bean mixture can also be served as a vegetarian dish over polenta or as a side dish to a main course.

750g (1½ pounds) broad beans, podded
1 tablespoon olive oil
1 small red onion (100g), thinly sliced
2 cloves garlic, crushed
2 medium tomatoes (380g), chopped finely
2 tablespoons finely chopped fresh flat-leaf parsley
1 tablespoon olive oil, extra
4 chicken breast fillets (800g)
60g (2 ounces) butter
2 tablespoons finely snipped fresh chives

1 Boil, steam or microwave beans until tender; cool, then remove grey skins.
2 Heat oil in medium frying pan; cook onion, covered, over low heat until very soft and starting to caramelise. Add garlic and beans; stir until heated through. Stir in tomato, and parsley; stir over low heat 5 minutes. Season to taste.
3 Heat extra oil in grill pan (or grill or barbecue). Cook chicken 5-7 minutes or until cooked through.
4 Combine butter and chives in small bowl.
5 Serve chicken on bean mixture; top with chive butter.

prep & cook time 40 minutes **serves** 4
note Bean mixture can be made a day ahead and gently reheated when required.

char-grilled chicken with broad beans and chive butter

Beetroot

Our grandmothers served beetroot, sliced and well-doused in malt vinegar, as a salad vegetable, otherwise it was seldom seen, except for the great Australian tradition that a proper hamburger had to include slices of canned beetroot along with the patty, tomato, iceberg lettuce and onion.

It wasn't until modern chefs discovered beetroot's earthy sweetness that it came into its own, served warm or cold as the perfect foil to duck, sausage, pork, hot or cold ham, corned beef, game and rich fish such as tuna and cured herring, and as a natural partner to bitter salad leaves, orange rind, sour cream, yogurt, walnuts, chives, horseradish, dill or the merest touch of a mellow vinegar such as balsamic.

The traditional red beetroot is being given a run for its money by the development of different-coloured varieties. They make interesting garden experiments and offer superior flavour. Golden beetroot, which turns from orange to yellow when cooked, and the white-fleshed 'albina vereduna' are both particularly sweet. An Italian variety, 'chioggia', has alternately reddish and white rings, like a red onion; and another variety, 'cylindra' is red and cylindrical, instead of round. This is very handy because it produces even-sized slices when cut. You may have to seek out specialist seed suppliers to find these unusual varieties.

In the garden

Beetroot grow in full sun but can survive some shade, in dappled light under a tree line or for half a day in the shadow of a fence. The soil should be prepared with decomposed manure, dug in well to break it up. Add blood and bone, pelleted poultry manure or any general fertiliser at planting time.

Seeds are knobbly clusters, like the seeds of silver beet or swiss chard, to which beetroot is closely related. Seeds can be planted from spring to early autumn in temperate and cool continental climates. It is said the sweetest bulbs are those that are exposed to the first frost of winter. In Mediterranean and subtropical gardens, plant after the hottest part of summer to prevent plants bolting to seed. In the tropics you can plant all year, though the wet season is probably risky.

Push the seed in to the depth of your first knuckle every 10cm (4") and cover them over. Water regularly and the seedlings will emerge in 2 weeks. Where 2-3 seedlings have grown from the cluster seeds, separate and transplant them into new rows or discard.

Seedlings are also available from your nursery. Plant them at suggested spacings into soil prepared as above. Regular watering will prevent the beets from becoming woody, and a spray with fish-based fertiliser or a soluble plant food every 2 weeks will supply nitrogen and all the trace elements to aid root development.

About 10 weeks after sowing, small bulbs are ready to be gathered as baby beets. If you want larger beets, leave them longer. As the beets sit on the soil surface you can assess their size without problems. Don't hill the soil over them. It's a good idea to harvest alternate beets as you need them. Those left in the row will have more space to expand. But don't be mistaken into thinking they'll last indefinitely; that tender flesh of youth can become leathery. Follow-up crops of beetroot can be planted every 4-5 weeks.

preserving the crop

STORING	Beetroot keeps for several days in the refrigerator. Never store leaves and bulbs together as the leaves cause the beets to shrivel and become soft. Beetroot with the leaves removed can be stored in a paper bag enclosed in a plastic bag in the refrigerator for about a fortnight.
FREEZING	Cooked and peeled beetroot can be chopped or sliced and frozen for up to 6 months (see Freezing, page 240). Thaw in the refrigerator and sauté in butter or oil and herbs, or serve in salads.

For the table

TO PREPARE

• Trim off leaves, leaving 2-3cm of stem attached. Do not trim the long, tapering root as this causes the colour to bleed out during cooking. Wash off any dirt.

• The leaves can be eaten, so reserve them if you wish, storing in cold water if you intend to cook them that day, or in a paper bag enclosed in a plastic bag in the fridge if you want to keep them for a day or two. They can be briefly steamed or boiled, wilted in a little oil in a frying pan or stewed with oil in a covered saucepan and used as a green vegetable or chopped for soups, stuffings, pasta sauces or salads.

• The traditional ways to cook beetroot are by boiling, baking or steaming until soft, trimming off the root and slipping off the skin after cooking. Today's chefs also char-grill wedges or small halves to retain their slightly crunchy texture.

• Beetroot can be grated raw and eaten as a crunchy salad ingredient, or heated in butter and a touch of good vinegar in a covered saucepan and served, still slightly crunchy, as a hot vegetable.

• Long-cooked beetroot, for example in a soup, may lose its bright colour and become brownish. To restore the colour, keep back a little raw or some lightly cooked beetroot, grate it and stir it in just before serving.

• Beetroot can be cooked in the microwave. Pierce the skin several times and wrap the beets individually in microwave-safe wrap and cook 20-30 minutes if large. Turn halfway through cooking.

TO SERVE

• Roasted beetroot are beautiful. Wrap individually in foil and cook with the Sunday roast. Do not peel until they are cooked.

• Roasted beetroot with a Lebanese-style garlic sauce makes a great side dish to strongly flavoured meats such as venison or rabbit.

• Beetroot makes an amazing dip. Roast without peeling, then peel, puree with a little sour cream and flavour with garlic, cumin and salt. Serve with toasted turkish bread or fresh vegetable crudités.

pickled beetroot

Use either caster or light brown sugar, and experiment with the spices to vary the flavour. You can also cook whole baby beets in this manner and the cooking time will be about 15 minutes.

6 medium beetroot (beets) (960g)
1 cup (220g) caster (superfine) sugar
4 cups (1 litre) cider vinegar
1 small cinnamon stick
8 black peppercorns
4 small dried red thai (serrano) chillies
1 teaspoon black mustard seeds

1 Trim beetroot, leaving 3cm (1¼") of the stem attached. Wash carefully. Add to a large saucepan of cold water; bring to the boil. Boil 45 minutes or until tender. Allow to cool in the cooking water, then drain, reserving ½ cup of the liquid.
2 Rub the skins off beetroot; slice or quarter beetroot and place in hot sterilised jars (see Bottling, pages 240-242).
3 Combine reserved cooking liquid, sugar, vinegar, cinnamon, peppercorns, chillies and mustard seeds in a large non-corrosive saucepan; stir over heat, without boiling, until sugar is dissolved, then bring to the boil. Pour over beetroot and seal while hot. Store in a cool, dark place for up to 6 months.

prep & cook time 1 hour 15 minutes (+ cooling)
notes Cider vinegar (apple cider vinegar) is made from fermented apples. It is available from supermarkets. Black mustard seeds, also known as brown mustard seeds, are more pungent than the white (or yellow) seeds used in most prepared mustards. They are available from supermarkets and specialty spice stores.

Spring Herbs

Throughout winter, the hardier members of the herb set will have survived to keep our food tasty. Come spring, tender perennials like chives, tarragon and vietnamese mint re-emerge and we discover self-sown seedlings of dill, basil, borage, parsley, coriander and nasturtium popping up. Most herbs grow well in pots, handy to the kitchen, but remember to feed and water them regularly.

In the garden

PARSLEY

Parsley is used by the handful both for cooking and for the 'sprinkle of chopped parsley' that adds charm to soups and salads, vegetables, scrambled eggs and omelettes, rice, buttered potatoes and many fish, meat and chicken dishes. Parsley stalks are more strongly flavoured than the leaves and are added to stocks, the cooking liquid for corned beef, and are used to infuse the milk for béchamel sauce. Parsley is available in curly-leaf or flat-leaf (also called italian or continental parsley) varieties; flat-leaf has a more concentrated flavour. Hopefully, parsley will have stayed productive through winter, in stunted form if your winter is very cool, but come the warmth of spring and longer daylight hours, the stems elongate and thicken. Parsley is a biennial plant (that is, it has a 2-year life cycle) and if you planted your parsley 2 years ago, it will probably start to seed this year. To start new supplies, sow seeds through the warm months in punnets, pots or in the ground. Soak the seeds overnight to speed up germination.

If you let parsley go to seed, in no time you'll have tall, green, flowery tops and the many seeds will settle throughout your garden and provide you with copious new plants. It's said you have to be particularly wicked to get returns of parsley, but perhaps what should be said is that you're very lucky.

CHIVES

Chives are small-growing, well-behaved members of the onion family. The grassy clumps stand 30cm (12") tall and have pink–mauve flowers in spring. Chives are equally happy in pots, garden clumps or as border plants. They like a sunny, well-drained spot but can also cope with shade. Don't attempt to grow chives in soggy conditions. They can be grown from seed or divided from a larger clump; otherwise buy a small pot from your nursery for an instant useable addition to your garden.

The soil should be richly manured. Liquid fertiliser should be given at least every month as you are growing a leafy plant. When the tips start to yellow, you know extra nourishment is needed.

As the cool weather approaches, the leaves will die down, even in subtropical gardens. Remember to mark the spot to avoid disturbing the clump during winter gardening. In spring the chives will re-emerge. They can then be lifted and divided. This strengthens cluster bulbs.

Garlic chives have strappy leaves, longer than traditional chives, and white flower clusters. The furled buds are used in Chinese stir-fries. These chives also have an excellent garlic flavour and don't scent the breath, hence their other name, 'society garlic'. They like the same conditions and grow in the same manner as normal chives.

Wild garlic, *Tulbaghia violacea*, can also be used in the same way.

preserving the crop

STORING	Herbs are best used straight from the garden, but can be wrapped in damp paper towel and stored in a vegetable storage bag in the refrigerator for several days. The flavour won't be as good so be generous when using.
FREEZING	All these spring herbs can be frozen (see Freezing, page 240). Coriander roots can also be frozen.
DRYING	Parsley, chervil and tarragon can all be dried successfully (see Drying, page 243) as can the flowers of chives and tarragon. Coriander loses its flavour when dried. Store coriander seeds in an airtight container in a cool, dark, dry place.

continental, italian
or flat-leaf parsley

curly parsley

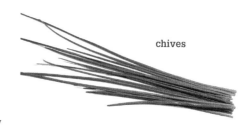
chives

CHERVIL

Chervil is a delicate, lacy herb with a fresh, slightly anise flavour. This is an unusual herb because it grows happily in shade; not deep shade, but filtered sun is preferred. It is also happy in a large pot, making it very convenient for small city gardens. In both gardens and pots, chervil needs to be kept moist.

Chervil is fern-like both in its appearance and growth. In good conditions, it will grow for about 18 months before running to flower and seed. Gather some seeds and plant immediately. (If it's the middle of winter, wait until spring.) Its leaves are fine, so harvest gently with scissors to avoid pulling out the plant accidentally.

TARRAGON

Tarragon, or *Artemesia dracunculus*, is a tender, delicately flavoured perennial sometimes called the 'King of Herbs'. French tarragon is the desirable, subtly flavoured herb, while russian tarragon has a coarser taste.

Buy a pot in spring or ask a neighbour for some newly emerging offshoots (there will be an abundance). Plant in a spot at least 1 square metre (1 square yard) in full sun in soil that has been well manured with blood and bone or a controlled-release fertiliser. Water well until established. Tarragon multiplies like mint so keep your spade handy to control its spread or confine it in a large pot.

CORIANDER

This herb is a parsley-like annual (often called chinese parsley) that prefers to burgeon when the weather is cooler (spring, autumn and even through mild winters). Coriander's worst characteristic is running to seed, particularly in summer when it sometimes bolts. Just when you've got a row of seedlings up, or planted out seedlings into a sunny spot, they suddenly change leaf shape to develop fern-like foliage and a flower on top. Save the seeds. They can be ground or used whole in cooking, or kept for future planting.

To avoid premature seeding, try planting during cooler conditions and giving large doses of high nitrogen fertiliser (soluble types are usually high in nitrogen) to encourage leafy growth rather than flowers and seeds. Snip off leaves as required. This will thicken the plant. Pull out whole plants when bunches or roots are needed. This will thin the row or cluster and allows the remaining plants to grow more robust.

Vietnamese mint, which grows all through summer and all year in frost-free areas, is a reasonable flavour substitute for coriander.

coriander

french tarragon

chervil

For the table

TO SERVE

- Toss the whole leaves of freshly harvested herbs through salads for an instant flavour boost.

- Roll a boned loin of pork or veal in chopped mixed spring herbs (tarragon, chervil, parsley and chives are all good); add some brown sugar and a few caraway seeds. Wrap tightly in plastic wrap and refrigerate overnight. Roast as normal.

- Chervil is one the four *fines herbes* (the others are parsley, tarragon and chives), the classic French herb blend, that flavours omelette aux fines herbes (herb omelette).

- *Fines herbes* is particularly good in egg dishes, sauces, salads and soups. It is also good used as a garnish or sprinkled on salads, fish, cream soups or cooked vegetables.

- Chervil is used in salads or sprinkled over vegetables. It goes well with egg, chicken and cheese dishes. Add a handful of chervil leaves to a gruyère soufflé, for instance.

- Chives are delicate, so snip them with scissors, rather than chopping with a knife, which will mince them.

- Chives can be snipped over buttered carrots or potatoes, omelettes or scrambled eggs and cream soups.

- Chives add a slight onion flavour and are great in cheese and egg dishes as well as salads and dips. The flowers are edible and look beautiful in salads.

- New tarragon growth has the most flavour. Add fresh at the end of slow-cooked dishes as it becomes bitter if cooked.

- Chopped tarragon combines with white wine vinegar, egg yolks and butter for a béarnaise sauce that is served on roast beef.

- Mix chopped tarragon leaves with soft butter, shape into a roll with plastic wrap and place in the refrigerator, ready to be sliced onto chicken, fish or vegetables.

- Soft, slender tarragon leaves have an affinity with eggs, chicken and sauces for fish.

- Tarragon is famous as a vinegar flavouring. Use a quality white wine vinegar and store for 1 month.

- Flat-leaf parsley tends to holds its flavour better and performs best in salads while curly-leaf parsley is best used as a garnish. Sprinkle gremolata (parsley, lemon rind and garlic) over rich casseroles such as lamb shanks and osso buco just before serving.

- Coriander is an incredibly useful herb because every part of the plant is edible. Its pungent aroma is magical to many. Add the chopped leaves and ground seed to guacamole. The dried seeds are used whole or ground in both sweet and savoury dishes. Add the leaves and the chopped root to stir-fries and curries.

- Spark up your nachos with a fresh coriander salsa.

- Coriander leaves are essential to hundreds of Asian, Latin American and Middle Eastern dishes; add stems to dishes during cooking to contribute their warm sage/lemon/anise flavour, and the roots are used in cooking chicken and in soups.

coriander crisps

coriander crisps

1 cup (150g) plain (all-purpose) flour
¼ cup (35g) self-raising flour
1 teaspoon ground coriander
1 teaspoon ground cumin
60g (2 ounces) butter
1 tablespoon lemon juice
¼ cup (60ml) water, approximately
1 egg white
1 tablespoon sea salt flakes

1 Preheat oven to 200°C/350°F.
2 Process flours, spices and butter until combined.
Add juice and enough of the water to make ingredients
cling together.
3 Roll dough on floured surface to 3mm thick; cut into
triangles. Place on oiled oven trays. Brush with egg white;
sprinkle with salt.
4 Bake about 10 minutes or until golden and crisp. Cool
on wire racks.

prep & cook time 20 minutes **serves** 6-8
note Crisps can be stored in an airtight container
for up to 2 weeks.

herb dip

125g (4 ounces) cream cheese, chopped
½ cup (125g) sour cream
2 cloves garlic, crushed
1 tablespoon finely chopped fresh parsley
1 tablespoon finely chopped fresh tarragon
1 tablespoon finely chopped fresh chervil
1 tablespoon finely snipped fresh chives

tomato salsa

2 medium tomatoes (380g), chopped finely
½ small red onion (50g), chopped finely
1 fresh small red thai (serrano) chilli, chopped finely
½ teaspoon ground coriander seed
1 tablespoon finely chopped fresh coriander leaves
  (cilantro)

1 Combine ingredients for herb dip in small bowl;
mix well. Season to taste. Cover, refrigerate 2 hours;
remove from refrigerator 10 minutes before serving.
2 Combine ingredients for tomato salsa in small bowl.
3 Serve with coriander crisps (see opposite).

prep time 10 minutes (+ refrigeration) **serves** 6-8
notes Herb dip can be made up to a day ahead. Store,
covered, in the refrigerator.
Tomato salsa is best made close to serving.

top: herb dip; front: tomato salsa

summer

Summer garden diary

Water becomes scarce and your garden will almost certainly need your help to avoid drying out. Maintain a schedule of regular watering. Water in the cool of the day (early morning or late afternoon) to minimise evaporation and leaf burn.

Don't let fruit or vegies fall and lie on the ground – this encourages pests.

Install a watering system, especially if you are planning a long holiday. Pots, in particular, dry out very quickly so need careful and constant moisture monitoring.

The heat is thick around us; it slows us down. The pace of living becomes languid, less urgent. A shady verandah invites us to sit, sip a long cool drink, to read, to sleep. We plan expeditions to the nearest watering hole. Long afternoon shadows are cast across the lawn. We come home from the beach sunburned and tired. Mad dogs and Englishmen ... it's just too hot to do anything.

Not so in the garden. Summer gardens don't slow down; they speed up. Everything grows like mad; leaves develop, fruits ripen overnight, vines unfurl before your eyes. The garden threatens to take over. Insects and diseases multiply to take advantage of the bounty.

Spread mulch around beds to retain soil moisture and protect roots. Plant 'thirsty' plants together to make thorough watering easier. Irrigate with furrows between plants so that water goes directly to the roots. Avoid growing those plants that you find too demanding for your cultivating conditions. Remember to take care of yourself. Don't work in the middle of the day and always wear protection against the sun, even in the mornings and evenings. Do only the essential maintenance tasks and leave the heavy garden jobs for autumn or winter.

pick now	*plant now*
most gardens artichokes, beans, beetroot, cabbage, capsicums, carrots, chillies, cucumbers, eggplant, leeks, lettuce, potatoes, radish, silver beet, squash, sweet corn, tomato, wombok, zucchini	most gardens basil, beans, cabbage, lettuce, parsley, potatoes, silver beet
cool gardens broad beans	cool gardens coriander, peas
subtropical gardens salad crops, summer vegetables, passionfruit	subtropical gardens corn, cucumber, tomatoes, zucchini
tropical gardens ginger, mangoes, water chestnuts, mildew-resistant vegetables grown in pots protected from the 'wet'	late-summer crops for winter asian greens, broccoli, cabbage, cauliflower, leeks, onions

All your careful spring preparations pay dividends as summer fruits and vegetables burgeon around you.

Most important of all, gather your harvest when it's at its peak. Enjoy the summertime treasures you and your garden have produced.

Tomatoes

What's a summer vegetable garden without tomatoes? The first ripe tomato of the season is a guaranteed thrill for every gardener. It will probably be only enough for a single sandwich or perhaps a salad, but it will taste like ambrosia. What flavour! What perfume! As summer progresses, and your tomatoes swing into full production, you'll harvest armfuls each evening. And you'll have the opposite situation of what do you do with the sheer volume? Luckily, tomatoes are easy to preserve, so you'll be able to capture this rich, ripe aroma of summer. That is, until next summer when you once again await that first tomato.

Round tomatoes are the kind seen most often at the greengrocer's. They have been developed as the perfect tomato from the trade's point of view: brightly coloured, uniform in shape, thick-skinned so that they can be transported without damage. From the customer's point of view, they're a mixed lot, sometimes good if they have truly been, as the sign may proudly say, vine-ripened, but often disappointing.

Oxheart tomatoes are an old-fashioned tomato. They are thin-skinned and don't keep well, and they don't look thrilling, being pink rather than red and often misshapen, but, in their natural season, they're juicy and flavoursome.

Egg or plum tomatoes are less juicy and more fleshy than others so they are best for cooking and drying. Roma is the best-known variety and is available either full-sized or miniature.

Cherry tomatoes are miniature varieties. They are decorative and usually well-flavoured, and are used both raw and lightly grilled, fried or roasted. Teardrop-shaped miniatures, usually yellow teardrop, are delicately sweet and sharp, and red or yellow grape tomatoes are smaller again than cherry ones.

Green tomatoes are considered a separate vegetable from ripe ones and are valued for their tartness and crunchy texture. They are grilled, baked, used in Indian and Mediterranean vegetable dishes and relishes and, for the famous dish of the American south, dipped in cornmeal and fried in bacon fat.

Kumatoes are a 'black' tomato variety, originally from the Galapagos Islands, with striking, nearly-black skin and dark-patched pink flesh.

Dried tomatoes may be completely dried to make them shrivelled, dark and chewy with a strong, savoury taste that is different from fresh tomatoes, or semi-dried to make them shrivelled but still tender, red and tasting like fresh tomatoes, but more concentrated. Drying can be done in the sun over two or three days (bringing them in each evening) or in a low oven over 8-10 hours (see Drying, pages 65, 243).

In the garden

Tomatoes need well-drained soil with plenty of manure or compost dug in before planting. They also require the complete fertiliser of your choice, be it chemical or organic, to really develop well.

Tomatoes generally require full sun, but in hot climates with daily temperatures over 35°C (95°F) the fruit can get sunburnt without some shade after midday. Tomatoes cannot stand frost.

Nurseries sell seedlings, and grafted plants are available with disease-resistant rootstock. You can also buy seeds to raise in pots or trays in warm, frost-free gardens or under glass or house protection in cold zones while frosts continue and the soil is cold. Seedlings take about 6 weeks to mature to transplantable size. If they develop too fast and the conditions aren't yet right, move the

preserving the crop

STORING	Tomatoes are best stored at room temperature for up to a week. They can also be stored in the refrigerator for 3-4 weeks.
FREEZING	Tomatoes can be frozen, but they won't hold their shape when thawed, making them useful only in cooked dishes. The best way to freeze tomatoes is to peel, seed, chop and pack the pulp into small containers (see Freezing, page 240). Stir in chopped fresh basil for dishes that call for fresh herbs. Freeze for 6-8 months.
DRYING	For drying advice, see page 65; also see Drying, page 243.

cherry tomatoes

kumato

egg, roma or
plum tomatoes

seedlings to 15-20cm (6-8") pots until the garden is ready. Small fruiters produce grape-like clusters in a range of shapes and colours. These usually show more resistance to fruit-fly and the 'bush' forms, that is, those that don't grow tall and don't need staking, are the best for growing in pots. They will need a rich potting mix and regular watering.

You'll also find many volunteer seedlings will appear from last season's dropped fruit or compost. Transplant them if needed but remove them if you want to concentrate on specific varieties.

Plant your seedlings in a prepared sunny position. Space them about 1m (3') apart, but if space is limited they can be spaced at 50-60cm (20-24") intervals when staked. Hammer in strong stakes at planting time to avoid disturbing the roots later. Close planting requires regular watering and fertilising. Tomatoes develop large root systems, so give them as much space as you can. Make furrows between the plants so the roots can be easily soaked. Avoid overhead hosing as it encourages leaf viruses and diseases. A good soaking every couple of days will keep your tomatoes growing well.

Plants can be let to ramble naturally (they have a wide spread) or controlled on stakes by removing the side growths (from leaf axils) when they are about 3cm (1") long. These can be planted in pots or in another part of the garden for a second crop. Don't remove the differently shaped flower spikes (you'll see the buds). Keep tying the plants to the stakes in loose figure-of-eight ties and break off the tip to halt growth when it reaches the top of the stake.

The flower stems will start to appear in 6-12 weeks and the fruit will form if there is good air movement to distribute the pollen and night temperatures are over 10°C (50°F). The tastiest fruit are those that ripen on the plant. Tomatoes can be grown under glass if conditions are too cool, but buy appropriate varieties and make sure there is good ventilation.

PESTS AND DISEASES

If fruit-fly is a problem, use non-toxic, bio-insecticides but be sure to read and follow the directions. Some gardeners wrap paper bags around the ripening fruit, but to be effective, the bags must be in place when the fruit is still green. Harvesting tomatoes early while still green can also reduce fruit-fly strike but flavour will suffer. Pyrethrum-based sprays are a safe treatment for thrips, white fly and tomato caterpillar. There are also proprietary chemical treatments for the many fungal blights that tomatoes are heir to, but Bordeaux spray may be an alternative. Drop any infected or diseased fruit in hot water, burn it or seal in plastic bags to bake in the sun. Don't compost any fruit infected by fungal blights as the spores don't die in the process.

Lastly, don't be put off by these dire warnings. Most gardeners raise terrific crops, and most tomato plants produce something, even in dire straits.

green tomatoes

oxheart tomatoes

vine-ripened tomatoes

For the table

TO PREPARE

• For the best taste, leave tomatoes on the vine for as long as possible to allow their flavour to fully develop. When picked, store at room temperature. They will be much sweeter than those stored in the refrigerator as cold dulls their flavour. Tomatoes can last up to a week at room temperature in hot weather and 3-4 weeks in the refrigerator.

TO SERVE

• Serve freshly sliced tomatoes with a scattering of shredded fresh mint, ground black pepper and a drizzle of olive oil as an accompaniment to easy summer dinners such as grilled fish, barbecued meats or chicken.

• Cherry tomatoes wrapped in long thin slices of lebanese cucumber, secured with a toothpick and served with pesto-flavoured mayonnaise make great summer finger food.

• For a quick lunch, toss halved teardrop and cherry tomatoes in a vinaigrette dressing. Serve on warm damper with rocket and some strong cheddar cheese.

• A tip for school lunches – for non-soggy sandwiches, hold the tomato with the stem end up and slice through it to the base, not across the tomato.

DRYING TOMATOES

There are two methods: oven-drying and sun-drying. For either method, 'roma', or egg tomatoes, and cherry tomatoes have less juice and are therefore easier to dry (see also Drying, page 243).

Sun-drying needs good sun and low moisture. Place halved tomatoes, cut-side up, on wire racks in a deep baking dish and place in the sunniest possible position. Dry fresh thyme or oregano at the same time to add as extra flavour when bottling. Drying should take 3-4 days, the fruit becoming darker the longer it is dried. Bring indoors each night to avoid dew.

Oven-drying is faster. Prepare tomatoes on racks in oven trays, as above. Scatter thinly sliced cloves of garlic and oregano sprigs over the top. Cook in a very slow oven (100°C/210°F) for about 30 minutes, remove the oregano if completely dry and continue cooking tomatoes for another hour, then remove the garlic if crisp and dry. Reserve both herbs and garlic. Continue cooking tomato for a total of about 8 hours (5 hours for cherry tomatoes) or until they are quite dry (turn them several times while drying).

Pack tomato into hot sterilised jars (see Bottling, pages 240-242), adding the dried garlic and oregano; completely cover with warmed, good-quality olive oil. Leave about 1cm (½") between the lid and the top of the oil. Store in a dark, cool, dry place for up to 8 months. Drain before using, but keep the oil for cooking as it will add a boost of tomato flavour.

Semi oven-dried tomatoes are cooked for 2 hours only. They are delicious tossed through salads with olives and balsamic vinegar. They have a much shorter shelf-life – about 5 days if stored, covered, in a little olive oil, in the refrigerator.

simple tomato sauce

simple tomato sauce

⅓ cup (80ml) olive oil
4 small onions (320g), chopped finely
20 medium tomatoes (4kg)
8 cloves garlic, crushed
⅔ cup finely chopped fresh basil

1 Heat oil in large saucepan, add onions; cook, covered, over low heat, 20 minutes, stirring occasionally.
2 Meanwhile peel, seed and chop the tomatoes.
3 Add garlic to pan; cook, stirring occasionally, 5 minutes. Add tomatoes; bring to the boil. Reduce heat; simmer, uncovered, about 1½ hours or until mixture is the consistency of pasta sauce. Stir in basil; cook, stirring occasionally, 10 minutes then season to taste.
4 Pour sauce into freezer containers leaving 1-2cm (½-1") above sauce for expansion. Cover, cool in refrigerator, then freeze for up to 6 months or store in the refrigerator for up to 5 days.

prep & cook time 2 hours 30 minutes
makes about 7 cups

tomato bruschetta

cooking-oil spray
8 thick slices sourdough bread (200g)
400g (12½ ounces) mixed tomatoes, sliced
500g (1 pound) mozzarella cheese, torn
⅓ cup (80ml) olive oil
2 tablespoons coarsely chopped fresh basil
2 teaspoons finely chopped fresh chervil
2 teaspoons fresh tarragon leaves
1 tablespoon finely grated parmesan cheese
small fresh basil leaves, to serve

1 Spray bread slices with oil; toast, both sides, in grill pan. Top toasts with tomato and mozzarella; drizzle with combined oil and herbs.
2 Sprinkle bruschetta with parmesan; season and top with extra basil leaves to serve.

prep & cook time 15 minutes **serves** 4

tomato bruschetta

Beans

Come summer the good vegetable garden is full of beans, in both senses. The garden comes alive with summertime produce, and among the easiest to grow and most delightful of all garden crops is the bean family. Beans come in all shapes, colours and sizes; they grow anywhere in the sun; are perfect in small spaces and, best of all, are great to eat.

Green or french beans come in several varieties which differ only slightly in shape. Almost all have been bred to be stringless, but always check by nipping off an end with a thumbnail and test whether you can pull down a string; if you can, string each bean on both sides.

Baby beans are simply green beans picked very young for their beautifully fresh taste and tenderness.

Yellow beans, also known as wax beans, are a delicate yellow colour with a milder flavour than green beans.

Snake beans, also known as yard-long beans, are in peak supply in summer and autumn though their season may stretch for longer than this. They have a slightly stronger taste than ordinary green beans but are interchangeable with them in recipes.

Roman beans, also known as continental beans, are in season from later summer into winter. They are flat and a paler green than ordinary green beans, with the seeds giving the edge of the pod a wavy appearance. Their flavour is robust and they usually need stringing.

Runner beans, also known as flat beans, are similar to ordinary green beans but are flatter and coarser unless picked young.

Borlotti beans, whose peak season is autumn, have pink-streaked pods and seeds. They are always podded and only the seeds cooked; they lose their pink streaks in the cooking process. Mealy in texture, they take much longer than green beans to become tender.

In the garden

Beans need well-manured and lightly limed soils and a frost-free summer. Plant seeds when the soil has warmed up and frosts have finished; add a complete garden fertiliser. Beans also need sun and protection from wind. Push the seeds down to your second knuckle into pre-moistened soil, or make a 3cm (1¼") deep furrow and drop them in 10-15cm (4-6") apart. Cover and they will emerge in about a week. A layer of compost, lucerne hay or leaf mulch will protect the roots, maintain soil moisture and suppress weeds. Beans require regular watering once the pods start to develop or they'll grow misshapen and stained.

Pick regularly when the pods are thin and the beans are tiny or fully formed. Detach the pods gently, preferably with scissors to avoid snapping the stems. Should you miss some and the pods become wavy with enlarged seeds, pick and shell them and cook the seeds fresh. They take about 20 minutes to soften and can be served on their own, added to sauces or served with whole beans. After a few months the leaves will crinkle, lose colour and drop off. Cut off stems 10cm (4") above the soil and add all stem and leaf matter to the compost. Collect missed dried bean pods for next season's planting. Dig in the roots as they contain nitrogen.

You can also leave beans to dry on the vine until straw-coloured. Finish drying them under cover, then pod and store in an airtight container. While most bean varieties have white seeds, borlotti develop white and pink-streaked seeds, purple beans have pale green seeds and many climbers have brown seeds. Dried beans need to be soaked before cooking.

Annual beans

These are planted each spring. They grow, flower and fruit through summer and die down when the weather cools. Climbers will happily twist their way 2-3m (7-10')

preserving the crop

STORING	Beans are best picked as close to serving as possible. They can be stored in the refrigerator for a day or so, but never in plastic as they go mouldy rapidly.
FREEZING	All beans are suitable to freeze for up to 6 months. Blanch before freezing (see Freezing, page 240). Cook borlotti beans before freezing. Do not thaw beans before use. If adding to cooked dishes, add in the final stages.

borlotti beans

snake beans

yellow beans

skyward over fences and walls, around lattice, stakes, tripods, netting, even wander up and over tall flowers and shrubs. Tripods can also be used in large pots if space is limited. Dwarf beans grow to 50cm (20") tall. They form bushes, don't require support, and are good as borders. They are, however, not as productive as the climbing varieties.

Runner beans

These are perennial beans and are best suited to areas where summers are cool. Their other name is 'seven-year beans' as they reshoot in spring for a number of years. They won't form pods where summers are always hot. Pick the pods when only 15cm (6") long and before the seeds have swollen. If left on the vine, they become tough and the plant doesn't produce extra flowers and beans. Both annual and runner beans come in all shapes, sizes and colours. Purple or yellow-podded types are available as well as red-, purple- or pink-flowered forms. Some pods are flat and others are rounded; some have strings and others are stringless; some are short at about 12cm (5") long while others, such as snake beans, reach 50cm (20"). The beans within can be the usual green, yellow, purple or streaked with red.

PESTS AND DISEASES

White flies are a common pest. They suck the plant juices and weaken them, and can be seen hovering when the leaves are disturbed. Spray with non-toxic soap sprays or use one of the alternative treatments given on page 17. Leaf abnormalities include halo blight (halo spots on pale leaves) which is death to the plant (burn or seal leaves in plastic bags to dispose), and rust spots and powdery mildew, both of which can be treated with proprietary fungicidal sprays or bicarbonate of soda spray (see page 17).

For the table

TO PREPARE

• Green beans and yellow beans can be cooked whole or sliced, snake beans need to be cut into shorter lengths and roman beans may need stringing. Borlotti beans are always shelled and only the seeds are cooked; mealy in texture, they take about 30 minutes to become tender.

• Like all green vegetables, beans should be cooked in plenty of lightly salted, boiling water with the lid off so that volatile vegetable acids leached into the water will be driven off, as otherwise they will change the beans' bright colour to a sad brownish green. Beans should be cooked only until they are tender but still quite firm. For salads, remove early and cool in iced water.

• Microwave beans in a microwave-safe dish with a tablespoon of water, for 3-5 minutes on HIGH (100%).

• Children enjoy snacking on beans fresh from the garden. Asking them to pick the beans is one way of making sure they eat their greens.

TO SERVE

• Toasted nuts make the perfect accompaniment to any bean. Toss beans in a little brown butter and add a sprinkling of nuts.

• Try beans with chopped basil and garlic with a squeeze of lemon juice – added at the last minute as lemon juice will discolour the beans.

• Combine beans with a tarragon-flavoured vinaigrette and serve warm or at room temperature.

• Borlotti beans and tomatoes seem to be made for each other. Simmer them in the Simple Tomato Sauce recipe (page 66) for a great vegetarian treat. Pan-fried pancetta can be added for meat-eaters.

salade niçoise

200g (6½ ounces) baby green beans, trimmed
500g (1 pound) whole baby new potatoes
2 tablespoons olive oil
1 tablespoon lemon juice
2 tablespoons white wine vinegar
4 medium tomatoes (600g), cut into wedges
4 hard-boiled eggs, quartered
425g (13½ ounces) canned tuna in springwater, drained, flaked
½ cup (80g) rinsed, drained caperberries
½ cup (60g) seeded small black olives
¼ cup firmly packed fresh flat-leaf parsley leaves

1 Boil, steam or microwave beans and potatoes, separately, until tender; drain. Rinse under cold water; drain. Cool, then halve the potatoes.
2 Whisk oil, juice and vinegar in large bowl; add beans, cooled potatoes and remaining ingredients, mix gently.

prep & cook time 30 minutes **serves** 4
note Caperberries are the fruit formed after the caper buds have flowered; caperberries are pickled, usually with stalks intact. Available from delicatessens and some larger supermarkets.

salade niçoise

prosciutto-wrapped bean bundles

prosciutto-wrapped bean bundles

200g (6½ ounces) green beans, trimmed
200g (6½ ounces) yellow beans, trimmed
8 slices prosciutto (90g)
60g (2 ounces) butter
1 tablespoon rinsed, drained baby capers
1 tablespoon lemon juice
⅓ cup coarsely chopped fresh flat-leaf parsley

1 Cook beans in medium saucepan of boiling water until just tender. Rinse under cold water; drain. Divide beans into eight equal bundles.
2 Top one slice of prosciutto with one bean bundle. Wrap prosciutto over beans; continue rolling to enclose beans tightly. Repeat with remaining prosciutto and beans.
3 Cook bean bundles in heated oiled large frying pan until prosciutto is crisp. Remove from pan; cover to keep warm.
4 Melt butter in same pan; cook capers, stirring, 1 minute. Stir in juice.
5 Serve bundles drizzled with caper mixture and sprinkle with parsley.

prep & cook time 30 minutes **serves** 8
notes Capers are the grey-green buds of a warm climate shrub. Sold dried and salted or pickled in a vinegar brine, from delicatessens and major supermarkets.
Prosciutto is a cured, air-dried, pressed ham; usually sold thinly sliced from delicatessens and major supermarkets.

Cucumber

Cucumbers belong to a large extended family, the cucurbits, which includes the warm-season wanderers: cucumbers, squash, zucchinis (or courgettes), marrows, pumpkins and melons. Like any worthwhile gathering of relatives, the family also includes some diverting members such as loofahs for the bath and gourds for decoration.

Telegraph or continental cucumbers are long and narrow with thick skin and are less juicy than other varieties.
Green or green ridge cucumbers are thick-skinned and long with large seeds that can be bitter, so are often removed.
Apple or white cucumbers may be longish or round and have large seeds, which may be removed before eating, if preferred. They are mild and juicy and many people feel they are more digestible than other cucumbers.
Lebanese cucumbers have thin, tender skins and small, soft seeds. They can be eaten peeled, partly peeled to give green and white stripes, or unpeeled. They are sweet and juicy; the seeds do not need to be removed.
Baby lebanese cucumbers, very tender with almost no seeds, are sold as qukes.
Gherkins or pickling cucumbers are hard with tough, knobbly skins. Small ones are pickled whole, large ones are cut into chunks for pickling.

In the garden

Cucumbers are a true summer crop: they demand full sun and are killed by frosts. They also demand soil rich in organic matter (manure, compost, decomposed leaf litter). The more, the better. Add lime or dolomite to reduce acidity and a complete garden fertiliser. In mild zones, two crops are possible by planting in both late winter and mid-to-late summer.
Shape the soil into mounds 50cm (20") apart, creating a furrow around each to allow water to reach the roots easily. Push 3-4 seeds into the mounds just below the surface. For bush or compact varieties, halve this distance or plant them in pots 30-50cm (12-20") wide and deep and packed with a rich potting mix.
Seedlings will break through in a week or so, depending on the temperature of the soil. Reduce to the healthiest 2 plants per mound once the leaves have started to form. Turn the vines to grow in opposite directions. If growing indoors, grow pairs of seedlings in egg cartons or grow-pots so they can be planted later directly into the soil without disturbing the roots.
To save space, train cucumber vines up netting, lattice, wire or tripods where their tendrils support them. Another space-saving technique is to cut off the stem after several fruit have formed. Side shoots will form and flower.
Keep cucumbers very well watered while flowering and fruiting. Each plant carries both male and female flowers. Male flowers have a prominent pollen-laden stamen in the centre. Females carry a tiny embryonic fruit behind each flower, the centre of which is rounded. In summer there are more male flowers than female; in spring and autumn there's an equality of sexes. Bees carry the pollen between the flowers, but if bees are in short supply, brush the pollen from a male flower onto several female flowers. Cucumbers are best picked when small when their skins are soft and the flesh is juicy. Pick early and often and more fruit will be produced.

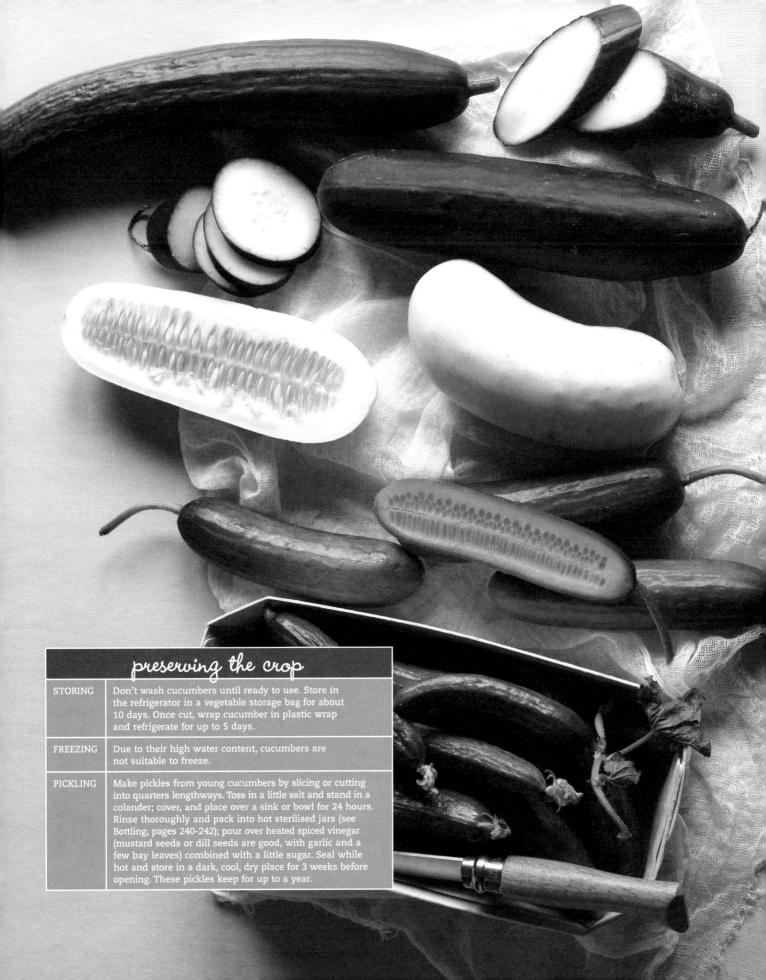

preserving the crop

STORING	Don't wash cucumbers until ready to use. Store in the refrigerator in a vegetable storage bag for about 10 days. Once cut, wrap cucumber in plastic wrap and refrigerate for up to 5 days.
FREEZING	Due to their high water content, cucumbers are not suitable to freeze.
PICKLING	Make pickles from young cucumbers by slicing or cutting into quarters lengthways. Toss in a little salt and stand in a colander; cover, and place over a sink or bowl for 24 hours. Rinse thoroughly and pack into hot sterilised jars (see Bottling, pages 240-242); pour over heated spiced vinegar (mustard seeds or dill seeds are good, with garlic and a few bay leaves) combined with a little sugar. Seal while hot and store in a dark, cool, dry place for 3 weeks before opening. These pickles keep for up to a year.

green cucumber

lebanese cucumber

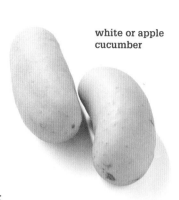

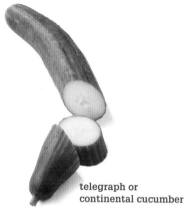
white or apple cucumber

telegraph or continental cucumber

PESTS AND DISEASES

Cucumbers can be stricken by downy mildew that discolours and eventually kills the leaves. It usually appears at the end of summer and signals the end of the productive season. Proprietary sprays are available and alternative treatments (see page 17) can be used. Do not compost the diseased leaves but burn or wrap them up before putting into the garbage.

Damping off is a condition where the stems of seedlings rot and the plants topple over. To combat it, do not plant the seedlings too deeply, make sure all organic matter is well rotted and don't overwater in the early stages. Leaves are often skeletonised by the larvae of the 28-spotted orange and black ladybird that grazes on the under-surface. These immature ladybirds are greenish-yellow with black spines and just over 0.5cm (¼") long. Crush them by hand or use a food-safe spray if there are fruit and bees about.

For the table

TO PREPARE

• There's no need to peel cucumbers if they are picked young. If left longer, you can either peel them or run the tines of a fork along their length, breaking the skin as you go.

• To crisp ageing cucumbers, cut into thick slices, sprinkle with salt, place in a colander over a sink or large bowl; add some ice-cubes and cover. Stand for about an hour; rinse thoroughly in cold water and pat dry.

TO SERVE

• Sauté cucumber in butter and add a sprinkle of green onions or chives.

• Cucumber cups filled with prawns in a Thai peanut sauce are a refreshing starter.

• Make a warm or cold soup from pureed cucumber, well-flavoured chicken stock and a little cream. Add dill to garnish.

• The traditional cucumber sandwich is a must at all tea parties. They should be made on fresh bread (white or brown) using butter, not margarine. And, as all good hostesses know, the crusts should be removed.

• Wrap smoked ocean trout or salmon around cucumber sticks with a thin spread of wasabi for Japanese-style finger food.

• Finely sliced cucumber tossed with mirin, chopped fresh dill and some horseradish cream makes a wonderful bed for char-grilled fish steaks.

• Make fresh Vietnamese spring rolls from matchstick-thin slices of cucumber, daikon, red capsicum and carrots.

• Combine with soaked rice noodles and snow pea sprouts and wrap in rice paper rounds. Serve with a light soy and sesame oil dipping sauce. You can add grilled chicken, fresh prawns or chunks of rare roast beef if desired.

• Cucumbers are 95 per cent water, so are refreshing in salads. Use a vegetable peeler to shave long thin strips from a couple of carrots; place in a bowl with a thinly sliced cucumber, a couple of large handfuls of bean sprouts and some finely chopped fresh coriander. Toss with a lemon vinaigrette.

• Tzatziki is the traditional cucumber and yogurt dip from Greece. Combine yogurt, grated cucumber, a crushed garlic clove, a squeeze of lemon juice and some fresh mint in a bowl. This goes well with most meat dishes.

chicken and cucumber salad

chicken and cucumber salad

200g (6½ ounces) chicken breast fillet, sliced thinly
1 clove garlic, crushed
1 tablespoon lemon juice
1 teaspoon finely chopped fresh oregano
¼ teaspoon sweet paprika
2 slices wholemeal lavash bread (120g)
cooking-oil spray
cucumber salad
1 telegraph cucumber (400g), halved lengthways,
    sliced thinly
1 large green capsicum (bell pepper) (350g), sliced thinly
4 medium egg (plum) tomatoes (300g), seeded,
    sliced thinly
1 tablespoon coarsely chopped fresh dill
1 tablespoon coarsely chopped fresh oregano
¼ cup (60ml) white wine vinegar
2 teaspoons white sugar

1 Combine chicken, garlic, juice, oregano and paprika
in medium bowl. Cover; refrigerate 30 minutes.
2 Toast bread; break into large pieces.
3 Spray heated medium frying pan with cooking-oil;
cook chicken in pan until cooked through.
4 Combine ingredients for cucumber salad in large bowl.
Add chicken and bread to salad; toss gently.

prep & cook time 25 minutes (+ refrigeration) **serves** 4

chilled yogurt, cucumber and mint soup

3 medium green cucumbers (510g), peeled,
    grated coarsely
1 clove garlic, quartered
1 tablespoon lemon juice
1 tablespoon coarsely chopped fresh mint
500g (1 pound) greek-style yogurt

1 Place cucumber in sieve over medium bowl. Cover;
refrigerate 3 hours or overnight.
2 Reserve cucumber liquid in bowl; squeeze excess
liquid from cucumber.
3 Blend or process cucumber, garlic, juice and mint
until mixture is smooth; transfer to large bowl. Stir in
yogurt then add reserved cucumber liquid, a little at
a time, stirring, until soup is of desired consistency.
4 Divide soup among glasses; top with mint. Serve
with toasted turkish bread, if you like.

prep time 10 minutes (+ refrigeration) **serves** 4

chilled yogurt, cucumber and mint soup

Salad Greens & Edible Flowers

No more does a salad consist of a lettuce leaf and a slice of tomato, and nor is it a forgotten side dish. Today's salads are sophisticated combinations of leaf, colour, flower, shape and texture. Add an exotic dressing and tasty treats are yours – in both summer and winter. Delicious to eat, salad greens make glorious decorative additions to the edible garden. Grow them in pots, as borders and edges, or among the flower beds. And, while a bed of lettuce makes an excellent winter crop in subtropical and tropical gardens, their delicate leaves won't survive frosts.

Iceberg lettuce has stiff, crunchy, pale leaves that are good for shredding, serving in wedges with a creamy dressing, using as cups for fillings such as prawns or chicken salad, and for sang choy bow, the delightful Asian dish of savoury minced pork in a lettuce-leaf cup.

Cos lettuce is a robust, strong-flavoured long lettuce that stands up well to heavy dressings and other substantial ingredients such as eggs, fish or bacon. Regular cos have a lot of wastage because the outside leaves are coarse, but baby cos have little wastage.

Butter lettuce is a soft-leaf lettuce that forms a loose heart. Its mild-tasting light-green leaves are an attractive background in both looks and flavour for fresh herbs.

Mignonette is a type of butter lettuce, but with green and reddish/bronze leaves.

Oak leaf lettuce has loose, soft, ruffled green or red-flushed leaves that look lovely with other leaves in a tossed salad. It is often described as a cut-and-come-again lettuce because you can take leaves as you need them without affecting the plant.

Coral lettuce is named for its tightly crinkled leaves. It comes in green or red-flushed varieties. It is a soft-leafed lettuce, but its frizzy mouth-feel makes it seem less tender than other soft lettuce.

Rocket is also known as arugula and is available both wild and cultivated, and as very young or baby rocket. Its flavour has been described as roast beef with a peppery tang. Wild rocket is the hottest, cultivated rocket is less peppery because it was grown more quickly and baby rocket is the mildest.

Chicory is a family of bitter-leafed plants including two closely related plant groups of culinary interest whose common names, chicory and endive, have come to be so much interchanged that the same plant may be known as chicory in one country and as endive in another. Three plants, radicchio, witlof and curly endive, are all members of the chicory family, but only curly endive belongs to the endivia branch of the family and is therefore botanically classed as an endive. Its flat-leafed variety is called endive in Britain, chicory in Australia, escarole in America and chicorée scarole in France.

Curly endive, also called frisée for its loose tangle of frizzy leaves, is available in full-size and baby form. It is a bitter green, though only mildly so in the tender baby leaves, which are usually sold as part of the baby-leaf mixture called mesclun.

Witlof, also called belgian endive, is a long, slender plant with crunchy, tightly furled leaves. It tastes mild and fresh with a touch of the characteristic bitterness of the chicory family, stronger in the red-tipped variety than in the pale green. It is grown in the dark to keep it white and to minimise bitterness.

Radicchio is a sturdy chicory that comes in numerous varieties, some with red and green leaves and some with red and white leaves. The different kinds are often called after their places of origin, such as round-headed 'verona' and elongated 'treviso'.

Mizuna, also called mitsuba, is a leafy Japanese herb with a crisp, aromatic flavour, used in salads, sandwiches, soups and savoury custards, and also as a garnish.

preserving the crop

STORING	Salad leaves and edible flowers are best picked as you need them – they keep much better in the garden. If you have to store them, wash salad leaves, not flowers, thoroughly in cold water, wrap in a damp clean tea towel and keep in the refrigerator for about 5 days at the most. Vegetable storage bags and lettuce keepers will extend their refrigerator life.
FREEZING	Salad leaves and edible flowers can't be frozen due to their high water content. The thawed-out sludge is of no use to anyone.
DRYING	Edible flowers can be dried (see Drying, page 243) but they will lose their flavour and colour, so use instead for pot pourri or non-culinary purposes.

rocket

baby cos lettuce

baby endive

Lamb's tongue, also called lamb's lettuce, mâche and corn salad, has small, tender, velvety leaves. It is sold in punnets and is available from autumn into spring.

Cress The tiny cress seedlings that are sold mixed with mustard seedlings in punnets are a cultivated variety known to growers as garden cress. Both kinds of seedlings, which are related, belong to hot-flavoured families, but the effect is minimal in these baby plants. Mustard and cress are snipped over salads, used as a garnish and go into egg and cress sandwiches, which rate along with cucumber sandwiches as a classic offering at a proper English afternoon tea (which the English never call afternoon tea, but simply tea).

Watercress grows in clear water. It is a member of the same family as mustard and has the hot flavour characteristic of the family, though watercress tastes fresh and peppery rather than mustardy. The watercress sold in shops is cultivated and is less hot than wild watercress because it has been grown more quickly.

In the garden

Except in the coldest areas, lettuces can be grown year-round, but it's important to choose varieties that are suitable for the season in which they'll grow. Severe frosts will ruin the leaves of summer varieties planted out of season and summer heat will cause cool-season lettuces to bolt to seed and become bitter too early. To prevent this, select varieties that can cope with warm weather. Your local nursery will be able to advise. Lettuces must grow fast. They need rich, well-prepared soil. Spread 10cm (4") layer of chicken manure over a sunny, well-drained site a month before planting and cover with another layer of leaf mould, mushroom or well-matured garden compost. Dig all this into the soil

at the end of the month and rake level and smooth. Sprinkle seeds thinly over the surface and rough up the soil to distribute, or sow thinly in 1cm-deep (½") furrows made in the prepared soil. If planting in a seedling tray, cover with 0.5cm (¼") of seed-raising mixture or sand. Water lightly and the seeds will sprout in a week or less. Lettuce seeds will not germinate when the soil is over 30°C (85°F).

Thin tray-raised seedlings to 20-30cm (8-12") apart. Transplant these or purchased seedlings into the garden at the same spacings when their true leaves form. This is best done in the cool of the day when the sun has lowered. Water lightly but thoroughly.

Mulch well to keep weeds down and protect roots, but leave the stems clear to prevent fungal stem rot. Lettuce needs regular watering and nitrogen-rich liquid fertiliser every 2 weeks. Lettuce can be grown in a heated glasshouse during winter in frosty zones.

Hearting lettuce

These lettuces are the most familiar of all the salad lettuces. They grow slowly and produce large leaves that curl inwards and enwrap each other to form a central ball. The leaves are light green and crisp and remain cup-shaped when removed from their embrace, making them useful as containers in dishes such as sang choy bow. They also tear apart easily.

'Great lakes' and 'iceberg' are two hearting lettuces that won't bolt in warm weather. 'Butterheads' are softer and looser. Harvest leaf by leaf until the heart has fully formed, then harvest it whole. 'Cos' or 'romaine' varieties grow tall and have tapering oval leaves that form a loose heart. These keep better than most in the refrigerator, and are essential for Caesar salads.

butter lettuce

radicchio

cos lettuce

Loose-leaf lettuce

With these lettuces we see the full range of colour and texture possibilities, such as the softly frilled 'salad bowl' and the much-divided 'oak leaf', the tightly frilled 'coral' or 'lollo' and the neatly packed 'mignonette' varieties. All are available in green or bronze-pink tones. There is also a red-leafed 'cos' and a yellow-leafed variety named 'australian yellow leaf'.

Salad greens

These are the more strongly-flavoured leafy salad greens that enjoy the same growing conditions as the better-known lettuces but are in less demand. They are easy to grow in any garden as they take up little space, are ready to harvest in no time and are fun to experiment with.

Rocket, or arugula, has a nutty, peppery flavour. The leaves develop from the centre and are divided like dandelion leaves but have round edges. The surface is smooth and glossy. Rocket is easy to grow from seeds sown 10cm (4") apart. Cluster planting in a pot or garden is also useful, with further plantings each month. Avoid planting during the hottest months as rocket now earns its name and runs straight to seed.

The leaves can be harvested leaf by leaf within a month. The plants will continue to thicken as long as they're well watered and fed. Pick off flower stems to stop early flowering, but when replacements are growing, let a couple of plants bloom prettily, as they do, and collect the seeds for future plantings. With luck you'll find self-seeded volunteers all over the garden.

Mizuna, like rocket, prefers cooler conditions for generous leafy growth. The leaves are heavily dissected and almost fern-like in appearance and its pointed tips are soft. Its flavour is not as strong as rocket, but it has its own almost grass-like taste. Leaves can be gathered in 20-30 days.

Radicchio comes in two guises. It can be lanky, loose-leafed and green with splashes of red, or tightly furled resembling a red cabbage. Both varieties have an almost bitter flavour. Radicchio combines well with other flavours but is often preferred on its own. Most green varieties re-sprout when cut 2.5cm (1") above the ground and develop into the red-hearted form in cool weather. Always keep radicchio well watered and fed.

Endive is grown in the coolest months. It, too, has a strong and sometimes bitter flavour. The more familiar loose-leafed frilly form requires regular water and mulching to prevent its roots from drying out and bitterness developing in the leaves. Gather a few leaves at a time while they are young but if you want to harvest the whole head, partially cover it with a plate or pot saucer for 3 weeks beforehand for a less bitter taste. Its blue flowers guarantee repeat crops as it self-seeds generously.

EDIBLE FLOWERS

Edible flowers are the special province of the cook's garden. After all, one rarely buys flowers to eat, and your kitchen garden can easily yield a plentiful supply of unusual and striking blooms and petals to team with greens for an individualised and unique salad mix. Wash all flowers very well. Dry them gently. Take care when gathering blossoms that you don't harvest concealed bees as well. Make sure you have not used any pesticide or fungicide sprays, that your neighbour's sprays have not drifted into your garden, or that pets or birds have not left their marks.

So, what's safe to eat?

iceberg lettuce

green oak lettuce

red oak lettuce

Calendula (*Calendula officinalis*) Its peppery orange or yellow petals are eaten raw in salads, on rice or in curries.

Chrysanthemum The petals are similar to calendula and can be used similarly.

Day lily (*Hemerocallis* varieties) These last only a day and colours include yellow, pink, cream, mauve and bronze. Pull off their green sepals and use the blooms whole or shredded in salads, batters or as garnishes.

Elderflower (*Sambucus nigra*) The small, white flowers form on a large head in spring, and the berries ripen to black in autumn. The flowers can be used to flavour Champagne or to garnish punch; the berries are used to make wine and jellies.

Fruit blossoms (*Citrus, Malus, Prunus*) The petals of cherries, plums, peaches, apples, crab apples and all the citrus blossoms make lightly-flavoured and pretty garnishes on cakes or sweet pies. Citrus flowers can also be crystallised or steeped in gin or vodka to make a citrus essence. Wash well to remove any chemical sprays and residues.

Geranium and pelargonium flowers and scented leaves These can be used as garnishes on sweet or savoury dishes. The scented leaves will release flavour when added during cooking; citrus or peppermint varieties are the most useful.

Grevillea flowers Often honey-laden, grevillea flowers make a striking garnish and can be used to flavour ice-cream. Some leaves can cause a rash when handled so gather carefully.

Herb flowers Basil, parsley, mint, marjoram, chives and the like can be added as garnishes just before serving,

but not during cooking. Blue borage flowers can be crystallised or frozen in ice cubes to add a pretty touch to drinks.

Honeysuckle (*Lonicera* varieties) Remove the calyx and shred the petals of the sweetly perfumed varieties for a lightly honeyed, fragrant addition to ice-cream, milk desserts or icing.

Lavender The flowers of any scented lavender variety can be milled into sugar, added to ice-cream, biscuits or jams.

Marigolds (*Tagetes* varieties) These are the familiar, strongly aromatic group of flowers with bright yellow, orange or bronze petals. Their strong flavour and colour are used like calendula.

Nasturtiums Both the flowers and soft, young leaves are edible with a slight peppery taste and are good in salads.

Rose Loose petals and whole flowers can be used for garnishes, crystallised or steeped in honey (for a flavoured spread) or in alcohol (for rose essence). Roses are also used to make jams, jellies and other preserves. Dark-coloured blooms hold their colour best during cooking. Beware of bought roses as they are likely to have been sprayed with pesticides and other chemicals.

Vegetable flowers The blooms of peas, beans and seeding lettuce varieties can be added to salads. Male zucchini and pumpkin flowers need to have their bitter stamen removed. They can be stuffed, then battered and fried. They can also be spread as a garnish on a quiche or frittata before baking.

Violet, viola and pansy flowers Their velvet petals and deep colours look beautiful when crystallised and also look good in salads.

lavender

marigolds

zucchini flowers

For the table

TO PREPARE

• At the risk of being repetitive, it is important to remember to pick edible flowers carefully, wash thoroughly and to make certain no chemical sprays have been used.

TO SERVE

• The centres of firm, big-hearted lettuce can simply be quartered and drizzled with blue cheese dressing.

• The French make a light and tasty soup from shredded lettuce simmered in chicken stock with a little rice.

• Mizuna is elegant mixed with pear slices and enoki mushrooms, and drizzled with hazelnut oil vinaigrette. Sprinkle with chopped toasted hazelnuts.

• Witlof is used in salads and also made into delicate hot dishes, usually braised in butter and chicken stock to serve with veal, chicken or ham, or blanched, wrapped in ham and baked under a blanket of cheese sauce to be served as a first course or lunch dish.

• Radicchio has robust, bitter leaves that can be torn or shredded for salads, or wedges can be cut for braising or barbecuing.

• Try crisp prosciutto, teardrop tomatoes, prawns and rocket tossed in a spicy lime dressing.

• Add torn rocket leaves to pasta and toss with a chilli-tomato sauce.

• Chicken pieces marinated in red curry paste then grilled or barbecued are great served with mixed salad leaves, including mint. Add a squeeze of lime juice to finish.

• Mix soft lettuce leaves with rocket and a few peach slices. Serve with a berry vinaigrette.

• Halve radicchio heads, place in an ovenproof dish, add a slurp of olive oil and season with sea salt and cracked black pepper. Cook in a hot oven for 20 minutes, turning halfway through cooking. Serve hot or at room temperature with grilled meats.

• Make a bitter salad from shredded witlof, radicchio and radish; dress with an orange vinaigrette and serve with roasted meats such as pork or duck.

• Serve cos lettuce with a lemon pepper vinaigrette; add hard boiled eggs and shavings of parmesan cheese.

• Puree a mango with basil, lemon juice and olive oil. Use as a dressing over curly endive with edible yellow flower petals such as marigolds.

• Edible flowers, such as rose petals and violets, can be painted with beaten egg white and dipped in caster sugar for beautiful dessert decorations.

green salad with fennel & herbs

1 baby cos lettuce (180g), shredded finely
200g (6½ ounces) rocket (arugula), trimmed
100g (3 ounces) watercress, trimmed
5 green onions (scallions), chopped finely
1 small fennel bulb (200g), sliced thinly
¼ cup coarsely chopped fresh dill
½ cup loosely packed fresh mint leaves
½ cup (80g) roasted pine nuts
red wine vinaigrette
¼ cup (60ml) olive oil
¼ cup (60ml) red wine vinegar

1 Place ingredients for red wine vinaigrette in screw-top jar; shake well.
2 Place salad ingredients in large bowl with vinaigrette; toss gently.

prep time 15 minutes **serves** 8

flower salad

250g (8 ounces) mixed lettuce leaves
½ cup edible flowers or petals (see note)
raspberry vinaigrette
2 tablespoons raspberry vinegar
½ cup (125ml) light vegetable oil

1 Make raspberry vinaigrette.
2 Toss rinsed, dried leaves and flowers in large bowl; drizzle with vinaigrette. Season to taste.
raspberry vinaigrette Combine ingredients in screw-top jar; shake well. Season to taste.

prep time 5 minutes **serves** 6
note Experiment with a variety of seasonal flowers and greens. Mix mild greens with a garnish of stronger-tasting flowers and vice versa. Suggested flowers include violas, calendula, culinary herb flowers, pineapple sage, dianthus, day lilies and roses. If the flowers are large, use only their petals.

green salad with fennel & herbs

flower salad

Capsicum

Throughout the world these vegetables are known by a variety of names. We refer here to the sweet or mild capsicum (also known as peppers) that have a fleshy skin and make a crisp crack when first cut. Their strong flavour and sweetness becomes more pronounced when cooked. Some have a mild, peppery bite and others a touch of spiciness. If you want to avoid any heat whatsoever, choose capsicum with thick skin but always check first by tasting a finger-dip of the juice. The shape of capsicum varies. Some are long balloons, others large or narrow, tapering cones and some are small, apple-sized balls. Colours include yellow, gold, orange, green, red or purple-black, depending on the variety and their ripeness. All capsicum start life green.

In the garden

Capsicum demand similar growing conditions to tomatoes; that is, a frost-free, well-drained, well-watered, sunny site with deeply dug soil that has been well supplied with a complete fertiliser. Capsicum also like the addition of lime or dolomite to lower the soil's acidity.
Seedlings can be started indoors if there's any threat of late-winter frosts. The seeds will germinate in 2-3 weeks. Mixed-seed packets are available so you can experiment with different-coloured fruits. You can also buy seedling punnets from nurseries and share your excess with friends. Plant 50cm (20") apart and mulch well between the plants but not against their stems. Capsicum also grow well in large pots. In tropical and mild subtropical gardens, last-year's plants may have survived as scrawny shrubs. Give them a tidying prune as the weather warms and apply a complete plant food to kick-start them again.
As the plants grow, the stems thicken and the leaves conceal most of the creamy-white blossoms. Later the first fruits will become visible, drooping below the leaves. Heavily laden plants need stakes to keep them upright. Harvest the fruit as you need them, but remember that early fruits will not be as sweet as those that reach maturity in 3-4 months after planting. While conditions remain warm, capsicum will continue to flower but be prepared to lose the last remaining fruits if frosts strike.

PESTS AND DISEASES

Capsicum are subject to fruit-fly attack, which can ruin a crop, so use a non-toxic, bio-insecticide. Always destroy the infected fruit and don't let it rot into the soil where the maggots pupate.

For the table

TO PREPARE

• Capsicum adds brilliant colour and an interesting sweet flavour to many dishes. Raw capsicum has a crisp, juicy texture and a fresh taste. Cut capsicum in half lengthways, remove the seeds and white ribs, and slice or cut up as required. Halves may also be left whole for stuffing.

• For capsicum rings, slice horizontally and pull away seeds and ribs.

• If capsicum is to be stuffed whole, cut a lid off the top and pull out the seeds and ribs, then stuff and cook as the recipe directs.

• To skin a capsicum, spear on a long-handled fork and hold over a gas flame, or char-grill, or place close to a very hot overhead griller (broiler), turning until the whole skin is blackened and blistered. Enclose in a plastic or paper bag to steam for about 10 minutes, then rub the skin off under cold water. Ripe capsicums are easier to skin than green ones.

preserving the crop

STORING	Store whole capsicums in the refrigerator crisper, where they will keep in good condition for a few days. Store cut capsicum in a paper bag enclosed in a plastic bag in the refrigerator, where it will keep well for a few days but will gradually soften and collapse if stored for too long.
FREEZING	Capsicum doesn't freeze well.

TO SERVE

• Capsicum can be used fresh in salads, stir-fried or sauteed, and they can be halved, hollowed out and stuffed. They're also good grilled on kebabs, or char-grilled, peeled and stored in olive oil.

• Capsicum is a must in the traditional ratatouille and, if roasted and peeled, capsicum pieces are terrific added as a colourful layer in a vegetable lasagne.

• Stuff capsicum with a mixture of cooked rice, tomatoes and tuna. Roast until the capsicum are tender and serve with a tiny dollop of pesto.

• Garnish salads with a fine, jewel-like scattering of finely diced red, green and yellow capsicum.

• Puree peeled red capsicum with oregano, olive oil and lots of roasted garlic and use as a dip or serve over sauteed chicken, fish or beef.

• Make a warm salad of red and green capsicum roasted with garlic. A small amount of balsamic vinegar added at the end of roasting is about all you need.

• For a refreshing starter, mix shredded red, green, purple and yellow capsicum and daikon, and add a dressing of chilli and coriander. Serve on top of rocket leaves with crisped lavash bread.

• Combine capsicum with apples to make chutney. Flavour with peppercorns and coriander seeds. Make sure you use cider vinegar to bring out the apple flavour.

• A roasted capsicum and tomato sauce is excellent served over pasta or as a sauce for roasted meats. It can also be used as a dressing for a roasted vegetable salad.

• Slice capsicum and stir-fry with snow peas, baby corn and green onions; add some ginger and rice vinegar. Serve over steamed fish.

• Top a pizza base with slow-fried onions and tomatoes. Add roasted and peeled capsicum strips. Use a mixture of colours, if desired. Sprinkle with crumbled goat's cheese and dot with olive paste. Bake in a very hot oven and serve with a rocket and parmesan salad.

roasted capsicum and goat's cheese terrine

3 large red capsicum (bell pepper) (1kg)
1½ cups (360g) ricotta cheese, chopped coarsely
250g (8 ounces) firm goat's cheese, chopped coarsely
¼ cup finely chopped fresh chives
2 tablespoons lemon juice
1 clove garlic, crushed
spinach and walnut pesto
¼ cup (20g) finely grated parmesan cheese
100g (3 ounces) baby spinach leaves
¼ cup (25g) roasted walnuts
1 clove garlic, quartered
¼ cup (60ml) olive oil
2 tablespoons lemon juice
1 tablespoon water

1 Preheat oven to 240°C/475°F. Grease two ¾-cup (180ml) petite loaf pans. Line base and two long sides of both pans with a strip of baking paper, extending 5cm (2 inches) over sides.
2 Halve capsicums; discard seeds and membranes. Place on oven tray; roast, skin-side up, about 15 minutes or until skin blisters and blackens. Cover capsicum with plastic wrap for 5 minutes then peel away skin. Cut capsicum into strips; line bases and two long sides of pans with capsicum strips, extending 2cm (¾ inch) over edges.
3 Combine remaining ingredients in medium bowl; spoon cheese mixture evenly into pans, pressing down firmly. Fold capsicum strips over to enclose filling. Cover; refrigerate 1 hour.
4 Meanwhile, make spinach and walnut pesto.
5 Carefully remove terrines from pans; sprinkle with extra chopped fresh chives and serve with pesto.
spinach and walnut pesto Process cheese, spinach, nuts and garlic until chopped finely. With motor operating, gradually add combined oil, juice and the water in a thin, steady stream; process until pesto is smooth.

prep & cook time 45 minutes (+ refrigeration) **makes** 2

Eggplant

Known also as aubergine, eggplant is another member of the tomato family. Eggplant is the hero of Middle Eastern cuisine, and a major player in the cooking of India and the countries around the Mediterranean, providing bulk, fleshy texture and a world of wonderful flavours for meals that may include little or no meat. It is also the great sponge of the culinary world. Eggplant readily absorbs flavours as well as vast quantities of oil. It has grey, downy leaves and stems, mauve flowers and the fruit are either bulbous and egg-shaped, thin and finger-like or tiny, round balls. They may be dark, shiny purple, white, streaked with purple and white or even green, depending on the variety. Eggplant is an interesting but slow-growing summer crop in the garden.

Common, or regular, eggplant are the oval purple ones in various sizes. Unless otherwise stated in a recipe, these are the ones to use.

Baby eggplant, also known as finger, japanese, oriental and lebanese eggplant, are long and slender. They are thinner-skinned and a little sweeter than common eggplant and do not need to be disgorged.

Thai pea eggplant are slightly larger than a green pea, and of similar shape and colour; they grow in clusters like grapes. They are rather seedy, and more bitter than the larger thai apple eggplant, with which they can be substituted in many Thai recipes.

Thai apple eggplant are hard and of golf ball size. They are usually pale green traced with white in colour, but can also be purple with a white blush, or a creamy white colour. They look like small unripe tomatoes and are very popular in both Thai and Vietnamese cooking. They are crisp and tart in flavour with lots of bitter seeds that should be removed before using.

In the garden

Eggplant grows in similar conditions to tomatoes. However, it takes a minimum of 3-4 months for the fruit to ripen and the plants will die at the first touch of a frost. For fruit to form, eggplants require night temperatures of 20°C (68°F). This can be engineered in cool zones by planting them against a protective, sun-baked wall. Allow 8 weeks to raise seedlings ready for transplanting. Seedlings are also available from nurseries. Plant them 60-75cm (24-30") apart in warm, well-prepared soil in a sunny site where water is able to drain away quickly. Protect seedlings from late frosts with mulch or plastic wraps. Eggplant does not need as much water as tomatoes and capsicum, so a deep soaking once a week will suffice. Watch the growing tips for signs of wilting, which indicates they need extra water.

Once five large fruits (or five clusters on smaller varieties) have developed, remove any extra flowers as this is all the fruit the plant can carry.

Harvest the eggplants when the skin is still shiny and yields to finger pressure. The riper the fruit, the less bitter their taste.

In tropical and mild subtropical gardens, the plants live through winter to produce again next year but prune them in autumn or early spring to generate new growth. Also give them a boost of extra fertiliser and a protective mulch. Plant new vigorous seedlings the following year.

preserving the crop

STORING	Eggplant is highly perishable in extremes of heat and cold; store for a day or two in a plastic bag in a cool, not cold, place.
FREEZING	Eggplant can be sliced or chopped, blanched and cooled, and then frozen for up to eight months (see Freezing, page 240). Use in casseroles and baked dishes on thawing.
PICKLING	Baby eggplants can be blanched in brine, drained and packed into hot sterilised jars (see Bottling, pages 240-242). Pour spiced vinegar over them with a little sugar; add some chillies and sprigs of dill to enhance the flavour. Store in a cool, dark, dry place for at least 3 weeks before opening. They can be kept for up to a year. Refrigerate after opening.

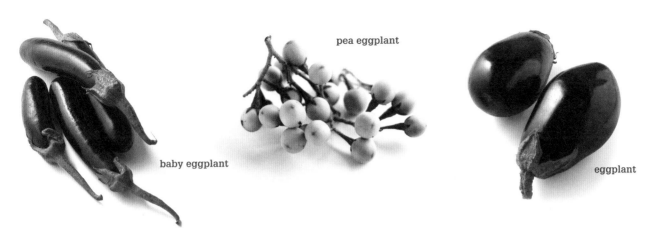

baby eggplant

pea eggplant

eggplant

eggplant parmigiana

2 large eggplants (1kg)
vegetable oil, for shallow-frying
½ cup (75g) plain (all-purpose) flour
4 eggs, beaten lightly
2 cups (200g) packaged breadcrumbs
3 cups (750ml) bottled tomato pasta sauce
1 cup (100g) coarsely grated mozzarella cheese
¼ cup (20g) finely grated parmesan cheese
⅓ cup loosely packed fresh oregano leaves

1 Using vegetable peeler, peel random strips of skin from eggplants; discard skins. Slice eggplants thinly.
2 Heat oil in large frying pan.
3 Coat eggplant in flour; shake off excess. Dip in egg, then in breadcrumbs. Shallow-fry eggplant, in batches, until browned lightly. Drain on absorbent paper.
4 Preheat oven to 200°C/400°F.
5 Spread about one-third of the pasta sauce over base of greased 2.5-litre (10-cup) ovenproof dish. Top with about one-third of the eggplant, one-third of the cheeses and one-third of the oregano. Repeat layering.
6 Bake parmigiana, covered, 20 minutes. Uncover; bake about 10 minutes or until browned lightly.

prep & cook time 1 hour **serves** 6

For the table

TO PREPARE

• Common eggplant, unless young and freshly picked, are usually disgorged before using (salted to draw out their bitter juices); this also reduces the amount of oil the eggplant will soak up when cooking. Cut up the eggplant as required for the recipe and place in a colander, sprinkle generously with salt and leave for 30 minutes or so, then rinse and dry thoroughly. Baby and pea eggplant do not need to be disgorged.

TO SERVE

• Roast an eggplant in a moderate oven for about 1 hour; leave to cool. The skin will be easy to remove and the flesh will have a slightly smoky flavour. Puree with flavourings, oil and lemon juice and you have the perfect dip. It can also be used as a sauce for thick-fleshed fish, such as tuna.

• Make eggplant chips by finely slicing an eggplant; pat dry before frying – this helps prevent the oil from splattering fiercely.

• Char-grill eggplant slices and serve tossed with rocket leaves; drizzle with tarragon vinegar and a sprinkling of mint or basil.

• Top turkish bread with slices of fried eggplant, olives and parmesan cheese. Pop in a hot oven for about 15 minutes or until hot and you have a great substitute pizza.

• Thick char-grilled eggplant slices can be used as a base for lamb steaks or even in place of the bun in a lamb burger.

eggplant spread

moussaka timbales

¼ cup (60ml) olive oil
1 medium brown onion (150g), chopped finely
2 cloves garlic, crushed
500g (1 pound) minced (ground) lamb
400g (12½ ounces) canned diced tomatoes
1 tablespoon tomato paste
½ cup (125ml) dry white wine
1 teaspoon ground cinnamon
¼ teaspoon ground nutmeg
¼ cup coarsely chopped fresh flat-leaf parsley
¼ cup (40g) roasted pine nuts
2 small eggplants (460g)

1 Heat 1 tablespoon of the oil in large frying pan; cook onion and garlic, stirring, until onion softens. Add lamb; cook, stirring, until lamb changes colour. Stir in undrained tomatoes, paste, wine and spices; bring to the boil. Reduce heat; simmer, uncovered, about 20 minutes or until liquid has evaporated. Cool; stir in parsley and nuts.
2 Meanwhile, using sharp knife, mandolin or V-slicer, slice eggplant lengthways into 3mm (⅛ inch) thin slices. Mix eggplant slices with remaining oil; cook on heated grill plate (or grill pan) until browned lightly. Cool.
3 Preheat oven to 180°C/350°F. Grease six-hole ¾-cup (180ml) texas muffin pan. Line pan holes with eggplant slices, overlapping slightly and extending 4cm (1½ inches) above edge of hole. Divide lamb mixture among eggplant cases. Fold eggplant over to enclose filling.
4 Bake about 10 minutes. Stand timbales in pan 5 minutes before serving, top-side down. Sprinkle with extra chopped fresh flat-leaf parsley, and serve with tzatziki, a Greek dip made from yogurt, diced cucumber and garlic.

prep & cook time 1 hour 15 minutes **makes** 6

eggplant spread

1 large eggplant (500g), peeled, chopped coarsely
2 tablespoons vegetable oil
1 clove garlic, crushed
¼ cup (70g) tahini
2 tablespoons lemon juice
¼ teaspoon paprika

1 To disgorge the eggplant, place in a strainer, sprinkle with salt then stand 30 minutes. Rinse under cold water; drain on absorbent paper.
2 Heat oil in medium saucepan; cook eggplant and garlic, stirring, over low heat about 10 minutes or until eggplant is tender.
3 Blend or process eggplant mixture, tahini and juice until smooth.
4 Transfer mixture to serving dish; sprinkle with paprika. Serve with crisp fresh vegetables and warm pitta bread.

prep & cook time 30 minutes (+ standing) **serves** 4
notes Can be made two days ahead; keep, covered, in the refrigerator.
Tahini is a rich sesame seed paste available from Middle-Eastern food stores, delicatessens and health-food stores.

moussaka timbales

Zucchini & Squash

Zucchini, courgettes to some, have the most delightful leaves: they are large, deep green and robust-looking with very attractive white mottling. They may look lush, but don't grow zucchini too near your garden paths as the leaves are rough and brittle to brush against. Squash are a little more restrained in their growth habit and do not sprawl so wide. The flowers of both zucchini and squash are edible, as well as the fruit.

In the garden

Like cucumbers and other members of the cucurbit family, zucchini and squash require similar conditions: a frost-free growing time and full sun. They also demand soil rich in organic matter (manure, garden or spent mushroom compost or well-decomposed leaf litter). Add a complete fertiliser and lime or dolomite to reduce acidity.

Wait until the soil has warmed and there is no threat of frost before planting. Shape the soil into mounds and push in 3-4 seeds to just below the surface. Both zucchini and squash ramble, so plant about 1m (3') apart to allow room to spread. Seedlings will emerge in 1-2 weeks. Once leaves have formed, thin the cluster to the two healthiest seedlings and turn them to grow in opposite directions. They will ramble, but they are less leggy in full sun.

If established indoors, grow seedlings in egg cartons or grow-pots to plant directly into the soil when ready. They don't like their roots to be disturbed.

Keep both zucchini and squash well watered during the growing season. An irrigation soak is preferable to splashings with a hand-held hose and will reduce the possibility of mildew developing.

Each plant carries both male and female flowers, which are bright yellow and trumpet-shaped. They start to appear in 6-8 weeks. Female flowers carry the embryo fruit attached to their bases and have a rounded centre. The male flowers have only a stem behind and a prominent pollen-laden stamen in their centre. Bees usually carry the pollen but if they're not active, brush the pollen from a male flower onto the female centre to guarantee fruit formation. When there is an excess of male flowers, they can be gathered and eaten. Plants remain productive for 2-3 months.

ZUCCHINI

Zucchini varieties come in various colours and shapes: cylinders of light green, dark green and yellow, balls of light green and dark green, and elongated straight and crooked-neck forms. Don't leave them on the vine for too long or they will become watery and their skins will harden. Pick when small when their flesh is juicy and their seeds are small. If your crop is abundant, remember that the male flowers can be eaten: harvest the morning they open and take indoors. Remove the stamen and let the flowers close up. They can be stored in an airtight container in the fridge for a few days until you have enough to eat.

SQUASH

Squash vary in colour from bright green to yellow with green tops to variegated forms. All small varieties are interchangeable with zucchini in recipes.

Button squash are currently very popular and great for small gardens. Harvest when fully shaped but still small, otherwise, their seeds and skins harden and the blossom end rots. Compact varieties are well suited to pots.

Large white or green-skinned squash are available, as is the unusual spaghetti squash, which grows into a large melon with spaghetti-like stranded flesh. These larger varieties are picked when their skins harden.

preserving the crop

STORING	Store zucchini and squash in the crisper drawer of the refrigerator for up to 5 days. Do not wrap in plastic as this makes them sweat and go mouldy. Wash before using, not before storing.
FREEZING	Because of their high water content, zucchini and squash don't freeze well.
PICKLING	Slice thinly and brown quickly in a pan with garlic and fresh herbs (parsley and mint work well). Heat some tarragon vinegar with a little salt and a few peppercorns. Place warm zucchini into hot sterilised jars (see Bottling, pages 240-242) and pour over warmed vinegar mixture. Seal immediately and store for a week before using. Great in antipasto platters.

green zucchini

yellow zucchini

zucchini flower
with stem

PESTS AND DISEASES

Like the whole cucurbit family, zucchini and squash are prey to mildew, which discolours their leaves and eventually kills the whole plant. It is caused by high humidity, rainfall and excessive watering. Proprietary sprays are available and for alternative treatments, see page 17. Do not compost diseased leaves; burn or wrap and place in the garbage. Yellow-green ladybird larvae can graze on the underside of leaves and skeletonise them. Crush them by hand or use a food-safe spray if there are fruit and bees about.

For the table

TO PREPARE

• Add both zucchini and squash to boiling water for a couple of minutes or steam until their colour is bright and they are just tender, about 5 minutes.

• Harvested when young, zucchini flowers can be stuffed then deep-fried, oven-baked or steamed to make a delicious appetiser. The stem of the zucchini is the baby zucchini attached to the flower.

• Zucchini are delicate and delicious when treated properly, watery and flavourless when boiled too long. In fact, the smallest members of the squash family (including patty-pan squash) are best if not boiled at all but steamed, fried, or baked with or without a stuffing such as minced meat or cheese sauce.

• Large white or green-skinned squash are always seeded, and can be sliced and steamed, or stuffed with a meat mixture and baked slowly.

TO SERVE

• Both zucchini and squash go beautifully with spices and rich flavours and are happy sliced into ratatouille, curry or risotto so long as they are added late in the cooking so that the slices will be just softened.

• They are excellent coarsely grated and mixed with herbs for a salad to go with a grill, or grated and tossed in foaming butter with a touch of nutmeg just until hot.

• Zucchini flowers are a summer treat to dip into batter and deep-fry or stuff with a savoury mixture, coat with egg and breadcrumbs and pan-fry.

• Fill zucchini flowers with fetta, ricotta, basil and pine nuts, dip in a light batter and deep-fry in batches until the batter is crisp and golden.

• Stuff zucchini flowers, with stems attached, with a mixture of ricotta and parmesan cheeses, lemon rind and juice, some chopped mint and roasted pine nuts; twist the tops to enclose filling. Steam in a large bamboo steamer about 20 minutes or until the zucchini stems are tender.

• Bake hollowed-out zucchini boats filled with minced lamb flavoured with yogurt and cumin for a healthy dinner.

• Cook squash until just tender, then toss in melted butter over low heat until coated.

• Cook spaghetti squash whole, then cut in half, pick out the seeds and add the spaghetti-like flesh to pasta sauces and casseroles.

char-grilled summer vegetables with herbed yogurt dressing

summer squash salad

500g (1 pound) yellow patty-pan squash, halved
500g (1 pound) green patty-pan squash, halved
200g (6½ ounces) baby new potatoes, unpeeled, halved
⅓ cup (80ml) olive oil
2 tablespoons lemon juice
1 clove garlic, crushed
1 tablespoon finely chopped fresh dill
250g (8 ounces) cherry tomatoes, halved
1 cup loosely packed fresh flat-leaf parsley leaves

1 Boil, steam or microwave squash and potatoes, separately, until tender; drain.
2 Combine warm squash and potatoes with remaining ingredients in large bowl.

prep & cook time 30 minutes **serves** 4

char-grilled summer vegetables with herbed yogurt dressing

4 finger eggplants (240g)
2 medium zucchini (240g)
250g (8 ounces) pumpkin
1 medium red capsicum (bell pepper) (200g)
1 medium yellow capsicum (bell pepper) (200g)
1 medium green capsicum (bell pepper) (200g)
¼ cup (60ml) olive oil
1 bunch rocket (arugula)
herbed yogurt dressing
¾ cup (210g) reduced-fat yogurt
1 tablespoon finely snipped fresh chives
2 tablespoons finely chopped fresh flat-leaf parsley
1 tablespoon finely chopped fresh mint
1 clove garlic, crushed

1 Make herbed yogurt dressing.
2 Cut eggplant, zucchini and pumpkin into 5mm (¼") thick slices. Cut capsicum into 2cm (1") strips.
3 Brush vegetables with oil; cook on heated oiled grill pan (or grill or barbecue), turning once, until just soft. Layer vegetables with rocket; serve with dressing.
herbed yogurt dressing Combine ingredients in small bowl; refrigerate until required.

prep & cook time 30 minutes
serves 6-8 as a side dish; 4 as a main course

summer squash salad

Rhubarb

What a marvellous, old-fashioned vegetable garden regular rhubarb is. This handsome perennial is the original cut-and-come-again garden plant and deserves a well-loved spot in the edible garden. Rhubarb belongs to the same family as sorrel. Rhubarb is also the favourite resting place of snails after they have created havoc among the vegetable seedlings, so inspect rhubarb plants regularly and squash the culprits there and then.

In the garden

Rhubarb needs very rich soil and full sun or at least sun for half a day. Add large quantities of manure and a nitrogen-rich fertiliser like pelleted poultry manure. Rhubarb also likes regular watering, but needs a well-drained site or its roots will rot. A position somewhere near the garden hose, a leaky tap or a dripper outlet on an irrigation system is ideal.

The small leaves unfurl from tightly crinkled bundles and soon resemble elephant ears. The stems thicken, lengthen and multiply as the plant expands to cover 1m (3') or more of the garden. It can be grown in a large pot but take care to keep it well watered to prevent wilting. Start to harvest the outside leaves as soon as there are five or so replacement stems unfurling in the centre of the plant. Pull each stem down and twist sideways to break it off with a snap. Wash well to remove dirt, cut off the leaves and add them to your compost.

Give regular extra feeds with liquid fertiliser and break off any flower stems that form. When rhubarb starts to die back for the winter, mulch with manure and compost ready for the following spring and to protect from winter frosts. In areas where winters are mild the plant may not die back fully. Divide the root mass every couple of years (these make terrific presents for friends and potted plants to sell at local stalls). Do this at the end of winter.

Rhubarb with red stems is the most familiar and most coveted variety among both gardeners and cooks. If you want a red-stemmed variety, only buy named crowns in winter as these will be divisions from plants that are known to have red stems. Seedlings sold in punnets at nurseries may grow into plants with red, pink or green stems – there can be no guarantee of the stem colour with plants grown from seeds. However, don't worry too much about the colour as the green-stemmed and pinkish-stemmed varieties have the same flavour and are just as good to eat.

For the table

TO PREPARE

• Never eat the leaves as they are poisonous (however, the stems are not, be they red, pink or green). Remove and discard all leaves, trim the root ends, wash stalks and, unless they are very young and tender, string them by running a vegetable peeler or small, sharp knife firmly from top to bottom down each rib. Cut into slices or lengths as directed.

• Add to a heavy-based pan with sugar and cook, over low heat, stirring constantly. Rhubarb contains a lot of moisture and will leach much of this out as it cooks, so only a spoonful of water should be added with the sugar for cooking.

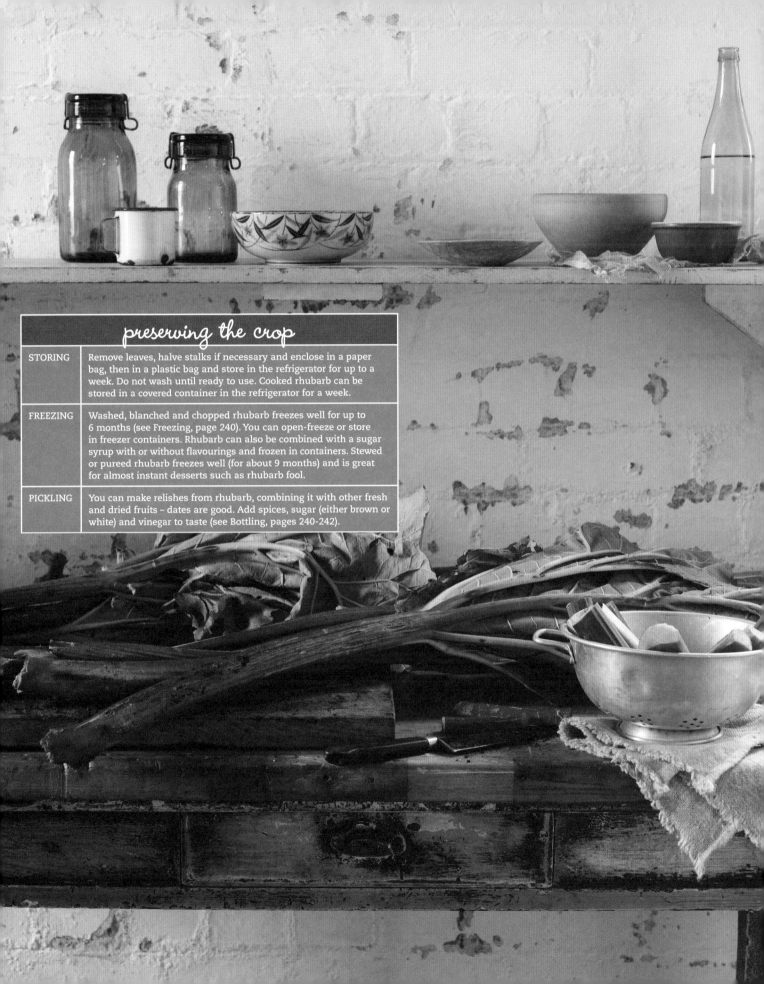

preserving the crop

STORING	Remove leaves, halve stalks if necessary and enclose in a paper bag, then in a plastic bag and store in the refrigerator for up to a week. Do not wash until ready to use. Cooked rhubarb can be stored in a covered container in the refrigerator for a week.
FREEZING	Washed, blanched and chopped rhubarb freezes well for up to 6 months (see Freezing, page 240). You can open-freeze or store in freezer containers. Rhubarb can also be combined with a sugar syrup with or without flavourings and frozen in containers. Stewed or pureed rhubarb freezes well (for about 9 months) and is great for almost instant desserts such as rhubarb fool.
PICKLING	You can make relishes from rhubarb, combining it with other fresh and dried fruits – dates are good. Add spices, sugar (either brown or white) and vinegar to taste (see Bottling, pages 240-242).

TO SERVE

• Its ribbed pink or red stalks are always cooked, which changes their tart, earthy flavour to refreshing sharpness and their crispness to tenderness. Often paired with apples, it has always provided the basis for sweet, stewed fruit desserts when they were essential family fare.

• Rhubarb has a special affinity with orange and ginger and is usually eaten in a sweet context – pies, tarts, muffins, strudels, cakes, ice-cream or a fool.

• Rhubarb can also be used for the savoury part of the meal, for example with sliced orange and watercress to serve with ham, pork or poultry, or combined with apple and ginger in a sweet/sharp jelly to serve with turkey, pork or duck.

• Make a compote with stewed rhubarb, plumped dried figs and apples to serve with anything from breakfast pancakes to a plain cake.

• If you want rhubarb to fall to a puree, cook it without sugar until soft, then sweeten to taste with white or brown sugar – process for a completely smooth texture.

• For rhubarb that holds its shape, cover the pieces with sugar syrup in a microwave dish and microwave in short bursts, checking after each burst until tender but still holding its shape.

• The old favourite, rhubarb fool, is made by mixing stewed rhubarb with whipped cream and a little cardamom – the only foolish thing is to not try it.

• Rhubarb bakes beautifully under a crumble topping. Orange segments and pears and your favourite spice will add extra interest.

• Arrange uncooked rhubarb over a firm cake batter before baking. It will sink and create an attractive top. Brush the warm cake with melted butter and sprinkle over cinnamon or ginger sugar – great as muffins, too.

• Add cooked rhubarb to home-made ice-cream. It will dye the ice-cream a pretty pink and the flavour is to die for.

rhubarb, apple and berry galette

2½ cups (375g) plain (all-purpose) flour
2 tablespoons caster (superfine) sugar
200g (6½ ounces) unsalted butter, chopped
¼ cup (60g) sour cream
½ cup (125ml) milk
¼ cup (40g) icing (confectioners') sugar
rhubarb apple filling
10 medium rhubarb stems (750g), chopped coarsely
2 medium granny smith apples (300g), peeled, cored, chopped coarsely
250g (8 ounces) strawberries, halved
1¼ cups (275g) caster (superfine) sugar
1 teaspoons vanilla extract
⅓ cup (50g) plain (all-purpose) flour

1 Process flour, sugar and butter until it resembles fine breadcrumbs. Add sour cream and milk and process until mixture forms a smooth ball. Wrap in plastic and refrigerate 30 minutes.
2 Meanwhile, make rhubarb apple filling.
3 Preheat oven to 200°C/400°F.
4 Cover a large pizza tray (30cm/12" across) with baking (parchment) paper. Roll out pastry to form a rough 37cm (15") circle. Place dough on baking tray, pile filling onto pastry leaving 5cm (2") around edges. Bring pastry edges over filling and pleat to form an open pie. Sift icing sugar over galette.
5 Bake galette in oven 1 hour 10 minutes or until the pastry is crisp, the filling is broken down and the juices have evaporated (juices from the fruit will probably run onto the tray, but don't worry as they will become toffee by the end of the cooking time).
6 Cool on tray 20 minutes, then slide onto a wire rack. Serve warm or at room temperature with ice-cream or custard.
rhubarb apple filling Combine ingredients in large bowl; stand about 10 minutes or until the fruit looks moist.

prep & cook time 1 hour 40 minutes
(+ refrigeration and cooling) **serves** 8-10
note Galette can be made several hours ahead. Store, covered, at room temperature.

Sweet Corn

Originally used as flour and stockfeed, sweet corn has now been bred to be a treat for humans. And what a treat it is: sweet, juicy and chewy. Those who grow sweet corn at home know how tender and sweet it can be when eaten fresh. The all-important sugar starts to convert to starch as soon as a cob is picked, hence sayings such as 'walk slowly to pick it; run back to the kitchen to cook it'. It is remarkable what a difference even just a couple of hours makes to home-harvested corn – imagine what happens to sweet corn that is harvested, sent to market, distributed then arranged on a grocer's shelves. You can understand why freshly picked cobs from the garden taste superior to corn from the shop.

In the garden

Corn must grow without frost, so plant seeds indoors if spring where you live is not to be trusted. If you use peat or grow-pots, you can nestle the seedlings directly into the soil leaving the young roots undisturbed. Where growing conditions are milder, plant seeds directly in the garden as the soil starts to warm – the second month of spring is a good time. In the tropics corn can be grown year-round, although not having plants maturing during the wet season is always a good idea.

Always plant corn in full sun and out of strong winds. Make sure the soil is rich in organic matter and add a complete plant food 2 weeks before planting.

Corn must be grown in blocks rather than rows, so the pollen from the male tassels at the top of each plant can dust the female silks on other plants as they appear on the immature cobs. The cobs form between the leaves and the stem, and there can be 2, 3 or 4 to each stem. Plant seeds 40-50cm (16-20") apart in a block, clusters or circles (never in a single straight line).

Corn also requires regular deep watering for the plants to develop fully. Test with your finger that the water is soaking down deeply. This also lets you check that stilt roots are developing. These are extra support props and a means of drawing up more water and nutrients. Hill up extra soil around these roots. The furrows created also become irrigation channels to flood the plants once or twice a week.

Spray the plants with liquid fertiliser every 2 weeks.

In 3-4 months cobs should be ready to harvest. There are two indicators of readiness: the silks will turn brown and the cobs will stand out from the stem. Pull down the top part of the husks and press a fingernail into the kernels. The grains should be soft and the juice creamy, not watery. When ready, pull down the cob and twist to snap it from the stem. You can eat corn raw from the plant but if you'd rather cook it, do so straight away. Where conditions remain hot, plant a second crop in early summer.

If you want baby corn cobs for Asian dishes, you can peel back the young silks and pick the immature cobs when you think they're right. However, baby corn is actually a specialised cultivar and if you want to grow this crop, you'll need to seek out special seed.

PESTS AND DISEASES

Watch for aphids on the stems and hose off, crush by hand or use a spray. Ear worms can bore into the cobs from the top, chewing first at the silks. Bio-insecticides based on bacteria toxic only to caterpillars will safely control these or try one of the home-made remedies (see page 17). Alternatively, crush the corn tops with your fingers at the first sign of an attack.

preserving the crop

STORING	The watchword with sweet corn is, don't store it but use it the day you pick it as its sugars start to turn into starch as soon as it is picked. If it is going to be a few hours before you cook it, put it in the vegetable crisper of the refrigerator. If you must store it longer, leave it in the husk and store in a paper bag enclosed in a plastic bag in the refrigerator. It will last about 2 days, after which it will start to become dry and starchy.
FREEZING	If freezing, the cobs can be left whole, cut into 7.5cm (3") lengths or cut into kernels. All need blanching before freezing (see Freezing, page 240). Freeze for up to 6 months.
PICKLING	Corn relish is an old favourite, and also a good way to preserve a large crop. Cut off the kernels. Simmer with capsicums, onion, sugar, vinegar and flavourings for 30 minutes. Stir in plain (all-purpose) flour combined with powdered mustard and turmeric (it keeps the golden colour) and a little cold water. Boil for 5 minutes. Pour into hot sterilised jars (see Bottling, pages 240-242) and seal while hot. Store in the refrigerator for about a month.

corn

baby corn

polkadot corn

For the table

TO PREPARE

• Boil or barbecue whole or cut the kernels off and use in soups and salads.

• Microwave corn cobs in their husks for 3-4 minutes each.

• To boil corn cobs, remove the green husk and the fine strands of silk. Bring a large saucepan of water to the boil (don't add salt as this toughens the corn), add the cobs and boil for 4-6 minutes. Overcooking will toughen, not soften, the kernels.

• To barbecue, pull back the husk but leave it attached. Remove the silk, fold the husk back over the cob, tie with string and dip into water, then barbecue over hot coals, turning two or three times, for about 15 minutes. The string will burn off and the husk will be charred; remove it before serving with butter, salt and pepper.

• When cutting corn kernels from the cob, cut the cobs in half crossways to make them easier to handle and the kernels less likely to end up all over the kitchen.

• Make stock from the denuded cobs. Simmer with traditional stock ingredients such as peppercorns and bay leaves. Use the stock in corn-flavoured soups, casseroles and risottos.

TO SERVE

• Boil or barbecue whole and enjoy as corn on the cob with salt, pepper and butter.

• Discard the silk from the cobs; drizzle cobs with a little flavoured oil, re-wrap in the husk, pile into a large baking dish, cover loosely with foil and bake in a very hot oven for 10 minutes or until tender.

• Remove the silk from inside the cob and replace with a smear of your favourite flavoured butter. Re-wrap in its husk and barbecue until tender.

• Use the kernels in soups and salads.

• Add corn kernels to a pancake batter for corn fritters. Serve with crispy bacon or sausages, roasted tomatoes and rocket.

• Cut cob into thick slices and add to beef or chicken casseroles for the last 20 minutes of cooking.

• Crush kernels until slightly creamy and add to a cheese soufflé mixture.

• Chicken and corn marry very well. Stir-fry chicken and add a handful of corn kernels to the wok a few minutes before the end of the cooking time.

chicken and sweet corn soup

cooking-oil spray
2 trimmed corn cobs (500g), kernels removed
4cm (1½ inch) piece fresh ginger (20g), grated
2 cloves garlic, crushed
4 green onions (scallions), sliced thinly
1 litre (4 cups) water
1 litre (4 cups) chicken stock
1 chicken breast fillet (200g)
1 teaspoon light soy sauce
1 egg white, beaten lightly

1 Lightly spray heated large saucepan with oil. Cook corn, ginger, garlic and half the onion, stirring, until fragrant. Add the water and stock; bring to the boil.
2 Add chicken; reduce heat. Simmer, covered, about 10 minutes or until chicken is cooked. Cool chicken in broth 10 minutes. Remove chicken; shred meat finely.
3 Return broth to the boil; add chicken and sauce. Reduce heat; gradually stir in egg white.
4 Serve soup sprinkled with remaining onion.

prep & cook time 40 minutes **serves** 4
note Light soy sauce is a salty-tasting sauce used in dishes in which the natural colour of the ingredients is to be maintained; it is not a salt-reduced soy sauce.

chicken and sweet corn soup

corn fritters

corn fritters

1 cup (150g) self-raising flour
½ teaspoon bicarbonate of soda (baking soda)
1 teaspoon ground cumin
¾ cup (180ml) milk
2 eggs, separated
2 cups (330g) fresh corn kernels
2 green onions (scallions), sliced finely
2 tablespoons finely chopped fresh coriander (cilantro)

1 Sift flour, soda and cumin into medium bowl. Gradually whisk in milk and egg yolks until batter is smooth.
2 Beat egg whites in small bowl with electric mixer until soft peaks form.
3 Stir corn, onion and coriander into batter; fold in egg whites.
4 Pour 2 tablespoons of the batter for each fritter into heated oiled large frying pan; spread batter into round shape. Cook fritters about 2 minutes each side. Remove from pan; cover to keep warm.
5 Repeat step 4 to make a total of 18 fritters. Sprinkle fritters with coriander; serve with some tomato chutney.

prep & cook time 40 minutes **makes** 18

Summer Fruit

Fruit is superb in summer: richly coloured, plentiful and sweetly perfumed. With so many vegetables available all year round, summer fruits remain one of the few truly seasonal taste delights. We look forward to the shiny brightness of the first-season cherries, the wafting aroma of peaches, the dusty gleam of plums and the lush juiciness of gooseberries. Their delights are also fleeting. Summer fruits have a short season so harvest your garden's fruits with speed and dedication. Preserve, bottle, freeze or pickle your fruits to extend their perfection into winter.

Berries

Berries do best in areas with cool-to-cold winters, a gentle spring and a warm and very sunny summer. Those gardeners who can grow berries easily don't realise how much the climatically less-blessed envy them, despite the fact that many berries are barbed with thorns and it's often a backbreaking and hazardous task to harvest berries and keep the vines under control.

Strawberries

Strawberries make pretty border plants and are happy among herbs and flowers. There are strawberry varieties to suit cold winter zones, some that produce high-yielding subtropical crops and others for temperate zones.

Buy virus-free plants in summer and dig them into rich, free-draining soil. A straw mulch (hence the name 'straw' berry) protects them during winter, suppresses weeds and keeps the fruit clear of the soil. Terracotta strawberry pots save space, but they do need a lot of maintenance, in particular regular watering and extra fertiliser in each pocket.

The first summer is their establishment year. Cut off any runners, feed in late summer and autumn and cut off the leaves at the same time. Come spring, strawberries really get growing. Fruit may be early or mid-season ripening. Slugs, snails and birds will also rush to the harvest. Pellets and traps will deter slugs and snails, and nets will help stop the birds.

Plant out new runners during the third year in a new, well-prepared site for crops the following year. Pull out old plants. In the tropics, strawberries should be treated as annuals and replanted each year.

Alpine strawberries look frail, but don't be deceived by their looks or name; they grow in most climates and, while their fruit is small, it is highly flavoured.

Raspberries

Raspberries come in red, the major variety, and also in gold, black and white varieties. They are the most intensely flavoured of all berries, with the perfect blend of sharp, sweet and aromatic flavour notes. Raspberry flowers develop at the top of tall, thorny canes. Different varieties fruit throughout summer, even into autumn. New canes, with some roots attached, can be planted in autumn or early spring when leafless. Buy canes from a nursery or collect from friends thinning their thickets. Mulch well and add plenty of manure for abundant spring growth. Raspberries are invasive so be prepared for boundary trims with a sharp spade each spring. Each autumn cut out the dead canes and thin the rest to 5-6 canes to each plant.

preserving the crop (berries)

STORING	Pick berries just before using. If you have to pick them early, place berries gently, not touching each other, in a single layer on a plate or oven tray lined with two layers of absorbent paper, cover with plastic wrap and store in the refrigerator for up to two days. Avoid washing.
FREEZING	Berries can be frozen as purees (see Freezing, page 240). Don't sweeten in case you want to make a sauce for chicken or other meats. The puree keeps, frozen, for up to a year.
PICKLING	We are all familiar with berry jams, but most berries contain only a small amount of pectin, which is needed to set jam. However, berries can be combined with apples, have lemon juice added, or be cooked using jam sugar, all of which increase the pectin level. Spoon hot jams into hot sterilised jars and seal while hot (see Bottling, pages 240-242).

blueberries

blackberries

tayberries

Blackberries and 'friends'

Blackberries and 'friends' are trailing berries and, like raspberries, are thorny horrors, although there are some thornless cultivars. 'Friends' include tayberries, loganberries, boysenberries and youngberries. Tayberries are a cross between blackberries and red raspberries. Boysenberries, loganberries and youngberries are all descended from the raspberry and the blackberry. The boysenberry, a cross between a youngberry and a dewberry (cultivated blackberry), tastes much like a raspberry but is much larger than either of its ancestors. The loganberry, a raspberry/blackberry cross, is more acid than a blackberry, less intensely flavoured than a raspberry, and seedless. The youngberry is a cross between a dewberry and a raspberry, tastes rather like a loganberry and looks like an elongated blackberry.

Blackberries, like raspberries, are thorny horrors, although there are some thornless cultivars. Blackberries have become weeds in some countries, and must be poisoned and removed. To be safe, choose an approved cultivar that doesn't spread (see your local nursery).
Attach the trailing canes to a trellis and cut off at ground level after fruiting. Tie up each new cane as it develops. This will keep the plant easy to harvest and stop it becoming a dense thicket.

Gooseberries

Gooseberries grow on a spiky shrub and, if destined for cooking only, the globular, light-green fruit are picked in late spring. In summer they ripen to a perfumed, sweet, soft fruit that is eaten fresh.
Plant cuttings or plants in well-manured soil in late autumn or winter. As gooseberries are very spiky, it's best to keep them thinned during winter and to remove any suckers to make harvesting less hazardous.

Blueberries

Blueberries grow on a thornless shrub that colours delightfully in autumn. The berries ripen over late summer and into autumn. They need peaty, acid soil to do well. If you can offer this, plus a cool-to-cold winter, they are the berry for you. You can also grow them in pots with the right soil mix.

Currants

Currants grow in grape-like clusters (red, black or white) on shrubs. Redcurrants and blackcurrants have nothing to do with the wrinkly black currants, which are dried grapes, but belong to a family that also includes gooseberries. Plant in autumn, winter or spring when plants are available from nurseries. Give them a protective mulch come winter if the weather is very cold. Blackcurrants fruit on new wood, so cut all the stems back in winter to 10cm (4") above the soil. Red and white currants fruit on old stems so prune only as needed to shape and control the shrubs. Each spring give all currant varieties a rich dressing of manure and a complete plant food, kept clear of the stems. Repeat in late summer.

For the table
TO PREPARE

• For most purposes, remove the green calyxes from strawberries, though they may be retained as a little "handle" for strawberries that are to be eaten in the fingers, such as those that have been half-coated with

red currants

strawberries

raspberries

chocolate or those to be dipped in a sauce such as sour cream sweetened with brown sugar.

• Gooseberries need topping and tailing. Other berries need no preparation except to remove any stalks. Do not wash berries until just before using.

• Don't cook berries in aluminium pans as this can affect their colour and flavour; always use non-reactive pans such as stainless steel, Pyrex glass, titanium or enamelled cast-iron.

TO SERVE

• Strawberries are the classic summer berry to eat with lightly whipped cream.

• Sprinkle strawberries with brandy or orange-flavoured liqueur, or drop them into a glass of sweet sparkling wine.

• Raspberry jam that is baked rather than boiled is superbly flavoured.

• Raspberries are lovely eaten raw with a dusting of icing sugar and thick or whipped cream.

• Use raspberries, with whipped cream, for filling and topping a sponge cake, or in pastries, ice-creams, sorbets and puddings of every kind.

• Blackberries make excellent pies, jams and jellies.

• Gooseberries are good eaten just as they are when they are ripe and red-flushed, otherwise they benefit from cooking or macerating with sweet wine or liqueur. Lightly cook, mash and fold into thick or whipped cream to make a great fruit fool.

• The flavour of blueberries, which can be a trifle bland, is improved by standing with a sprinkle of sugar and lemon juice for a few hours; the same treatment works for any other berries that are found to lack flavour.

• Blueberries are best lightly cooked, just until the juice runs, or in cakes and muffins.

• Berries can make great-tasting, colourful vinegars for salads and sauces. Pour good-quality white wine vinegar over fruit; add cardamom pods or cinnamon sticks, cover and stand for 2 days. Discard the fruit and spices and pour the flavoured vinegar into hot sterilised bottles (see Bottling, pages 240-242). Store in the refrigerator for up to 1 year. The vinegar becomes sweeter as it ages.

Passionfruit

The passionfruit is not only a delicacy in itself but has the quality of bringing out the flavours of other fruits. Its tough shell encloses magnificently perfumed, intensely-flavoured, tangy-sweet pulp with embedded black seeds that are usually eaten. The common variety, which is also the most fragrant and best-flavoured, is small, round and purple-skinned, while panama passionfruit, a large, round, light purple/red-skinned cultivar, is almost as good. There is also a long, yellow variety known as banana passionfruit, which is somewhat less intense and tangy in flavour, and a round, yellow-skinned variety, which is less perfumed than the common one.

Although native to tropical America, passionfruit (or granadillas) grow well in temperate zones. They enjoy life in tropical and subtropical gardens, though it can be a battle to grow them without protection in cooler areas; in frost-prone climates, a heated glasshouse is the only way. Their dark evergreen vines look handsome scrambling over fences and walls, and their flowers are spectacular. Seedlings and grafted plants are available during spring and summer. Plant in a sunny site protected from harsh winds and against a trellised wall, pergola or archway to climb over with access underneath for harvesting. Be

passionfruit

apricots

prepared for this area to become 'hallowed' ground as passionfruit don't like their surface roots disturbed and must be kept well watered and mulched. This is particularly true of grafted plants because, where roots are damaged, the vigorous understock will shoot up and very quickly overcome the grafted vine. Soil should be rich in organic manure or compost, and given extra dressings of complete garden fertiliser each spring and late summer. The vine grows quickly in warm weather. Direct the stems where you want them to climb and cut out any that are superfluous. The tendrils will cling to any support. Watch out for their spreading ways and prune, as necessary. In their first winter they'll slow down and perhaps drop some leaves. Don't prune or disturb them while they're resting. The following spring the vine will get marching again and buds and flowers will develop. The flowers are green, purple and white extravagances with a tiny, immature fruit among the stamens and anthers. Bees and the breezes will do their duty and, by early summer (late summer in cooler areas), the first season's crop will be ready to drop off the vine.

As soon as the fruit is finished, prune the stems as it's the new growth that bears flowers. A passionfruit vine will crop well for several years and then start to fade. Then it's time to plant a replacement vine, either as a seedling raised from dropped fruit or a new grafted specimen.

PESTS AND DISEASES

Aphids will mass on tender new shoots. They can be hosed or crushed if you can reach them, or sprayed with harmless insecticidal soap spray. See page 17 for alternatives to chemical sprays. Passionfruit is also attacked by a virus that produces woody-skinned fruit. It can't be treated, and vines should be pulled out to limit its spread. Healthy plants and grafted plants will usually be disease-resistant.

PRESERVING THE CROP

STORING Once picked, passionfruit keep well at room temperature for a week or more. For longer storage, they will keep in the refrigerator crisper for 2-3 weeks, but will gradually shrivel and become mouldy if kept much longer. Passionfruit lasts for about a week at room temperature.

FREEZING Passionfruit is one of the few fruits that maintain their sharp-sweet flavour after freezing. Freeze the pulp in ice-cube trays, then transfer to a freezer bag.

TO SERVE

• Passionfruit makes an excellent fruit curd, and takes beautifully to creamy flavours: its tang comes through strongly in mousses, ice-creams and, most famously, against the meringue-and-cream richness of the favourite Australian dessert, pavlova.

Stone Fruit

All stone fruits belong to the *Prunus* family. They turn on a glorious blossom display in spring, bring forth their divine fruit in high summer, offer another colour burst in autumn when their leaves turn, and then stand stark and structural through the winter.

They all demand similar growing conditions: a cool-to-cold winter, a warm summer, rich soil and a good supply of water. They are ideally suited to Mediterranean (winter rainfall) climates as long as extra water is available during dry summers. In temperate and cool temperate gardens, late-spring frosts can ruin early blossoms. Some cultivars with low chilling requirements are more suited to mild subtropical zones. Ask your nursery for recommendations.

The spring blossoms are very delicate, so don't plant where strong winds can shatter them before the bees have had a chance to visit. Apply a complete garden

cherries

yellow peaches

plums

fertiliser (a proprietary blend or combined pelleted poultry manure and fish emulsion fertiliser) twice a year in early spring and late summer. In winter when the trees are dormant, add a generous mulch of manure as well.

PESTS AND DISEASES

There are a number of diseases that await stone fruit. The leaves may be twisted and deformed by leaf curl, a fungus disease that can only be treated when the tree is dormant. Pick off and burn any affected leaves during summer and autumn, and give the tree extra fertiliser to promote new leaf growth in summer. Rake up the leaves regularly but don't compost them. During late winter, as early buds swell, spray with a fungicide like Bordeaux mixture. Don't spray too late as it will burn the leaves. Aphids cause a similar wrinkling, but are visible on the stem tips. Crush by hand or hose off.

Fruit-fly is another major pest. Spray with a bio-proprietary insecticide or one of the non-chemical alternatives on page 17. Boil or burn the infected fruit and collect all fallen fruit to ensure the grubs can't pupate in the soil.

Apricots

A perfect tree-ripened apricot, luscious, sweet and aromatic, is food for the gods. They are justifiably famous for the golden jam they produce. Apricots do best where the summers are long and hot, but are reasonably adaptable to site as there are varieties to suit coastal, highland and inland zones. They are self-fertile and, with their rounded leaves and white blossoms, they are beautiful in spring.

Prune to control their height and spread. Reduce the central sections to open out the tree to gain more sunlight and air movement around the fruit.

Fruit damaged by fruit-fly is still useful for making jam.

Cut out the damaged sections from the fruit and drop the waste into boiling water. Leave to cool. This can then be safely composted. The useable sections of the fruit can be weighed and made into jam, as usual.

Cherries

Cherries are the first summer fruit on the scene. They must endure a cold winter or fruit will not set, and the following summer should be warm with periodic rain. Late frosts will ruin a whole year's crop as will heavy rain when the fruit is almost ripe but they do require regular watering so the fruit develops evenly.

Cherries are usually self-sterile; that is, they need two or more varieties for fertilisation of the blossoms to occur. However, 'stella' and 'morello' can be grown on their own as they don't need another pollinator.

Cherries develop into large trees and may be too large for a home garden but they do have delightful blossoms and an elegant shape. They require almost no pruning except to clear low-hanging branches.

Peaches and Nectarines

Peaches come in yellow and white varieties, both of which can be either clingstone or freestone, defined by whether the flesh separates cleanly from the stone. White peaches are scented and luscious, while yellow peaches, especially freestones, are easier to peel and stone.

Like peaches, nectarines are one of the joys of summer. They are, in fact, a variety of peach, not a cross between a peach and a plum as is often believed. They can be either clingstone (when cut, the flesh clings to the stone) or freestone (when cut, the flesh will fall or twist cleanly away from the stone), and white- or yellow-fleshed. White nectarines are more fragile than yellow but worth it for their lusciousness and marvellous perfume with flavour to match.

Peaches and nectarines are synonymous with summer with their strong perfume and rich colouring. Different varieties of peaches and nectarines are ready for picking throughout the season. In very cold climates, peaches need a snug site near a sunny wall or, even better, espaliered against it. In warm-temperate or subtropical areas, enquire at your nursery for recommended low-chill varieties. Specially-developed dwarf forms are ideal for pots because regular varieties won't usually crop in confined conditions. Peaches are self-fertile, so a single tree can be planted as a garden feature, to mark a corner of the vegetable garden or shade the chicken shed. Remember not to plant where it will cast too long a shadow over vegetables in summer. Thin the juvenile fruit and leaf shoots if heavily massed, and leave a 20cm (8") space between each for large, juicy fruit. In winter, prune out crossing branches and old wood. Trim low-hanging branches and those that are too high from which to harvest any fruit.

Regularly clear debris from under the tree, especially after birds attack and the fruit falls. Commercial growers pick their fruit early, but tree-ripened fruit is everybody's dream. Netting the tree may help deter birds.

Fruit-fly damaged peaches may still be used for jam. They can be treated in the same way as fruit-fly-infected apricots.

Plums

Plums are the most varied of all the stone fruits. The fruit can be narrow or fat, oval or cricket-ball sized; some are green-fleshed, others purple, yellow or red. Their skins are mostly glossy, but a few are powdered with a white bloom. There are varieties to suit warm-temperate, Mediterranean and cool-climate gardens, and they are more tolerant of heavy clay soils than any other stone fruit. They don't grow in swamps, but are happy at the water's edge.

Most plums are self-sterile and need a pollinator to form fruit. Two varieties that self-pollinate are cherry plums, mostly grown for their spring blossoms, and the variety called 'santa rosa', if you want just one tree. You can even buy different varieties grafted onto the one tree. Pruning is not necessary for plum trees but remove any branches growing across pathways or scrape the ground.

Fruit-fly damaged plums may still be used for jam. They can be treated in the same way as fruit-fly-infected apricots.

Plums are among the relatively few fruits that continue to ripen properly after harvesting, though they must be fully mature when picked.

PRESERVING THE CROP

Storing apricots Keep ripe apricots in a covered container in the refrigerator and use them within a day or two; for fullest flavour, allow them to return to room temperature before eating.

Drying apricots Dried apricots (see Drying, page 243) will keep well in the cupboard for months.

Storing cherries Keep in a covered container in the refrigerator for about a week.

Storing plums Perfectly ripe plums can be kept at room temperature for a day, but should be refrigerated and used within a few days as they deteriorate quickly. Store slightly unripe plums at room temperature until fully ripe, which may take up to a week, then refrigerate and use within a few days.

For the table

TO PREPARE

• The thin skins are usually left on plums for cooking, especially for poaching, as the skins are softened by the cooking and can easily be pulled off, leaving a perfect, glossy surface behind; if the skin is red-blushed it will also give a pretty rosy flush to the flesh.

• To easily remove plum skins, dip the fruit briefly into boiling water, then into cold water, and slip them off.

• Some dark varieties of plum are good for cooking, especially jam, but are too tough-skinned or dry to be good for eating raw; however, in general, both soft-fleshed and firm-fleshed plums are good for eating out of hand, and both kinds are used for cooking.

• Apricots do not need skinning, but are usually split and the stones removed before cooking.

• Nothing can surpass the pleasure of eating a perfectly ripe, unadorned peach on a summer day, but these fruit also respond well to poaching or grilling, combining with other fruits, baked with a rich stuffing or in a creamy tart or butter cake, layered with cream and meringue or served in the old-fashioned way with home-made custard.

preserving the crop (peaches)

STORING	Pick only enough peaches for a few days at a time. Keep them at room temperature until they are soft; this can be hastened by enclosing them in a paper bag. Once soft, store in the refrigerator crisper for a day or two. Bring to room temperature before eating.
FREEZING	Process overripe peaches with a little sugar until pureed. Freeze in ice-cube trays and transfer to a freezer bag.

• To eat a peach out of hand, first rub the downy skin smooth under cold running water. To peel, pour boiling water over, leave up to 30 seconds, depending on ripeness, then drain and pull skin off. As the cut or peeled flesh darkens very quickly, brush with lemon juice if not to be used or served immediately.

• Peaches are best poached in their skins as the skin gives a pretty rosy flush to the flesh and the cooking softens it so that it is easy to pull off, leaving a perfect, glossy surface behind.

• Cherries can be stoned by halving and digging out the stone, or by using a special cherry stoner, available from kitchen shops or professional kitchen equipment shops.

TO SERVE

• Stone fruit poached in their skins retain their bright colours and are easier to peel afterwards.

• For a beautiful upside-down cake, place chopped stone fruit in the base of a cake pan along with brown sugar and butter, and top with a plain cake batter. Cook as normal and let stand for 5 minutes before turning out.

• A summer fruit platter is the perfect finish to a barbecue. Arrange slices of fresh peaches, apricots, nectarines, plums and mangoes on a large platter; drizzle over passionfruit pulp and sprinkle with chopped pistachios.

• Poach any stone fruit in a white wine sugar syrup with a little stem ginger; cool the fruit in the syrup and serve with a dollop of crème fraîche or mascarpone cheese.

• Cherries can make great-tasting, colourful vinegars for salads and sauces. Pour good-quality white wine vinegar over halved fruit and add cardamom pods or cinnamon sticks, if you like. Cover and stand for 2 days. Discard the fruit and spices and pour the flavoured vinegar into hot sterilised bottles (see Bottling, page 240-242). Store in the refrigerator for up to 1 year. The vinegar becomes sweeter as it ages.

• Poach peaches in a low-joule lemonade or ginger ale for a great summer treat for slimmers.

• Process overripe peaches with a little sugar until pureed. Freeze in ice-cube trays and transfer to a freezer bag. For a refreshing water-ice, puree as many cubes as you need.

• Uncooked white peaches are the right peaches for a Bellini, the famous Italian summer drink that combines fresh peach flesh and sparkling wine; add peach puree to the bottom of a glass of Champagne. Yellow peaches, especially freestones which are easier to peel as well as to stone, are the better kind to use in cooking.

• Nectarines' thin, smooth skin doesn't need peeling if they are to be eaten out of hand, halved and grilled, or sliced and drizzled with passionfruit pulp or piled on buttered and sugared brioche for an ambrosial breakfast.

• Nectarines can be poached or peeled and used raw for a tart filling, cake, crumble, trifle, ice-cream or other summer treats, however, the flesh discolours very quickly after peeling or cutting, so should be brushed with lemon juice if not to be cooked or served immediately.

• For a hot, sweet soufflé either place chopped fruit in the base of the dish or add pureed apricots to a basic sweet soufflé mixture.

• Mediocre apricots are transformed into something quite delicious when cooked; their sharp-sweet flavour is particularly accommodating and will marry beautifully with pork, chicken, veal, lamb, duck and turkey, as well as other fruits, nuts and spices. Apricots have starred for centuries in Middle Eastern meat cookery and in the finest creations of European pastry chefs.

• Apricots are not only lovely to eat just as they are but are also ready to be gently poached or preserved in sugar syrup or wine, starred in pastries and cakes, studded through jelly or ice-cream, or pickled to go with lamb or pork.

• Plums can be pureed raw, or cooked and folded through sweetened whipped cream for a fruit fool, poached in a wine or plain sugar syrup with lemon or orange rind and spices, used for cakes or crumbles, or made into jams, chutneys or sauces to serve with cooked meats.

peach, papaya and raspberry juice

1 medium peach (150g), chopped coarsely
50g (1½ ounces) peeled, seeded, coarsely chopped
  red papaya
50g (1½ ounces) raspberries
¼ cup (60ml) water

1 Blend or process ingredients until smooth.

prep time 10 minutes **serves** 1

note Papaya (also known as pawpaw or papaw) is a
large, pear-shaped red-orange tropical fruit.

balsamic strawberries with mascarpone

peach, papaya and raspberry juice

balsamic strawberries with mascarpone

500g (1 pound) strawberries, halved
¼ cup (55g) caster (superfine) sugar
2 tablespoons balsamic vinegar
1 cup (250g) mascarpone cheese
1 tablespoon icing (confectioners') sugar
1 teaspoon vanilla extract
¼ cup coarsely chopped fresh mint

1 Combine strawberries, sugar and vinegar in medium
bowl, cover; refrigerate 20 minutes.
2 Meanwhile, combine mascarpone, icing sugar and
extract in small bowl.
3 Stir mint into strawberry mixture; divide among serving
dishes. Serve with mascarpone.

prep time 5 minutes (+ refrigeration) **serves** 4

sweet almond cherry tarts

sweet almond cherry tarts

1½ cups (225g) plain (all-purpose) flour
150g (4½ ounces) butter, chopped coarsely
⅓ cup (55g) icing (confectioners') sugar
2 tablespoons iced water, approximately
2⅓ cups (350g) cherries, seeded
2 tablespoons white sugar
almond filling
60g (2 ounces) butter, softened
⅓ cup (75g) firmly packed light brown sugar
1 egg
1 tablespoon plain (all-purpose) flour
1 cup (100g) ground almonds

1 Process flour, butter and icing sugar until mixture resembles breadcrumbs. Gradually add the water, if required, processing until mixture just comes together. Knead on floured surface until smooth, cover; refrigerate 30 minutes.
2 Preheat oven to 200°C/400°F. Grease four oven trays; line with baking paper.
3 Make almond filling.
4 Divide pastry into eight pieces. Roll each piece into a 15cm (6 inch) round on floured surface; place two rounds on each tray. Divide almond filling among rounds, leaving a 4cm (1½ inch) border. Top with cherries; fold over border. Sprinkle with white sugar.
5 Bake about 20 minutes or until pastry is browned lightly. Serve with thick cream or vanilla ice-cream, if you like.
almond filling Beat butter, sugar and egg in small bowl with electric mixer until smooth. Stir in flour and ground almonds.

prep & cook time 50 minutes (+ refrigeration) **makes** 8

grilled nectarines with passionfruit yogurt

grilled nectarines with passionfruit yogurt

You need about two passionfruit to get the amount of pulp required for this recipe.

8 nectarines (1.5kg), halved, stones removed
¼ cup (55g) light brown sugar
2 tablespoons orange juice
1 cup (280g) yogurt
2 tablespoons icing (confectioners') sugar
2 tablespoons passionfruit pulp

1 Preheat grill (broiler).
2 Place nectarines, cut-side up, on oven tray; sprinkle with brown sugar and juice. Grill until browned lightly.
3 Meanwhile, combine yogurt and sifted icing sugar in medium bowl; swirl in pulp. Serve nectarines with yogurt.

prep & cook time 20 minutes **serves** 4

Summer Herbs

Summertime is the very season for herbs – almost every herb is romping by summer. There will be generous supplies in the garden or in pots within easy reach of the cook's kitchen. The two herbs featured: basil and mint, are at their most pungent and flavourful in the heat of the summer sun.

In the garden

BASIL

Basil is the queen of the summer herbs. It originally came from India even though it is now synonymous with Mediterranean cuisine. Varieties are also used throughout Asia and are added to noodles, curries and soups.

Its strong scent evokes high summer and its lush, green leaves scattered over salads and pasta captures the essence of warm weather. Its leaves are also an honest indicator of the turn of the seasons, as they start to blacken and wither in cool winds.

Basil is a warm-season herb, but you might be lucky to find self-sown seedlings in your garden from last year. Otherwise, pots, punnets and seeds are readily available from nurseries throughout spring and summer.

Plant seedlings in a sunny site in a rich garden bed or large pot after all frosts and cold winds have finished. If spaced 15-20cm (6-8") apart they will support each other as they grow.

Basil is lovely planted near a path or steps where you accidently brush the leaves at each passing. Pinch out the flower heads as they start to form and gather sprigs by nipping back the top of the stem to a pair of leaves. This will thicken the plant.

Feed with a liquid fertiliser every 2 weeks, but spray late in the day to avoid leaf burn. Always wash the leaves before using. Slugs, snails, grasshoppers and caterpillars will want a share, but most pests can be seen and caught before they've done too much damage.

MINT

Mint grows in most climates all year round, although in very cool areas it will need protective mulch during winter. But in summer mint really romps, growing tall, flowering and extending invasive new stems underground to take control of your herb bed. The best form of control is confinement in pots or troughs. These can be dug into the garden with their rims above the soil, but always watch out for stems that escape over the edge.

The scent of mint is delightful and there are a number of varieties – common garden mint with its mild flavour and rounded leaves, apple mint with its furry foliage, spearmint with its glossy pointed leaves, and peppermint with slightly purple-toned leaves. 'Eau-de-cologne' is named because of its perfume and, although not used in the kitchen, it's lovely to brush past.

Mint loves water and grows best with regular supplies; it will, however, recover if forgotten. Mint is much more aromatic if grown in full sun, but it does tolerate partial shade. Flowers are mauve, cream or white. Give it a 'haircut' after it flowers.

Vietnamese mint or laksa herb grows in the same generous way as mint, but is not a mint at all. Its strong flavour is not dissimilar to coriander and can be used as a substitute. It is, of course, added to laksas. Cut away the midrib if it gets woody and replace plants each spring.

preserving the crop

STORING	Pick herbs as close to using as possible. Basil, in particular, is very fragile and blackens easily. Store in a plastic bag wrapped loosely in absorbent paper towel for up to 3 days.
FREEZING	Both mint and basil can be frozen (see Freezing, page 240) for up to 6 months. Freeze sprigs in a rigid container and pluck off the frozen leaves as you need them. Once frozen, basil and mint are best used in cooked dishes. Another good idea is to chop basil finely, mix with butter and freeze as a log. Slice off a portion as you need it.
DRYING	Dried basil has not much flavour and has limited uses in the kitchen. Dried mint (see Drying, page 243) is used widely in teas, often mixed with chamomile.

common garden or
round mint

sweet or common basil

purple basil

For the table

TO SERVE

• Basil is a must with tomatoes. Leaves are best torn, not cut, as they will go black. Scatter over tomatoes and drizzle with olive oil.

• Add basil to any dish. To fully enhance its flavour, stir in extra fresh leaves at the end of cooking.

• Basil pesto is justifiably famous. Stir into soups and stews at the last minute, or spread on crusty bread before toasting for bruschetta. A pizza base spread with pesto under the tomato base is delicious.

• Place whole basil leaves over the centre of a boned loin of pork, cover with seasoning, roll and roast. Also add basil to the gravy for extra flavour.

• A great dressing for a lamb salad is pureed basil, green apple, garlic, lemon juice and oil.

• Mint cooked with apples makes a traditional mint jelly. Cook apples until they go rosy pink, but don't strain the pulp through muslin or the result will be cloudy.

• Mint mixed with yogurt, garlic and seeded cucumbers serves as a dip or sauce over grilled fish or chicken.

• Wrap whole mint leaves, julienne vegetables and prawns in rice paper rounds and serve with a lemon grass and mint sauce.

• Freeze mint leaves in ice-cubes and add to long cool drinks during hot summer days.

• Add some mint to zucchini fritters and serve with simple tomato sauce (see page 66).

basil pesto

2 cups firmly packed fresh basil leaves
2 cloves garlic, quartered
⅓ cup (50g) roasted pine nuts
½ cup (40g) coarsely grated parmesan cheese
¾ cup (180ml) olive oil

1 Blend or process basil, garlic, nuts and cheese until chopped finely. With motor operating, gradually add oil in a thin, steady stream; process until smooth.

prep time 10 minutes **makes** 1 cup
note Pesto will keep, refrigerated, for up to one week; spoon into a screw-top jar and cover with a thin layer of olive oil. If you want to keep it longer, freeze in the same container. Pesto will never freeze solid because of its high oil content, so you can easily remove a little at a time.

autumn

Autumn garden diary

The delights of summer inevitably fade,

but with autumn comes the best conditions for working in the garden, clearing up debris, straggling leftovers and dried remains that can all be composted when not diseased. If you have mountains of fallen leaves, pile them in a corner with handfuls of nitrogen-rich fertiliser, weigh them down with netting or a tarpaulin and leave them to mature for you to use as a summer mulch.

DEEP DIGGING AND SPREADING AROUND MANURE OR COMPOST TO REVITALISE GARDENS BECOMES A PLEASURE IN THE COOL WEATHER. IF YOU'VE GOT AREAS THAT ARE BECOMING SHADED AS THE SUN DIPS, LEAVE THEM DEEPLY MULCHED WITH MANURE AND STRAW OR GRASS CLIPPINGS UNTIL THE SPRING.

Enjoy drying, preserving and storing your summer bounty.

Plant out ready-prepared or bought seedlings to guarantee winter supplies. It is often a good idea to keep a record of what grew where in the garden over summer, what was successful, what caused more trouble than it was worth and what was not a treat to eat.

Prune shrubs and trees that block sunlight or lean over too far. Perennial vegetables like artichokes, chillies, capsicums and asparagus benefit from pruning before being mulched for protection against frost. Check soil is well drained to stop root rot and stunted growth. Build up soil levels with mulch and compost.

Days begin to shorten and the first signs of autumn start to appear. Mornings and evenings are just that bit cooler, and a warm spot in the sun is soon a sought-out pleasure. There's no denying the altered slant of the sun and the changes in the garden as plants prepare for the approach of winter, more spectacular in some parts of the world than others, but observable everywhere, from the subtropics to the polar reaches. In the tropics there'll be lush new growth in response to the abundant rain, but elsewhere there's a sedate reduction, a battening down for the lean times ahead.

Globe Artichokes

Who would believe that a thistle could look and taste so good? Globe artichokes belong to the thistle family, and are the flower buds of a wonderful grey-leafed plant that contributes a stunning architectural element to any flower-bed or vegetable patch. Subtle they are not; artichoke plants are tall and dramatic and require almost 1m (3') of space all round for their branches to spread. Try them if you have the space.

In the garden

Provide artichokes with deep, well-manured soil and plant in spring in temperate climates or late autumn or winter in milder gardens. Well-rooted offshoots from an established plant may be available from friends or as plants from large nurseries or from mail-order suppliers, and these are usually a better option than growing from seed. The quality of plants raised from seed varies greatly, and you may be disappointed with the crop you get from seedlings. Artichokes are short-lived perennials, so once planted, they'll last 3-4 years. Treat them as annuals in frosty gardens by raising fresh seed indoors or under glass, and planting them out as soon as the frosts are over. Give artichokes side dressings of complete garden fertiliser or pelleted poultry manure to ensure strong growth and buds at each branch end.

Cut the buds when they are still tightly closed and about 5-6cm (2-2½") round. Don't leave the globes on the plant too long as a dry thistle top will develop and other buds will not form once flowering begins. If you reduce the number of buds on the stems as soon as they start to develop, you'll force fewer, but larger, globes.

After flowering, keep artichokes watered, and in autumn cut the stems back to 30cm (12") above the soil. Spread around a protective and nourishing mulch of lucerne hay and manure for the winter and to give them a good start come spring.

You can make new plants by detaching offsets from established plants in autumn, but only do this to those plants that have produced the best quality artichokes.

For the table

TO PREPARE

• When preparing artichokes there's no need to snip off the top third of the leaves unless you are bothered by their tattiness or they are the variety with a small spike at the end of each leaf. Always remove the tough bottom leaves. Rub any cut surface with a lemon as artichokes discolour rapidly.

• You may like to remove the choke. Pull the centre leaves apart and, using a teaspoon, dig out the hairy choke and some of the tiny inner leaves.

• Boil, steam or microwave until just tender. Always cook artichokes in a non-reactive pan, or your artichokes will blacken. The part you eat is the fleshy base of each leaf, dipped in melted butter or a sauce such as hollandaise, and also the tender heart, which is revealed after the leaves are removed.

• Baby artichokes may be eaten raw, braised or fried, while larger ones are boiled or braised, and trimmed considerably before cooking.

• If serving cold, drop cooked artichokes into a sink of iced water for a minute or two to stop the cooking process, then drain them upside down.

• When serving artichokes, provide each diner with a large napkin and a finger bowl of warm water with a lemon slice. Also, place larger bowls, within easy reach, for the discarded leaves.

preserving the crop

STORING	Artichokes start to deteriorate when they are picked, so are best eaten soon after harvest. They can be stored, unwashed, in a vegetable storage bag in the refrigerator for 2 days. Wash just before using.
FREEZING	Artichoke hearts can be blanched and frozen (see Freezing, page 240). Break away the outside leaves and blanch hearts in acidulated water; drain well. Freeze for up to 4 months.
PICKLING	Artichoke hearts can be cooked in spiced vinegar and stored in olive oil (see Bottling, pages 240-242) for about 3 months. Toss cooked hearts in herbs before covering with olive oil.

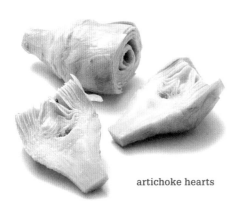

artichoke hearts

globe artichokes

TO SERVE

• Devotees of artichokes describe their flavour as 'nutty', 'smoky' or simply 'exquisite'. One of their flavour components (cynarin), has the unusual effect of making foods taste sweet after they have been eaten.

• Serve cold artichokes with tartare sauce, mayonnaise or a vinaigrette dressing.

• Most artichoke recipes call for dipping the leaves in sauces. The Italian sauce, bagna cauda, with anchovies is great but hollandaise goes just as well.

• Artichokes can be stuffed and baked. Try a mixture of breadcrumbs, pancetta and basil or oregano. Place stuffing between the artichoke leaves and bake. Drizzle with a flavoured mayonnaise and, again, add a few anchovies for their salty taste.

• Add cooked and quartered artichokes to salads, especially Mediterranean ones. Add a touch of mint to the vinaigrette for a refreshing flavour.

• Top chicken fillets with cooked artichoke hearts, pour over cheese sauce, sprinkle with parmesan and mozzarella and grill until golden and bubbling.

• Serve artichokes hearts on toasted focaccia. Drizzle with garlic oil.

• Do not discard the stem of young artichokes. About 15cm (6") is edible. Cook with the heads, then peel and slice, and add to dishes in the final stages.

artichoke, anchovy and chilli pizza

2 x 335g (10½ ounce) pizza bases
⅓ cup (95g) tomato paste
⅔ cup (80g) grated cheddar cheese
10 drained marinated artichokes (600g), quartered
10 anchovy fillets, drained
½ teaspoon dried chilli flakes
¼ cup (20g) finely grated parmesan cheese

1 Preheat oven to 220°C/425°F. Place pizza bases on oven trays.
2 Spread bases with paste; divide cheddar cheese between bases. Top with artichoke and anchovies; sprinkle with chilli and parmesan cheese. Bake about 15 minutes.

prep & cook time 25 minutes **serves** 4
note We used large (25cm/10 inch diameter) packaged pizza bases for this recipe. You can scatter 2 tablespoons of fresh oregano leaves over the pizza just before serving.

artichokes with lemon herb butter

80g (2½ ounces) butter, softened
2 teaspoons finely grated lemon rind
1 tablespoon finely chopped fresh flat-leaf parsley
2 teaspoons finely chopped fresh basil
4 medium globe artichokes (800g)

1 Combine butter, rind and herbs in small bowl. Place on piece of plastic wrap; shape into log, wrap tightly. Freeze until firm.
2 Meanwhile, remove and discard tough outer leaves from artichokes. Trim stems so artichoke bases sit flat.
3 Cook artichokes in large saucepan of boiling water about 40 minutes or until tender; drain.
4 Serve hot artichokes topped with slices of herb butter; accompany with lemon wedges.

prep & cook time 50 minutes (+ freezing) **serves** 4

artichokes with lemon herb butter

artichokes with lemon pepper hollandaise

1½ cups (375ml) water
1 cup (250ml) white wine
⅓ cup (80ml) olive oil
4 bay leaves
6 medium globe artichokes (1.2kg), trimmed
lemon pepper hollandaise
3 egg yolks
2 teaspoons finely grated lemon rind
1½ tablespoons lemon juice
½ teaspoon cracked black pepper
250g (8 ounces) unsalted butter

1 Combine water, wine, oil and bay leaves in large saucepan; bring to the boil. Add artichokes; simmer, covered, 30 minutes or until tender. Drain.
2 Meanwhile, make lemon pepper hollandaise.
3 Halve artichokes lengthwise; remove chokes. Drizzle artichokes with hollandaise to serve.
lemon pepper hollandaise Blend egg yolks, rind, juice and pepper until combined. Melt butter in small saucepan until bubbling. With motor operating, add hot butter to egg yolk mixture in a thin steady stream; blend until mixture is thick and creamy.

prep & cook time 40 minutes **serves** 6
notes Artichokes can be prepared an hour ahead. Hollandaise is best made close to serving; avoid adding the milk residue from the butter to the mix.

artichokes with lemon pepper hollandaise

Avocado

Avocados are the fruit of a family of large evergreen trees originating in Central and South America. Ripe avocados have soft, buttery flesh and a nutty flavour, and contain a high level of monounsaturated oil. Avocados were once exotic tropical fruits that few people knew how to peel, let alone grow and present at the table. Then there was a rush of extravagant uses from ice-cream to heated dishes. Now we've settled for the 'simple is best' belief, to take advantage of their rich smoothness and delightful green colouring.

In the garden

This elegant, evergreen tree grows to about 8m (25') and may be too large for the average garden. It also demands a warm and frost-free site. If in a well-sheltered position, an avocado tree can be coddled along in cooler conditions. Avocados display the most peculiar behaviour: in spring the flowers change sex on the same trees and, in subtropical and tropical areas, it is often necessary to grow two compatible varieties to achieve effective pollination. If you plan to grow a few, combine 'sharwil', a mid-season fruiter with 'hass', a late variety, and you will ensure effective pollination and an extended harvesting period. However, when grown out of the subtropics or tropics, the cooler conditions upset the plant's pollination system and a single tree usually provides all the avocados a household could want. Plant trees in spring to give them summer to get established. Like mangoes, avocado seeds might sometimes, very occasionally, sprout from compost heaps, but such trees can be unreliable and very slow to fruit. You are always best advised to buy a named avocado variety rather than risk disappointment with a seedling.

Apply a good dressing of complete garden fertiliser or pelleted poultry manure under the drip line in spring, summer and autumn every year, and water in well.

Avocados don't need pruning unless you're trying to keep the branches at a reasonable picking height. Avocados bloom in late winter and spring, and the fruit forms over summer. The fruit doesn't ripen on the tree. They are ready to pick when they've ceased expanding and have started to lose their glossy sheen. Store picked fruit indoors and it will ripen in 10 days or less. They are fully ripe when they just give to pressure at the stem end, otherwise you can leave the fruit on the tree until they fall to the ground, collect them and bring them inside to ripen.

Pests such as possums can be destructive, chewing the bark and eating the unripe fruit.

Hass is in season from late winter to early spring, has a lusciously creamy flesh free of fibre and with outstanding flavour. It is the only variety that changes colour as it ripens – its hard, pebbly shell changing from dark green to purple/black. Very occasionally, hass can be rubbery.

Shepard is in season from early autumn to the beginning of winter, is green-skinned, firm and mild-flavoured. It is much more resistant to darkening once cut, than other varieties. Replace the stone in the remaining fruit and cover tightly with plastic wrap. Some avocado fanciers find shepard too firm even when fully ripe.

preserving the crop

STORING	Allow avocados to ripen at home in the fruit bowl, hastening the process if necessary by enclosing them with a ripe banana in a paper bag. Once ripe, they can be kept in good condition for a day or two by refrigerating them, but don't refrigerate before they are ripe as this will damage their cellular processes and they will never ripen.
FREEZING	Avocados do not freeze and cannot be bottled, so must be enjoyed fresh.

hass avocado

fuerte avocado

sharwil avocado

Fuerte is in season from autumn to mid-winter and has a firmish buttery flesh with a rich flavour. Its smooth, thin green skin is easy to peel off. Very occasionally, fuerte can be watery.

Sharwil is in season in winter, has knobbly green skin, creamy-textured yellow flesh and a rich smoky flavour.

Reed is sometimes called the 'summer' avocado because it is in season from spring to mid-summer. It is very large with thick, rough, dark green skin and yellow flesh with a rich, meaty texture and buttery flavour.

Cocktail avocados are not a different variety but the unfertilised fruit. They are small and seedless, usually of good flavour, though occasionally a little too mild.

For the table

TO PREPARE

• You can speed up the ripening process by putting an avocado in a brown paper bag with a ripe banana. The ethylene gas given off by the banana helps ripen the avocado.

• Cut round the avocado lengthways, going right in to the stone, then pick it up in both hands and twist to separate the two halves. Many cooks remove the stone by placing that half on a board and, while steadying it firmly with one hand, stabbing a small, pointed knife into the stone and twisting to release it; a safer way is to cradle the half with the stone in your hand with the wider end away from you, and use the fingertips of your other hand to pry the stone up and out, starting from the wide end. You can then peel the skin back from the flesh, run a rubber spatula between the skin and flesh to scoop it out in one piece, or scoop out the flesh in spoonfuls.

• Cut avocado darkens very quickly, so it is best to prepare it only when you are ready to use it, or if you have to prepare it ahead of time, brush the exposed surfaces with lemon or lime juice. Mix juice through mashed avocado, and cover closely with plastic wrap. Leaving the stone in the half that is not used immediately is said to retard browning, but has only a limited effect.

TO SERVE

• Add slices of avocado, coated in lemon juice, to green salads where they will add a buttery texture and taste.

• The simplest way to enjoy its buttery, nutty flavour is to squash it onto bread or toast, season with salt and pepper and a touch of lemon juice, and eat it immediately.

• Avocado is good served as an accompaniment to ham or bacon, chicken, fish (including canned salmon and tuna) or shellfish; layer in a sandwich with any of these plus tomato and lettuce, or mix with them in a salad – but be sure to keep the avocado in large enough pieces for its subtle flavour to come through.

• In its homeland, avocado and corn are a favourite pairing, especially using corn tortillas to scoop up guacamole, the classic combination of mashed avocado, chilli, onion, lime juice and sometimes chopped coriander or tomato.

• The natural shape of an avocado half, with its large cavity where the stone was, makes it a perfect case for stuffing with hot or cold mixtures using any of the ingredients mentioned above.

• Avocado does not cook well because heating spoils both its texture and flavour. It can, however, take the slight warming imparted by a hot stuffing or hot bacon or chicken in a sandwich.

guacamole

2 medium avocados (500g)
½ small red onion (50g), chopped finely
1 medium egg (plum) tomato (75g), seeded,
  chopped finely
1 tablespoon lime juice
¼ cup coarsely chopped fresh coriander (cilantro)

1 Mash avocados in medium bowl; stir in remaining
ingredients.

prep time 10 minutes **makes** 2½ cups
note Serve guacamole as a dip with corn chips or torn corn
tortillas, or as an addition to nachos, burritos and fajitas.

tex-mex pizza

guacamole

tex-mex pizza

4 x 115g (3½ ounce) pizza bases
¾ cup (180g) refried beans
½ cup (130g) spicy tomato salsa
½ small red onion (50g), sliced thinly
½ cup (50g) coarsely grated pizza cheese
1 medium avocado (250g), sliced thinly
2 tablespoons fresh coriander leaves (cilantro)

1 Preheat oven to 220°C/425°F. Oil two oven trays.
2 Spread bases with beans; top with salsa and onion,
sprinkle with cheese.
3 Cook about 15 minutes. Top pizzas with avocado
and coriander.

prep & cook time 25 minutes **serves** 4
notes We used small (15cm/6 inch diameter) packaged
pizza bases for this recipe.
A Mexican staple, frijoles refritos (refried beans) are
sold canned in supermarkets. You will also find spicy
tomato salsa in supermarkets.

nachos

1 tablespoon olive oil
1 small brown onion (80g), chopped finely
1 clove garlic, crushed
400g minced (ground) beef
1 fresh long red chilli, chopped finely
35g (1 ounce) packet taco seasoning mix
400g (12½ ounces) canned diced tomatoes
1 tablespoon tomato paste
⅓ cup (80ml) beef stock
420g (13½ ounces) canned mexican chilli beans,
    rinsed, drained
¼ cup coarsely chopped fresh coriander (cilantro)
230g (7 ounces) corn chips, chopped coarsely
1½ cups (180g) coarsely grated cheddar cheese
guacamole
1 large avocado (320g), chopped coarsely
1 medium tomato (150g), chopped finely
½ small red onion (50g), chopped finely
1 tablespoon lime juice
1 tablespoon finely chopped fresh coriander (cilantro)

1 Heat oil in large frying pan; cook onion and garlic, stirring, until onion softens. Add beef; cook, stirring, until beef changes colour. Add chilli and seasoning mix; cook, stirring, until fragrant.

2 Add undrained tomatoes, paste and stock; bring to the boil. Reduce heat; simmer, uncovered, 15 minutes. Add beans; cook, stirring, about 5 minutes or until thickened. Stir in coriander. Cool 10 minutes.

3 Preheat oven to 200°C/400°F. Grease eight holes of two six-hole (¾-cup/180ml) texas muffin pans; line greased holes with two criss-crossed 5cm x 20cm (2 inch x 8 inch) strips of baking paper (parchment).

4 Combine corn chips and 1 cup of the cheese in small bowl; divide half the corn chip mixture among prepared pan holes, pressing down firmly. Divide beef mixture among pan holes; top with remaining corn chip mixture, pressing down firmly. Sprinkle with remaining cheese. Bake about 15 minutes or until browned lightly.

5 Meanwhile, make guacamole by mashing avocado in medium bowl; stir in remaining ingredients.

6 Stand nachos in pan 5 minutes. Using baking paper strips as lifters, carefully remove nachos from pan holes. Serve topped with guacamole; sprinkle with fresh coriander leaves and accompany with sour cream and lime wedges, if you like.

prep & cook time 1 hour **makes** 8
note Taco seasoning mix is found in most supermarkets; it is meant to duplicate the taste of a Mexican sauce made from oregano, cumin, chillies and other spices.

Pumpkin

These ragged but ornamental wanderers have developed throughout summer and by autumn or even early winter will be ready to harvest. Some pumpkins are coloured a subtle grey like the queensland blue or jarrahdale; others are deep green and flecked like the jap or turkish turban, and others are orange to cream like the butternut, jack little or red kuri. These all have a rich orange flesh, and are excellent to eat.

Huge, competition-size pumpkins are spectacular but are mostly used for stockfeed. The shapes and sizes of pumpkins are as varied as their colours.

Pumpkin is an obliging vegetable, ready to be baked with the roast, or mashed to go with the sausages or chops; it lends a warm sweetness to spicy Middle Eastern soups, meat or rice dishes, goes in vegetable or meat curries, teams with strong herbs such as sage or rosemary for stuffing ravioli or serving with gnocchi, and blends with other ingredients for healthy cakes or traditional pumpkin scones. Pumpkins are available all year round.

Butternut is a small, creamy beige pumpkin with thin, tender skin and nutty-sweet flesh.

Butter pumpkin has easily cut orange-pink skin and well-flavoured yellow flesh.

Crown prince is a large, hard-skinned blue-grey pumpkin with full-flavoured, deep orange flesh.

Golden nugget is a small, round pumpkin whose easily-cut skin, many seeds and mild-flavoured flesh make it ideal for hollowing out, stuffing and baking.

Hubbard is a full-flavoured, pear-shaped pumpkin recognisable by its hard, bumpy, dark-green skin.

Jap, or japanese pumpkin, also known as the kent variety, is small with easily peeled, mottled green and yellow skin and a sweeter flesh than most other varieties.

Jarrahdale is a large pumpkin with ribbed, firm, but not hard, skin and a sweet orange flesh.

Queensland blue is a large variety with hard, deeply indented skin and a dry, full-flavoured flesh.

Windsor black is large and flattish with almost-black green skin and well-flavoured flesh.

In the garden

Pumpkins belong to the same family as the large and diverse range of melons, cucumbers, zucchini and squash, and require the same growing and cultivation conditions (see pages 72 and 94).

If you have the space, let your pumpkins run wild over fences, sheds or trees. This will save ground space in the garden. Make sure the fruits don't get rubbed by trees or against fences, as the skin gets damaged and scarred. The developing fruits may need support as well if growing on a fence or high place.

Some suggestions are given on page 72 for controlling the spread of cucurbits generally. Some compact forms are available, usually marketed as 'bush' pumpkins that cluster around a central stem. These are ideal for growing in limited spaces or pots. Pumpkins must have regular water during their development, particularly when confined in pots.

Pumpkins are the only member of the large cucurbit group to be harvested after the vine has withered and after the attachment point has broken, or at least become woody and brittle. Dry and harden them in the sun if they have to be harvested earlier. They must be fully mature for good flavour, and the skin hardened to ensure they will keep.

Always check stored pumpkins regularly for signs of rot or pest damage. See pages 74 and 96 for the control of pests and diseases.

preserving the crop

STORING	Whole pumpkins store well in a well-ventilated place away from heat and sunlight for up to 2 months. Hard-skinned ones will often store for much longer than this; some old-timers say that storing in the open through winter improves pumpkins, making them sweeter. Once cut, remove the seeds, cover with plastic wrap and store in the refrigerator for up to a week.
FREEZING	Uncooked pumpkin is not suitable to freeze, however, pumpkin puree and pumpkin soup freeze beautifully (see Freezing, page 240).
PICKLING	With the addition of sugar, citrus rind and juice and flavourings, such as fresh herbs, pumpkin can be made into jam. Seal in hot, sterilised jars for up to 4 months (see Bottling, pages 240-242).
	Make chutney from pumpkin, apples and raisins with spices, vinegar and sugar; this keeps for up to 6 months.

butternut pumpkin

jap pumpkin

golden nugget

jarrahdale pumpkin

spiced pumpkin soup with cinnamon cream

1 tablespoon olive oil
1 medium brown onion (150g), chopped coarsely
1 clove garlic, crushed
2 teaspoons ground cumin
½ teaspoon ground coriander
1kg (2 pounds) butternut pumpkin, chopped coarsely
2 medium potatoes (400g), chopped coarsely
2 cups (500ml) water
1½ cups (375ml) vegetable stock
5cm (2 inch) strip orange rind
cinnamon cream
⅔ cup (160ml) thickened (heavy) cream
½ teaspoon ground cinnamon

1 Heat oil in large saucepan; cook onion and garlic, stirring, until onion softens. Add spices; cook, stirring, until fragrant. Add pumpkin, potato, the water, stock and rind; bring to the boil. Reduce heat; simmer, covered, 20 minutes or until vegetables are tender.
2 Meanwhile, make cinnamon cream.
3 Blend or process soup, in batches, until smooth. Return soup to same pan; stir over heat until heated through.
4 Serve bowls of soup topped with cinnamon cream.
cinnamon cream Beat ingredients in small bowl with electric mixer until soft peaks form.

prep & cook time 30 minutes **serves** 4

For the table

TO PREPARE

• Make pumpkin slightly easier to peel and still retain all your fingers by microwaving for a few seconds after cutting into pieces. Otherwise, call in some muscle.

TO SERVE

• Add chunks of roasted pumpkin to pasta sauces or, if you're keen, make your own ravioli from roasted pumpkin, sage and parmesan cheese.

• There's no need to add cream to pumpkin soup. Simply cook chunks in chicken or vegetable stock with added aromatics such as onion and garlic. Puree and serve with bacon and pan-fried bread. A little added orange rind and juice will bring out the natural sweetness of the pumpkin.

• Make a gratin from thinly sliced pumpkin, kumara (orange sweet potato) and potato. Pour over a little cream, sprinkle with herbs, breadcrumbs and cheese, and bake.

• Pumpkin makes great deep-fried chips, but watch carefully as they cook faster than potatoes.

• Like zucchini flowers, pumpkin flowers are edible. Remove the inside stamens and fill with a cheese mixture. Dip in a light batter and deep-fry until golden. Otherwise, use whole and add to frittatas.

• The seeds of pumpkin are also edible. Dry them and discard the shell. The kernels are known as pepitas and have a nutty flavour that goes well with browned butter. Serve over grilled fish.

• Cut the tops off mini pumpkins, add a dot of butter and drizzle with honey; replace the top and bake until tender.

spiced pumpkin and chickpeas

roasted pumpkin and rosemary risotto

When you cook a roast, cook extra pumpkin to add to salads or dishes like this.

1 litre (4 cups) chicken or vegetable stock
1kg (2 pounds) pumpkin, chopped coarsely
¼ cup (60ml) olive oil
1½ cups (300g) arborio rice
1 clove garlic, crushed
1 tablespoon rosemary leaves
150g (4½ ounces) baby spinach leaves
¼ cup (20g) coarsely grated parmesan cheese
¼ cup (60ml) pouring cream

1 Preheat oven to 180°C/350°F.
2 Bring stock to the boil in medium saucepan. Reduce heat; simmer covered.
3 Combine pumpkin and half the oil in baking dish; cook, in oven, about 40 minutes or until pumpkin is tender.
4 Heat remaining oil in large saucepan, add rice; stir 2 minutes or until rice is coated in oil. Add garlic and rosemary; cook, stirring, until fragrant.
5 Stir in ½ cup simmering stock; cook, stirring constantly over low heat, until liquid is absorbed. Continue adding stock, in 1-cup batches, stirring until liquid is absorbed after each addition.
6 Stir pumpkin, spinach, cheese and cream into mixture; stir over heat until hot. Top with parmesan flakes to serve.

prep & cook time 1 hour **serves** 4
notes Make risotto close to serving. Leftover risotto can be made into patties and pan-fried. Serve topped with crisp prosciutto and dollop with sour cream.
Arborio rice is a small, round-grain rice. It is well-suited to absorb a large amount of liquid, so is especially suitable for risottos. It is available from supermarkets.

spiced pumpkin and chickpeas

2 tablespoons peanut oil
500g (1 pound) pumpkin, into 1cm (½ inch) pieces
1 tablespoon chermoula spice mix
420g (13½ ounces) canned chickpeas (garbanzo), rinsed, drained
350g coarsely chopped spinach

1 Heat oil in wok; stir-fry pumpkin about 6 minutes or until almost tender.
2 Add spice mix; stir-fry about 2 minutes or until pumpkin is tender.
3 Add chickpeas and spinach; stir-fry until spinach wilts, season to taste. Serve with steamed jasmine rice and lemon wedges, if you like.

prep & cook time 15 minutes **serves** 4
note Chermoula spice mix (chermoula spice blend) is a North African spice blend that gives a spicy Moroccan flavour to food. It is a blend of cumin, paprika, turmeric, cayenne pepper, garlic, onion, parsley, salt and pepper and is available from specialty spice shops and most major supermarkets.

roasted pumpkin and rosemary risotto

Carrots

Why bother growing carrots? They're cheap and plentiful in the supermarket, after all. Yet these colourful and familiar vegetables are ideal for growing in backyard gardens. Their soft, feathery green tops look great among the other crops and they don't take up much space. There are even short, round varieties that grow happily in pots. Carrots have many uses: they are the indispensable vegetable for casseroles, stews, soups and stocks; they're delicious on their own, with chopped parsley, eaten raw, grated in salads, julienned in stir-fries, baked into cakes and are universally admired as a juice vegetable par excellence. There is plenty to do with your bumper crop of carrots.

In the garden

The delicate foliage of carrots is a clue to their fragile constitution. They are frost-tender, so don't plant in autumn where the winters are cold. Nor do they like hot, dry weather. Autumn and early spring are ideal times for sowing in Mediterranean, subtropical and frost-free temperate gardens.

Like all root crops, carrots like a soft soil mix. Break up all clods and reduce all organic matter to fine particles otherwise they'll be misshapen where the going's too tough. Add a general garden fertiliser or pelleted poultry manure as the soil is worked over. Drag through a trowel or press on a rake handle to form shallow furrows for the seeds. Carrot seeds are very fine and tend to stick together. They can be mixed with fine sand to distribute them evenly, otherwise, lightly roughen up the soil in the furrow after the seeds have been dropped in. Seedlings emerge in 2-3 weeks. Sometimes carrots are sown with radish seeds, which are much larger. Radishes germinate sooner, their leaves keep weeds at bay while the carrots are immature, and they are harvested well before they begin to compete with the carrots for root space.

Thin when the seedlings are tiny and again as small carrots start to form. These are the tiny foretastes of the gatherings to come. Leave 5cm (2") between the remaining carrots to allow enough room for their ultimate size. Keep well watered, weed-free and hill up the soil if the carrot tops start to show above the soil. Sunlight turns carrots green. They are still edible, but look less attractive.

Check their size after about 3 months. Pull out a carrot or run your fingers around the top under the soil. If it's the right size, take as many as you need for each occasion, leaving the others in the ground. However, don't leave the stragglers too long as they'll become woody. Sow follow-up plantings each month. Parsnips grow similarly.

For the table

TO PREPARE

• There is no need to peel carrots; they'll lose most of their vitamins if you do. Just wash thoroughly and remove the tops.

• Carrots can be boiled, steamed or microwaved, but don't overdo it – they should be crisp rather than limp.

• Children often prefer carrots raw, and when they're just pulled from the garden and washed, they have even more appeal.

preserving the crop

STORING	Store carrots in vegetable storage bags in the refrigerator. Baby carrots will keep for 2-3 days while larger carrots can be kept for about a week.
FREEZING	Carrots can be blanched and frozen whole, if baby, or otherwise sliced (see Freezing, page 240); freeze for up to 10 months. Grated carrot can also be blanched and frozen but doesn't keep as long. It's useful to have on hand to add to casseroles and stir-fries.
PICKLING	Carrots can be pickled. Cook for a very short time only, and pack into hot sterilised jars (see Bottling, pages 240-242); pour over a hot, spiced vinegar mixture and seal while hot. Leave for a couple of weeks before serving with antipasto platters or ploughman's lunches. They will keep for up to 6 months.

mature carrots

baby or dutch carrots

carrot cakes with cream cheese frosting

⅓ cup (80ml) vegetable oil
⅓ cup (75g) caster (superfine) sugar
1 egg
2 medium carrots (240g), grated coarsely
¼ cup (30g) finely chopped walnuts
¾ cup (110g) self-raising flour
¼ teaspoon bicarbonate of soda (baking soda)
½ teaspoon mixed spice
cream cheese frosting
20g (¾ ounce) butter, softened
60g (2 ounces) cream cheese, softened
¾ cup (120g) icing (confectioners') sugar

1 Preheat oven to 180°C/350°F. Grease 8 holes of a 12-hole ½-cup (125ml) oval friand pan.
2 Beat oil, sugar and egg in small bowl with electric mixer until thick and pale. Transfer mixture to large bowl; stir in carrot, nuts and sifted dry ingredients. Spoon mixture into pan holes; bake about 20 minutes. Stand cakes in pan 5 minutes before turning, top-side up, onto wire rack to cool.
3 Make cream cheese frosting.
4 Spread cold cakes with cream cheese frosting. Serve topped with halved walnuts, if you like.
cream cheese frosting Beat butter and cream cheese in small bowl with electric mixer until light and fluffy. Gradually beat in sifted icing sugar.

prep & cook time 40 minutes (+ cooling) **makes** 8

TO SERVE

• Start the day with freshly squeezed apple and carrot juice. Add pineapple juice for extra zing. Another popular combination is carrot, orange and beetroot.

• Grated carrots and fresh mint make an easy salad.

• Grated carrot can be added to potato cakes; serve with a dot of butter.

• Add grated carrot, squeezed out in kitchen paper, to a spicy apple cake. Eat while still warm.

• Carrots can be cut into julienne (matchsticks), stir-fried in oil until tender but still with a bit of bite, then tossed with shredded mint.

• Slice lengthways, brush with melted butter or oil and barbecue or char-grill for rich flavour and caramelised charred stripes.

• Cut into halves, then halve or quarter lengthways, brush with melted butter or oil and roast on a baking tray at 200°C/400°F, turning once or twice, until tender and caramelised.

• Gently cook whole small or baby carrots in a covered saucepan with melted butter, a little sugar, a little lemon juice and a spoonful or two of water until almost tender, uncover, turn up the heat a little and shake the saucepan to roll the carrots until the liquid evaporates and they are glazed; sprinkle with fresh parsley to serve.

orange and maple glazed baby carrots with hazelnuts

30g (1 ounce) butter
800g (1½ pounds) baby carrots, trimmed, peeled
2 teaspoons finely grated orange rind
¼ cup (60ml) orange juice
2 tablespoons dry white wine
2 tablespoons pure maple syrup
½ cup (70g) coarsely chopped roasted hazelnuts

1 Melt butter in large frying pan; cook carrots, turning occasionally, until almost tender.
2 Add rind, juice, wine and syrup; bring to the boil. Simmer, uncovered, until liquid has almost evaporated and carrots are tender and caramelised.
3 Serve carrots sprinkled with nuts.

prep & cook time 25 minutes **serves** 4

orange and maple glazed baby carrots with hazelnuts

dhal and carrot soup

1 tablespoon peanut oil
1 medium brown onion (150g), chopped coarsely
2 cloves garlic, crushed
1 tablespoon ground cumin
1 tablespoon ground coriander
2 teaspoons garam masala
5 medium carrots (600g), chopped coarsely
2 litres (8 cups) vegetable stock
1 litre (4 cups) water
½ cup (100g) brown lentils
½ cup (100g) yellow split peas
½ cup (100g) red lentils
2 tablespoons coarsely chopped fresh coriander (cilantro)

1 Heat oil in large saucepan; cook onion and garlic, stirring, until onion softens. Add cumin, ground coriander and garam masala, stirring, until fragrant. Add carrot; cook, stirring, 2 minutes.
2 Add stock and the water to pan; bring to the boil. Add brown lentils and peas; reduce heat, simmer, uncovered, 40 minutes.
3 Add red lentils; simmer, uncovered, 10 minutes or until tender.
4 Stand soup 10 minutes, then blend or process half the mixture until smooth; stir into remaining soup in pan. Stir in chopped coriander; serve with a dollop of yogurt and sprinkle with extra chopped fresh coriander, if you like.

prep & cook time 1 hour 15 minutes **serves** 8
note Garam masala is a blend of spices based on cardamom, cinnamon, coriander, cloves, fennel and cumin, roasted and ground together. It is available from specialty spice shops and major supermarkets.

dhal and carrot soup

Olives

Their home is land bounded by or close to the Mediterranean Sea. Most of the picturesque, gnarled specimens are hundreds of years old and still productive. Massive new groves are constantly being planted to cope with the expanding world demand for olive oil. It's impossible to imagine Spanish, Italian, Greek and Middle Eastern cuisines without olives and olive oil. Equally impossible to imagine is the Mediterranean without its characteristic groves of olive trees with their narrow, grey-green leaves and tough, gnarled bark. Olives vary in size and colour, but there are scores of cultivars that will provide you with just the type to suit your garden. Olives are not palatable straight from the tree. They have to be brined before use. They can then be bottled in brine or oil, pitted, filled or eaten salted.

Green olives are firm and tangy. They are available stone-in or stoned and stuffed, usually with pimiento (capsicum), almond or anchovy. They come in sizes from fingernail to cherry tomato; the biggest, sold as spanish or queen olives, are the best size if you want to stuff them yourself with something interesting such as tuna or preserved lemon. They are difficult to stone by hand, so if stoned ones are called for in a recipe, buy yourself a gadget known as a cherry-stoner or olive-pitter, which punches out the stone leaving a neat hole.

Black olives have a richer and more mellow flavour than green ones and are softer in texture. They are available plain, not usually identified by variety except for pointed kalamatas or small, wrinkled ligurians, and are also sold in many kinds of marinade from garlic or herbs to lemon and chilli.

In the garden

An olive tree's chief requirement is well-drained soil with enough depth of soil for its roots to hold, even though an olive tree is predominantly a surface rooter.

Keep olive trees well mulched (straw, decaying grass clippings, leaf mulch, even rocks) during hot, dry summers to keep moisture around the roots. For a productive life, olive trees need protection from winter winds. They grow to 4-5m (13-16') quickly.

Most olives can survive frosts, occasional snowfalls and hot dry summers as long as there is regular rain or watering from mid-autumn through until mid-spring. There are varieties that do well in subtropical and warm-temperate areas. Olive trees can also be grown in large pots for a dramatic display, though they will produce only a modest crop.

Discrete, fragrant olive clusters appear in early summer after their first 3-4 years' growth. The berries fill out over summer. They can be harvested green by running your hands down the fruit-laden stems. They are easier to pick when ripe and black because they naturally fall off. In olive groves, sheets are spread under the trees and the branches are shaken with a mechanical gripper that harvests the entire crop at once. For the home gardener, vigorously shaking the branches is sufficient to release the ripe olives. Pick up the olives from your dropsheet. You can also simply pick up the olives as they fall, and store the early arrivals in the refrigerator until you've got sufficient numbers for brining.

Ask at your nursery for recommended cultivars for your area or go on-line for mail order suppliers. One or a few olive trees make an interesting project for the keen gardener, and you can continue the ancient tradition of preserving olives at home. You will, alas, need a whole grove to keep your kitchen in olive oil for the year.

preserving the crop

STORING	Untreated olives should be kept for as little time as possible. Store in a vegetable storage bag in the refrigerator for about 2 days. Green olives should be stored in an airtight jar, black ones in a jar of olive oil with additions such as sliced garlic if you wish. Olives don't need refrigerating because they are salted, but if green ones are to be kept a long while, they may do better if refrigerated with a little freshly-made brine, and turned over from time to time to keep them moist.
PICKLING	Olives can be pickled (brined) and marinated (see page 154).
SALTED	All olives need to be preserved in brine before consumption (when bottling do not mix black and green olives). Olives can also be salted before use as this is a form of brining. Toss the olives in an equal weight amount of salt and place in a sieve or drainer. Weigh down and leave for a month at least. The olives will be dried and have a wrinkly skin and a salty taste (you can rinse before using).

dried black olives

pimento-stuffed green olives

ligurian olives

tomato, pesto and olive tart

500g (1 pound) red grape tomatoes
1 tablespoon balsamic vinegar
1 tablespoon olive oil
1 sheet puff pasty
2 tablespoons basil pesto
⅓ cup (55g) seeded black olives
1½ cups (360g) ricotta cheese

1 Preheat oven to 220°C/425°F.
2 Combine tomatoes in medium bowl with vinegar and half the oil; place on oven tray. Roast, uncovered, about 10 minutes or until tomatoes collapse.
3 Place pastry on oiled oven tray. Fold edges of pastry over to make a 5mm (¼ inch) border all the way around pastry; prick base with fork. Place another oven tray on top of pastry (to stop it puffing up); bake 10 minutes. Remove top tray from pastry; reduce temperature to 200°C/400°F.
4 Spread pastry with pesto; top with tomatoes and olives. Sprinkle with cheese. Bake about 10 minutes. Drizzle with remaining oil before serving.

prep & cook time 30 minutes **serves** 4
notes Substitute cherry tomatoes for the grape tomatoes. Balsamic vinegar, made from the juice of Trebbiano grapes, is a deep rich brown colour with a sweet and sour flavour. It ranges in pungency and quality depending on how, and how long, it has been aged. Quality can be determined up to a point by price; use the most expensive sparingly. It is available from most supermarkets.

For the table
TO SERVE

• Green olives or mixed green and black olives are good to serve with drinks or as part of an antipasto tray.

• A green olive is a classic addition to a martini.

• Black olives are a favourite snack, garnish or addition to a cheese board.

• Use black olives in pizzas and breads, pâtés, salads, pasta, risotto and hearty meat dishes.

• Black olives star in their own right as the soul of the famous Provençal relish, tapenade, which is piled onto sliced baguette or turkish bread, scooped up with torn lebanese bread or crudités, spooned onto bowls of soup, used for pasta sauces or served as a condiment with grilled meats and fish.

• Blend or process preserved pitted olives with anchovies, sun-dried tomatoes, capers and garlic for a spread that has to be tried to be believed. Spread on bruschetta and top with goat's cheese.

• Once olives have been brined, pack them into hot sterilised jars with lemon grass, chillies and coriander seeds for a fragrant Asian flavour.

• Wrap pitted preserved olives in a cheese pastry and chill for several hours. Bake them in a hot oven until golden and serve at room temperature with drinks.

• Puree preserved, pitted olives with parmesan cheese, garlic and oregano. Spread this paste over the base of a pizza, together with cheese and sun-dried tomatoes.

• Toss a few preserved olives over a watermelon and red onion salad; drizzle with orange juice and olive oil.

pickled olives

pickled olives

*Pickle, or brine, olives for about 5 weeks before using.
Don't mix black and green olives.*

1.5kg (3 pounds) black or green olives, unblemished
⅓ cup (75g) fine sea salt
1 litre (4 cups) water
½ cup (125ml) olive oil

1 Using a sharp small knife, make two small slits along
the length of each olive, through to the stone. Add olives
to 2-litre (8-cup) sterilised jars (see Bottling, pages 240-242)
until two-thirds full. Cover with water. Fill a small plastic
bag with water; tie securely and sit on top of the olives to
keep them submerged (scum will appear on the surface of
the water).
2 Change the water every day. Do this for 4 days for
black olives and 6 days for green olives.
3 To make brine, combine salt and the water in medium
saucepan; stir over heat until salt is dissolved; let brine
cool to room temperature.
4 Drain the water from jars; cover olives with brine. Pour
oil over olives and brine. Seal the jars.
5 Do not disturb for 5 weeks. Keep in a cool, dry place
for up to 6 months.

marinated olives

*This is the next step after the brining process and cannot
be completed unless you have first brined the olives.*

600g (1¼ pounds) drained black or green olives
1 clove garlic, sliced
2 lemon wedges
2 sprigs fresh thyme or rosemary
2 cups (500ml) olive oil

1 Combine olives, garlic, lemon and herbs in 1-litre (4-cup)
sterilised jar (see Bottling, pages 240-242). Pour in olive oil
to cover olives; seal well.
2 Leave for 2 weeks before using. Store in a cool, dark
place for up to 6 months and, once opened, refrigerate.

notes The flavourings of marinated olives can be changed
to suit your taste. For cajun olives: add chilli, garlic, black
peppercorns, mustard seeds and celery seeds.
You can also try packing sun-dried tomatoes with the olives
and adding sprigs of dried oregano and some garlic.

marinated olives

Autumn Fruit

Summer fruits are scented, sensual but oh-so-fragile. Autumn fruits are robust, dependable, earthily fragrant and often magnificently storable. Harvesting new-season fruit is always a delight, but the first bite of a nature-chilled crisp apple, licking the juice of a perfectly ripe pear, smelling the heady aroma of a sun-warmed rockmelon and tracing the convoluted intrigues of a sliced fig make the season sing. Twining vines of grapes and kiwifruit will drape themselves with golden hues before their leaves drop. They are both such ornamental fruits that they are able to dress the table purely in their own right. And when prepared for eating, they are even better.

Grapes

IN THE GARDEN

Grapes grow in most climates, except the subtropics and tropics. In the warmer months they prefer dry air rather than humidity and frequent rain, as these cause grapes to develop damaging fungal diseases of the fruit and leaves. If you want to try grapes in an area with humid, rainy summers, seek out varieties that can cope with those conditions. There are many grape varieties: red or white, seedless or seeded, for eating or wine. Your local nursery can advise on what grows well in your area. Grapes grow very easily from cuttings. Plant them in winter and mark the site as it's so easy to mow over the mere sticks or break them as you pass. They will grow very easily from cuttings taken from winter prunings, or buy dormant plants from the nursery in winter.

In early spring the buds become furred and fat. Once they burst into leaf, the new stems grow at a rapid rate. The tiny bunch-of-grape flowers are sweetly scented. Grapevine moth (or possums) may well come to dine on new foliage. Collect moths by hand or spray with a non-toxic bio-insecticide based on bacteria that affects only caterpillars. Without spraying, the vine will usually survive the attack but may be rendered unsightly. The new leaves can be used for dolmades (small parcels containing rice, vegetables or minced meat wrapped in grape leaves), but remember to wash off any sprays. In very dry weather, soak the roots once a week. The vine is a very generous climber and can create a sheltered dining area under a pergola in a single season, and will form a dense cover in 2 seasons.

Birds and bees will want their share, so pick the grape bunches regularly and keep the area beneath the vine clear of debris. Handle bunches gently so you don't remove any bloom and always cut, rather than break, the stems. Pruning is essential in late autumn or winter if the vine is to remain productive and shapely. For the home garden, growing it along a strong fence or as a standard will keep it low. Cut back hard to a leaf node on sturdy wood and remove all the cross-connecting stems. When training a grape vine to grow high, such as over a pergola, remove all side shoots until it has reached the desired height, and a thick trunk will develop. Treat the spreading top growth as described above.

In cold areas, grapes have to be kept in a conservatory. The vines are pruned and laid on the ground for filling with sap and speedy growth in the spring.

For the table

TO SERVE

• Grapes simply should be washed and enjoyed fresh.

• Serve with soft cheeses, rich terrines, ham or chicken salads, in fruit salads, and use to make jelly preserves.

• Serve on a cheeseboard with scissors for diners to cut off what they want, or already cut into small bunches.

• Thread frozen grapes onto toothpicks, and serve after a hot and spicy curry.

preserving the crop (grapes)

STORING	Store table grapes in a vegetable storage bag in the refrigerator for a week or so, bringing them to room temperature before eating.
FREEZING	Grapes can be frozen but must be eaten that way and not defrosted.
PICKLING	Pack grapes into hot sterilised jars (see Bottling, page 240-242); pour over a hot sugar syrup flavoured with spices and a high proportion of liqueur, then seal while hot and store for a couple of weeks before using. They will keep for about 6 months at room temperature; once opened must be refrigerated and used quickly. Serve with plain cakes or ice-creams.
BOTTLING	Grapes can be made into jelly but need the addition of apples or a setting agent. Pour hot jelly into hot sterilised jars (see Bottling, pages 240-242) and seal while hot. Store in a cool dry place for up to a year. Once opened they must be stored in the refrigerator.

white figs

purple figs

Figs

IN THE GARDEN

The gnarled framework of a fig tree stands starkly bare in winter in all but very mild climates. It will happily grow in a wide range of conditions, though it will need shelter from icy winds where it is very cold (below 5°C/41°F). Select a variety recommended for your area, either green (called white), brown or purple fruited, whatever pleases you most. The darkest fruits make the darkest jam. Little pruning is required, and fertiliser applied in spring and late summer will keep it happy.

Birds will no doubt invade during the fruiting season, so nets over the tree may well be necessary – try to keep the fruit well inside the netting. Fruit ripened on the tree is the sweetest.

For the table

TO PREPARE

• Remove the hard bit and any stalk at the stem end of fresh figs. The whole fruit is edible but can be peeled; for presentation, slit the skin downward into quarters, peeling it back like petals.

• Dried figs may be steamed to soften them before adding to a cake or pudding mixture.

TO SERVE

• Figs are a great snack to eat fresh as they are.

• They are also great served on a cheeseboard.

• Warm slightly and drizzle with a creamy gorgonzola cheese sauce.

• Serve as a starter or classic first course with prosciutto.

• Raw or grilled, they go well with hot or cold ham, pork or poultry.

• The Italian custom of placing room-temperature fruit on a bed of ice for serving suits figs perfectly.

• Poach or bake with sugar and a little water; add flavourings such as orange flower water or spices, then chill and serve with cream or ice-cream.

• Quarter and soak for a couple of hours in port, orange juice or an orange liqueur to make a simple, yet elegant, dessert.

• Dried figs are available as firm but soft whole fruit, or as glacé (candied) figs, or compressed into blocks for use in cakes and puddings.

PRESERVING THE CROP

STORING Fully ripe figs should be eaten the day you pick them. Place them in a single layer on a plate or tray and put them in the refrigerator. Remove figs an hour or so ahead of serving to bring them back to room temperature (the cold dulls their fragrance and flavour). If you have to hold figs for a day or so, store in a single layer, covered, in the refrigerator crisper.

FREEZING Figs are not suitable to freeze.

PICKLING The season doesn't last, so preserve their flavour by making jam.

DRYING Halved figs can be oven-dried (see Drying, page 243). Set the oven temperature at the lowest setting and leave overnight or until dried. Store in an airtight container in a cool, dry place.

caprese salad with figs

figs with mascarpone

1 cup (250g) mascarpone cheese
2 tablespoons ricotta cheese
2 tablespoons honey
1 tablespoon white sugar
½ teaspoon ground cinnamon
8 medium fresh figs (480g), halved

1 Preheat grill (broiler).
2 Beat combined cheeses in small bowl until smooth.
Stir in 2 tablespoons honey.
3 Combine sugar and cinnamon in another small bowl.
4 Dip figs, cut-side down, into sugar mixture; place on
oven tray, cut-side up. Grill until brown.
5 Serve figs with mascarpone.

prep & cook time 15 minutes **serves** 4

caprese salad with figs

4 large tomatoes (480g), sliced thinly
4 large fresh figs (320g), sliced thinly
25 cherry bocconcini cheeses (375g), drained,
   sliced thinly
½ small red onion (50g), chopped finely
¼ cup firmly packed fresh basil leaves
2 tablespoons olive oil
1 tablespoon balsamic vinegar

1 Overlap slices of tomato, fig and cheese on serving plate.
2 Sprinkle with onion and basil; drizzle with combined
oil and vinegar.

prep time 20 minutes **serves** 4

figs with mascarpone

preserving the crop (apples)

STORING	Store apples in the refrigerator in a vegetable storage bag to help retain crispness, although apples are best eaten at room temperature for full flavour. As a general rule, large apples do not store as well as smaller ones.
FREEZING	Blanched apple wedges can be frozen for up to 3 months (see Freezing, page 240) and are useful for adding to cooked desserts such as cobblers and pies. Do not thaw before using.
PICKLING	Apples make wonderful pink-coloured jellies. Place in hot sterilised jars (see Bottling, pages 240-242) and seal while hot. Store in a cool, dark place for up to a year. Add quinces to apple jelly as well. Apples are often added to chutneys and relishes as an extender to other fruits and vegetables and as a setting agent for jams and jellies.
DRYING	Apples can be dried in slices but need to be prepared in a salt or citric acid solution before drying (see Drying, page 243).

granny smith

pink lady

Apples, Pears and Quinces

IN THE GARDEN

These fruit, despite their differences, belong to the same family as the rose, cotoneaster and hawthorn berries, crab apples and loquats. They all retain a tiny flower remnant at the base of the fruit and prefer summers that aren't too hot and humid, and cool-to-cold winters. Some varieties tolerate other climates and these are useful to the home gardener, but major fruit production only takes place in ideal conditions.

Remember to consider summer shade and winter sun when planting fruit trees. They can be useful in your garden design, perhaps as a spreading feature, a solitary sentinel at the end of a path or as an espaliered screen.

APPLES

Apples like rich, deep soil and protection from strong winds that can shatter spring blossoms or damage young fruit. They don't like undrained soil; however, they do need regular watering for the fruit to fill out. Apples are self-sterile so you'll need two trees for pollination to take place. An answer for small gardens is a grafted tree where two or three apple varieties have been inserted into the one rootstock. These can be very useful for the home gardener, if a little weird-looking, because the varieties are usually early, middle and late maturing and will produce a continuing supply rather than a once-off glut. The other alternative for tiny gardens is to espalier against a wall or grow dwarf varieties, which are excellent in pots.

Keep your fingers crossed for no late-spring frosts during flowering or do what orchardists do, and turn on the sprinklers at nights when frosts are predicted. Chase off birds that attack new buds.

When the fruit starts to form, the clusters will probably include too many fruit. Some will drop off naturally but you may still have to reduce their numbers to create 10-15cm (4-5") spaces between each to provide enough room for good-sized fruit to develop. Leaving them all on will result in misshapen and skimpy apples, like the ones you find growing along roadways. Pick apples when the flavour's right and they are crisp and juicy.

Apples store well, so pick before they develop creeping skin and birds find them. Keep the ground under the tree clear to prevent disease. Don't leave fruit lying around and rake up diseased leaves. This will reduce the incidence of codling moth in next year's fruit, and fungal problems on the leaves. Apply your preferred complete fertiliser under the tree trunk to the drip-line, and water in well each autumn and spring.

Pruning is done during winter and is essential for espaliered apples to control and shape them. Pruning can also be useful on a full-sized tree to reduce the mass of branches and open it out, vase-like, to capture extra sun and allow air to circulate around the blossoms, leaves and fruit.

Braeburn is a New Zealand variety now grown around the world. A crisp, juicy, early-season dessert apple with outstanding 'old-fashioned' apple flavour. At its best when freshly picked but also stores well.

Bramley is a mid-to-late season heritage English apple with firm, very acid flesh. It is prized for cooking when you want the apple to 'fluff up'.

Cox's orange pippin is an old English early-season apple with a dense, sharp-sweet flesh; it's traditionally one of the best eating varieties and is also good for cooking, though some apple fanciers think some of the character has been bred out of them in recent years.

Fuji is a juicy, late-season Japanese variety that has become popular internationally. Very dense and juicy, with a distinctive flavour; it cooks well.

Jonathan is an old early-season variety with outstanding

fuji

golden delicious

red delicious

royal gala

sweet and tangy flavour when eaten fresh and is also good for cooking. It does not come well through lengthy storage so is in danger of being phased out of production.

Granny smith is an old, late-season Australian apple now popular world-wide. Excellent for cooking when you want a puree, as for apple sauce. Good eating, with tart, crisp flesh, when fresh, but can be disappointing as an eating apple out of season.

Golden delicious is a mid-to-late season apple; while it is aromatic, it is often thought as insipid for eating, but it performs well in cooking (when lemon juice can be added for tartness). When sliced, it holds its shape well for decorative tarts.

Red delicious is a mid-to-late season apple, sweet and juicy with the aromatic quality of the 'delicious' family. An immensely popular eating apple though a little flat in flavour for some tastes.

Pink lady is one of the great successes of the newer varieties. A late-season apple, with dense, fine, crisp flesh and an excellent sweet/tart flavour.

Royal gala is an early-season apple developed in New Zealand, with dense, juicy, sweet flesh. Excellent for eating raw and makes good baked or poached apples, but is not good for apple puree.

For the table

TO SERVE

• Apples are the perfect healthy snack for any time of day.

• Add to bread and cheese for the best of all lunches.

• At breakfast or brunch, freshly grated apple is the secret of sensational muesli.

• Sautéed apple slices are great companions to bacon or sausage.

• Chopped apple adds flavour and good nutrition to pancakes and muffins.

• Apple adds a fresh note to spicy soups such as lentil or curried parsnip, and crisp sweetness to a salad.

• Roasted or sautéed pieces added to a tangy sauce is the perfect foil to rich meats such as pork or duck.

• Apple jelly is a marvellous old-fashioned treat on bread, toast, scones or pancakes.

• Finely chopped apple with lemon juice, salt and perhaps a touch of chilli is an excellent sambal to serve with curry.

• And consider the glorious cavalcade of apple cakes, dumplings, sponges, fools, strudels, charlottes and that most beloved of all desserts, apple pie.

PEARS

Like apples, pears like rich soil and protection from winds. Also like apples, pears like well-drained circumstances but plenty of water, especially when the fruit is developing. During long, dry summer spells, you'll need to water to supplement nature.

Pear trees can be grown individually as they don't need a pollinator. They are usually taller and form a more pyramidal shape than apples. There's no need to prune them unless you want to reduce their height. They blossom earlier than apples and hence are more vulnerable to frost damage. So, if you have the choice of site, plant pears in your least frost-prone area. Their spring blossoms and autumn leaves are magnificent.

Pears are ready to harvest when they willingly break from the tree but are still hard. They ripen after picking, and this is their greatest disguise. Just giving in to pressure at the stem end is the most reliable clue to the readiness of pears as their outside appearance tells you

preserving the crop (pears)

STORING	Pears should be stored at room temperature until ripe; the process can be hastened by enclosing them in a paper bag with a banana or apple. Once ripe, they will keep for a day or so at room temperature or a little longer in the refrigerator; some will keep for longer, as noted above, but pears should be kept under observation as their period of perfect ripeness before they start to break down is brief. They need oxygen around them so should not be stored on top of each other or enclosed in a plastic bag at any stage.
FREEZING	Pears can be chopped and frozen but used in cooked recipes only. Pears will exude their juice which has to be cooked off.
PICKLING	Pears can be pickled with spices and vinegar. Pack into hot sterilised jars (see Bottling, pages 240-242), seal while hot and store in a cool, dry place for up to 6 months. Once opened, store in the refrigerator.
DRYING	Pears can be dried in slices but need to be prepared in a salt or citric acid solution beforehand (see Drying, page 243).

william pear

nashi

beurre bosc pear

very little. They turn from perfect to wasted in no time at all, but stewing or pickling can save a few.

Different varieties of pear have textures ranging, when ripe, from luscious and almost melting, to firm and slightly grainy to crisp and crunchy for the Asian pear, the nashi. All pears are unusual in that they ripen from the inside out and should not be allowed to ripen on the tree as they quickly become woolly and their core breaks down if picked ripe. They are best picked mature but still hard and ripened in a cool place over a few days.

Beurre bosc is a large pear with russet skin. When ripe, it is soft and juicy with a slightly and pleasantly grainy texture. It is good raw and also suitable for long cooking. It is available from early autumn through to early summer.

Cocktail pears are miniature green/gold pears with a crunchy texture; they may be eaten fresh or pickled. They are available in summer.

Corella is a small pear with a richly coloured green/red/golden skin and a rich flavour that keeps well. It is available from autumn through to spring.

Lemon bergamot is small to medium in size and is available from autumn to spring. They are ideal to use in desserts and cooking.

Nashi is a true pear of Asian origin. It is sweet, juicy and crisp when ripe. Unlike European pears, it is ripened on the tree and keeps well after picking. Nashi are easily bruised so are usually sold in protective netted sleeves. They are available from late summer to late winter and are at their peak in late summer-early autumn.

Packham's triumph, also known as packham, is a large, often bumpy pear that is slow to ripen but, when it does so, is very juicy with a sweet, subtle flavour. The skin may remain green when ripe or may change to light yellow. Used firm, it is a good cooking pear. It is available from autumn through to summer.

Red anjou is a medium-sized pear, available from mid-summer to autumn. Its white, fine-textured flesh makes this variety perfect for salads.

Red sensation is a 'sport' (spontaneous mutation) of the william pear, which has bright red skin when ripe. It is like the regular william in cooking, eating and storing quality. It is available from late summer to late autumn.

Winter nelis, also know as honey pear, are small, rough-skinned, long-keeping pears with a spicy, juicy flesh. It is available in winter.

William, also known as bartlett, is an aromatic, buttery pear with pale yellow skin, sometimes red-blushed, when ripe. Used firm, it is a good cooking pear. Once ripe, it is excellent raw but will not last long in good condition. It is available from summer into autumn.

For the table

TO SERVE

• A fine pear is equally at home with savoury dishes or sweet ones – it is as good poached in a red-wine syrup and served with ice-cream as it is with a glass of red wine, some bread and freshly cut parmesan, or with blue cheese, walnuts and a sweet dessert wine.

• Pears are good in salads, especially those with bitter leaves such as witlof, or peppery ones such as watercress.

• Quartered firm pears are excellent baked beside rich meats such as duck or pork as they roast, or grilled with pork chops or ham steaks.

• On the sweet side, pears can be used for a tart filling, a crumble or fruit salad.

• Poach and serve with zabaglione or a drizzle of Poire William (pear eau-de-vie or fruit brandy) and cream or, most famously, with vanilla ice-cream and hot chocolate sauce for Poires Belle Hélène, named for Offenbach's opera about Helen of Troy.

quince

green kiwifruit

yellow kiwifruit

Quinces

The large blossoms of quince in spring are handsomely restrained and the whole tree is attractive throughout the year. The fruit has a furry, golden skin, hard, white flesh and an exquisite aroma. Most flesh turns a beautiful rich pink, as if by magic, as it slowly cooks, and all produce a claret-red liquid as they reduce to a jelly. 'Appleshape' doesn't cook to pink but 'de bourgeaut', 'smyrna', 'champion' and 'rea's mammoth' can be relied upon to do so. 'De vranja' colours well and is resistant to fleck, a leaf-spotting fungus.

While apples and pears don't like damp soil, quinces are more tolerant but none of them likes very wet roots.

For the table

TO PREPARE

• This cousin to the apple is always eaten cooked as it is too hard and acidic to be enjoyable raw. It takes long cooking, but its glorious scent and lovely musky flavour are worth it. Its flesh is cream when raw, but turns deep pink as it is cooked.

• Quinces are covered with a rather sticky down, so this should be rubbed off under running water.

• Cutting the hard fruit takes a heavy knife and great care to keep your fingers out of harm's way.

• The skin can be removed with a vegetable peeler or small serrated knife. Drop each piece into water with a little lemon juice added as the flesh discolours quickly in contact with air.

TO SERVE

• Peel, slice and poach very gently in a sugar syrup for as little as 1 hour and up to 4-5 hours until the flesh has changed to a rich red colour or is soft. Store, covered with sugar syrup, in the refrigerator until required. Covered, they will last for about a week.

• It is the best of all fruits to use for the stiff fruit quince paste that is a popular addition to cheeseboards.

• Are excellent sliced, poached and served with cream.

• Cooked slices can be used as a tart filling, served beside a panacotta or crème caramel, folded through a plain buttercake batter or pureed for the delicious old-fashioned dessert called a 'snow', made with egg whites.

• Serve with pork, duck or roasted quail or chicken. Middle Eastern cooks often pair quince with meat in a casserole and use it in stuffings and rice dishes.

• Quince's other great gift is that it is high in pectin so it makes excellent jam or jelly.

PRESERVING THE CROP

STORING Quinces will keep well at room temperature, in a single layer not touching each other, for weeks. Refrigerate only if you want to keep them for much longer, and only in a lidded plastic box or other airtight container or they will perfume other food.

FREEZING Blanched quince wedges can be frozen for up to 3 months (see Freezing, page 240). Best used frozen, not thawed.

PICKLING The ever-popular jelly or quince paste keeps almost indefinitely in an airtight container. Quinces can also be pickled (see Bottling, pages 240-242).

fig and quince paste

quince and pistachio cake

This cake is delicious for afternoon tea or dessert. Try replacing the pistachios with toasted slivered almonds.

¾ cup (110g) caster (superfine) sugar
½ cup (125ml) orange juice
1 cup (250ml) water
2 cardamom pods, crushed slightly
3 medium quinces (990g), peeled, cored and sliced
pistachio cake batter
90g (3 ounces) butter, softened
2 teaspoons grated orange rind
1 cup (220g) caster (superfine) sugar
3 eggs
½ cup (75g) self-raising flour
1 cup (150g) plain (all-purpose) flour
¼ teaspoon bicarbonate of soda (baking soda)
½ cup (125ml) sour cream
¼ cup (60ml) orange juice
½ cup (75g) coarsely chopped roasted pistachios

1 Combine sugar, juice, the water and cardamom in medium saucepan; stir over heat, without boiling, until sugar is dissolved. Add quince; simmer, uncovered, about 1¼ hours until quince is soft and liquid almost absorbed; cool. Remove cardamom pods.
2 Make pistachio cake batter.
3 Preheat oven to 180°C/350°F.
4 Grease deep 22cm (8½ inch) round cake pan; line base with baking (parchment) paper. Arrange two-thirds of the quince over the base of the pan. Blend remaining quince until smooth. Gently fold quince puree into pistachio cake batter to give a rippled effect. Spread cake batter over quince in cake pan. Bake cake in oven about 1¼ hours.
5 Stand cake in pan 15 minutes before turning, top-side up, onto a wire rack. Cake can be served hot or at room temperature, with cream, custard or ice-cream.
pistachio cake batter Beat butter, rind and sugar in large bowl with electric mixer until lighter in colour. Beat in eggs, one at a time, until well combined. Stir in sifted flours and soda with combined cream and juice in two batches. Fold in nuts.

prep & cook time 3 hours **serves** 8-10
notes Cake can be made up to three days ahead. Cardamom is one of the world's most expensive spices; it has a distinctive aromatic, sweetly rich flavour and is available from specialty spice shops.

fig and quince paste

1kg (2 pounds) quinces
1 cup (190g) coarsely chopped dried figs
1 cinnamon stick
caster (superfine) sugar
¼ cup (60ml) lemon juice

1 Peel, core and quarter quinces; combine in large saucepan with figs, cinnamon and enough water to cover. Bring to the boil; simmer, covered, about 1 hour or until most of the liquid is absorbed. Discard cinnamon stick; process mixture until pulpy.
2 Measure mixture into same pan. Add 1 cup caster sugar to every 1 cup pulp; stir in juice, stir until sugar dissolves.
3 Cook, over very low heat, about 2 hours or until mixture leaves side of pan.
4 Oil and line deep 20cm (8 inch) round cake pan; pour quince mixture into pan. Stand at room temperature overnight until set. Serve as part of a cheese platter.

prep & cook time 3½ hours (+ standing) **makes** 4 cups

quince and pistachio cake

preserving the crop (kiwifruit)

STORING	Kiwifruit stores well at room temperature for up to a week. Store separately as the ethylene from other fruit (such as apples and bananas) ripens kiwifruit before you need them. Once they give a little when pressed gently, store in the refrigerator for several days. Like melons, they are best served cool but not too cold.
PICKLING	Jam and chutney can be made from kiwifruit. They must be peeled before use. Spoon the hot jam or chutney into hot sterilised jars (see Bottling, pages 240-242), and seal while still hot. Store for several months.

Kiwifruit

IN THE GARDEN

Once these small, brown furry vine fruits were known as 'chinese gooseberries' until farmers in New Zealand discovered they excelled at growing them and bred new, improved varieties. They are now marketed worldwide as kiwifruit and the 'chinese' name is all but gone. Kiwifruit is a luscious and particularly nutritious fruit, being high in vitamins, minerals and antioxidants, which is believed to be helpful in fighting heart disease, repairing DNA and protecting against cancer. It now comes in gold varieties as well as green.

Kiwifruit, with their downy coats, grow on an equally downy, deciduous vine that clambers upwards by twisting its strong stems around trellises, pergolas, verandah rails or through trees. A kiwifruit vine can be a useful alternative to grapes as a summer sun shield and will allow winter sun through as the leaves drop. For the best growth, kiwifruit need a long warm summer and a cool, frost-free winter. Their roots are shallow and fibrous, so keep them well watered right through summer. Spread a thick mulch of old manure, well-rotted compost or leaf mulch and the complete garden fertiliser of your choice each spring to protect the roots from drying out. There are male and female plants so you must plant a pair for the spring blossoms to pollinate. If you want to plant more than a pair for extra fruit, one male plant can cope with five rapacious females.

The large, rough leaves shield the developing fruit from the sun during summer. In autumn as the leaves fall, the low sun sweetens the fruit. Pick them as you need them before they drop off the vine.

For the table

TO SERVE

• Kiwifruit are very convenient to serve. You only have to peel them. They can also be spooned out like boiled eggs.

• Kiwifruit are best enjoyed as they are. They can be used as a snack, as a dessert with ice-cream, in fruit salads, on cereal or with yogurt for breakfast, or pureed for milkshakes or flavouring a creamy dessert.

kiwifruit, lychee and lime salad

2 kiwifruits (170g), cut into wedges
4 fresh lychees (100g)
1 tablespoon fresh mint leaves
1 tablespoon fresh lime juice

1 Combine ingredients in small bowl.

prep time 5 minutes **serves** 1
note Lychees are small fruit from China with a hard shell and sweet, juicy flesh. The white flesh has a gelatinous texture and musky, perfumed taste. Discard the rough skin and seed before using. Available from greengrocers.

honeydew melon

rockmelon

watermelon

Melons

IN THE GARDEN

These luscious summer and early autumn fruits are produced on a vine with leaves that are dry, leathery and prickly to touch. Their fruits are sweet and delicious with flesh in the most delightful range of colours: deep pink, soft orange, luminous limpid green or pale gold.

For general cultivation advice and soil preparation, see the sections on cucumbers and cucurbits on pages 72 and 94. We are familiar with the more common varieties of melons, such as watermelons, rockmelons and honeydew. Watermelon varieties are now available in different sizes and some have reduced numbers of seeds. There are varieties with light pink or white flesh, and some with unusual skins like 'moon and stars'. Rockmelons also come in an assortment of shapes, skin colours and sizes. The honeydews come in a variety of colours: some green, some white-fleshed.

For truly unusual varieties, try specialist mail-order seed suppliers and companies that specialise in heritage seeds. You can also save seeds from last year's favourite crops, and friends are always happy to share seeds.

Whichever melon variety you choose, plant them as early as possible in spring after frosts have ceased, as the fruits take about 4 months to mature. Follow the advice on pages 72 and 94 for soil care, spacing and seed planting. Nurseries will often carry seedlings. Each plant can comfortably support 4-5 melons, so cut back extra stems still growing once the fruits have formed, and break off any baby fruit in excess. This will result in good-sized, juicy melons.

A white patch on the skin of developing melons can indicate sunscald. If possible, wind some leafy stems over the fruit or erect a screen to protect the rest of the crop. They are ripe and ready to pick when fully expanded and firm.

Rockmelon is a netted or musk melon, with a raised netted pattern on the skin and smooth, sweet, richly scented flesh. In Australia and America, it is often, incorrectly, called a cantaloupe. It is available for much of the year but its season is from early summer into autumn.

Honeydew is classified as a winter melon, but it is at its best from late summer into autumn, though it remains available into winter. It has hard, smooth skin and pale, juicy, slightly crisp flesh, which is fragrant and delicately delicious when fully ripe, but can be rather tasteless otherwise. The main variety is the white (though actually greenish white, ripening to cream) honeydew, but there is also a golden variety, the yellow honeydew.

Cantaloupe is a group of small, round melons with rib lines marking the skin into segments. They include some of the best flavoured and most fragrant melons, but they are not well known in Australia as attempts to grow them in commercial quantities have not, as yet, been successful.

Jam melons have little flavour when raw, but make good jam when combined with a sharp-flavoured ingredient such as lemon, pineapple or ginger.

For the table

TO SERVE

• Melons have a great affinity with salty and spicy foods. Wrap pieces of rockmelon in prosciutto as a finger food. It's a well-known combination and never ceases to please.

• Slices of well-chilled melon finish an Asian-inspired meal beautifully.

• For a bit of a kick, try vodka over watermelon; gin over honeydew melon; and rockmelon drizzled with port is another great combination.

• Both rockmelon and honeydew can be served with ice-cream or creamy desserts, and used as an ingredient in ice-creams, mousses and sorbets.

preserving the crop (melons)

STORING	Jam melons will store at room temperature for months. Other melons, once ripe, should be stored in the refrigerator and eaten within a few days. Scented melons should be double-wrapped in plastic or stored in a lidded container, especially if they have been cut, to prevent them from perfuming other food.
FREEZING	Melons can be frozen in chunks (see Freezing, page 240), then pureed and served as a sorbet or water-ice.
PICKLING	Use watermelon rind in pickles flavoured with cinnamon sticks and allspice. Pack into sterilised jars (see Bottling, pages 240-242); seal while still hot and store in a cool, dry place for up to 6 months. Once opened, store pickles in the refrigerator.

Autumn Herbs

The full range of spring and summer herbs is generally available through autumn, but here we pay particular attention to those herbs seemingly designed for the dishes we associate with cooler weather. Rosemary teams up with roasted meats and barbecues, while lemon grass and chilli, those essential ingredients in Asian curries and soups, add heat and piquancy. All three are easy to grow in the garden or in pots.

Rosemary

This woody, evergreen Mediterranean herb has a strong, resinous fragrance and flavour. Rosemary is a tough shrub with thin, stiff, aromatic leaves or needles. Its basic form is stoutly upright and dense with pale mauve flowers at the stem tips during autumn and winter. Another variety is prostrate and drapes itself down walls or rocks, or spreads like a mat over the ground. Its flowers are sky-blue.

IN THE GARDEN

This plant likes a challenge: seaside sites, strong winds, dry rocky slopes, heavy snow or baking sun, and almost any type of soil. However, it won't survive soggy conditions and doesn't care for shade. It is the ideal plant for pots and can be formal enough to look and smell impressive on a sunny doorstep or stand shoulder to shoulder with a line-up of potted herbs along a pathway.

When the plant is still small, nip a few leaves at a time until it starts to expand. It does take its time. Rosemary lasts many years, seeing out successions of basil, chervil and parsley, and eventually becoming a sizeable shrub that will need repotting.

For the table

TO SERVE

• Add rosemary sprigs to a bottle of red wine vinegar along with a few peppercorns for a great salad dressing.

• For a smoky rosemary taste, add sprigs to the barbecue fire when barbecuing lamb or chicken.

• Its traditional partner is lamb; use sprigs to brush chops as they are grilling, or tuck it into roast lamb.

Lemon grass

Lemon grass is basic to South-East Asian cooking. Its stems are rich in citral, the substance that also gives lemon rind its fragrance and flavour, so it not only gives a fresh, sharp lemon flavour to a dish, but perfumes it too.

IN THE GARDEN

Lemon grass is exactly that: a grass. It's perennial and forms a dramatic dense clump of tall, weeping foliage. It also makes a great tufted display in a large pot. Like other grasses, it is hardy as well. Try not to plant it too close to paths or steps as the leaves are sharp to brush against, although its scent is delightfully aromatic. It grows best in full sun or just dappled shade in well-drained soil, and tolerates tropical right through to temperate climates. It even tolerates a windy site.

Give it a good soak around the roots every week in dry weather and, provided you don't use every cane that develops, in time it will form a large clump.

The leaves can be used fresh or dried as a tea, but they will become ragged and rust-spotted during winter. You can either ignore its looks or, in early spring, cut it back to 15cm (6") above the ground, leaving the stems to use while the new leaves push through the centre and unfurl.

For the table

TO PREPARE

• The pale lower and inner part of the stem is the part used in cooking. It is rather hard and fibrous and should be sliced very thinly crossways to break the fibres before chopping or grinding as the recipe directs.

STORING ROSEMARY	Store fresh stalks in a plastic bag in the refrigerator.
FREEZING ROSEMARY	Rosemary can be frozen for up to 6 months (see Freezing, page 240). There's no need to chop; freeze the stalks on a flat tray and, when frozen, transfer them to a plastic freezer bag; the needles will break off from the stems.
DRYING ROSEMARY	Fresh is best, but home-dried rosemary (see Drying, pages 243) keeps its flavour longer than commercially dried rosemary.
STORING LEMON GRASS	The fresher the better, so leave in the garden as long as you can. If you must store fresh lemon grass, cut as little as possible from the stalks, leaving the root end intact, wrap in damp paper towel in a plastic bag, and store in the refrigerator for a couple of days only.
FREEZING LEMON GRASS	Can be chopped and frozen in small batches (see Freezing, page 240). It will keep in the freezer for up to 6 months.
DRYING LEMON GRASS	Dried lemon grass is integral to some Asian dishes but don't keep for longer than a couple of months or you will be disappointed in the taste (see Drying, page 243).
STORING CHILLIES	Chillies should be stored in a cool, dry place for up to a week. Pack loosely so air can circulate through them.
FREEZING CHILLIES	Chopped fresh chillies can be frozen for about 6 months. Add them frozen to cooked dishes.
DRYING CHILLIES	Thread chillies onto a thread or string, and hang in an airy place to dry (see Drying, page 243). The heat intensifies on drying, so use with caution.

rosemary

lemon grass

• Peel away the tough outer layers to reveal the pale lower section of the stem; use a sharp knife to trim the base. If using in soups, syrups or casseroles, press the stem with the flat side of a large knife to bruise and release the flavour. If using in stir-fries, cut the pale section thinly across the fibres.

• While the white lower portion of the stem only is used in cooking, in Asia the leaves are often used to make lemon tea.

TO SERVE

• Use lemon grass as giant skewers for chicken and pork. Quarter the stalks before threading meat cubes onto them; cook on a ridged grill pan or barbecue.

• Complete stems can be lightly pounded to bruise them, tied in a knot and used as a bed on which fish or chicken is steamed or barbecued in foil, or added to soups or sauces during cooking; remove before serving.

• When making sweet chilli dipping sauce for fresh spring rolls, leave out some of the chilli and add chopped fresh lemon grass instead.

Chillies

The burning mouth from eating chilli is caused by a substance called capsaicin, which also reacts on skin. While this is not recommended, rubbing a cut chilli onto small area of skin can give an indication of the heat of a chilli. After 20 minutes, the skin may either blister, get a red mark or feel a stimulating buzz, thus warning the eater of its fierceness. To moderate the heat, halve the chilli lengthwise and scrape out the seeds and white membrane, which are the hottest parts; true chilli-lovers leave them in to get the maximum blast. Heat is not,

however, the only thing to look for. Fresh chillies vary in flavour and may be sweet, rich, fresh or mellow; and dried or smoked ones may have savoury or caramel notes. In general, green (unripe) chillies are juicier and stronger-flavoured than ripe ones, while ripe ones are sweeter and more fragrant. The capsaicin level increases from pollination until the fruit begins to change from green to its ripe colour: red, yellow, brown, purple, orange or sometimes a deeper green. As ripening continues, the level drops a little. Again, in general, the smaller the chilli the hotter it is.

Ancho is a poblano chilli dried until it is brownish red. It is mildly hot with a sweetish full-bodied flavour.
Banana can be yellow, lime-green and red; they are sweet and mild in flavour, and taste much like capsicum.
Cascabel, also called bola chilli, is a dried, round, moderately hot brown or red chilli.
Cayenne, the chilli from which cayenne pepper is made, is red and very hot.
Chipotle is a smoke-dried jalapeño chilli, deep red and very hot, with a smoky flavour.
Habanero is a short chilli rather like a tiny, pointed red or orange capsicum. It is one of the hottest of all chillies.
Jalapeño is a medium to hot red chilli with thick, juicy flesh and a complex, slightly sweet flavour.
Kashmiri is a large, mild red chilli used for its colour and flavour rather than its heat.
Mulato is, like ancho, a dried poblano chilli, but is dried to a brownish black and is sweeter than ancho.
Pasilla is a dried chilaca chilli (in its fresh form chilaca is a long, narrow chilli, light to dark green in colour, but is almost always used dried). Pasilla is dark brown with a mild to medium heat and a rich smoky flavour.

red thai chillies

yellow banana chilli

red banana chilli

Peri peri, also known as piri piri and pil pil, is a red/purple African thai red chilli (birds-eye chilli) used in the cooking of the ex-Portuguese colonies of Mozambique and Angola. It is also widely used in Portugal, especially in piri piri sauce. It is intensely hot.

Poblano is very dark green, almost black, when unripe and red or brown when ripe. A large, mild, heart-shaped chilli with very thick walls, it is widely used for stuffing.

Serrano is a round chilli that ripens from green to red to black. It is very hot.

Scotch bonnet is closely related to habanero and, like the habanero, is one the hottest of all chillies. It is a red chilli but is often used at its yellow and orange half-ripe stage. Its name comes from its shape, round and flattish with bumps, suggesting a Scottish tam o'shanter (which is a Scottish bonnet/hat worn by men; it's made of wool with a pompom in the centre).

Thai chillis, also known as birds-eye, are tiny, bright red and intensely hot. They are also available green, which are unripe chillies.

In the garden

Chillies are related to capsicums and grow under the same conditions; see page 84 for details. Most develop into spreading sub-shrubs 1m (3') or more tall and wide in a season. Chillies flower in spring and summer, and the chillies hang on the plants well into winter in mild gardens. Frosts and very cold winds will destroy them. You many be able to prune them down to 15cm (6") in autumn, and in cool and cold zones protect with straw or compost and manure over winter. If they survive an icy winter they will sprout again as the warm weather commences. However, in areas with cold winters, it's usually best to save some seeds and start plants anew in spring when frosts have finished. Seeds and seedlings are available from nurseries and dried seeds from varieties you have tried are often successful.

For the table

TO PREPARE

• Even a tiny amount of capsaicin left on your hands after cutting chillies can cause trouble hours later if you should happen to touch your eyes or nose. Ideally, wear disposable plastic gloves, available at chemists and supermarkets. Cut on a surface that can be thoroughly washed. Capsaicin is oily and hard to wash off, so thoroughly wash everything you have used, including your hands even if you were wearing gloves, in warm soapy water as soon as you have finished cutting.

• Even the invisible fumes from freshly cut chilli can cause choking and wheezing in some people, so if you have ever had any breathing problems, such as asthma, or an allergic reaction, get someone else to do the job, or failing that, use some form of prepared chilli such as chilli flakes or powder, chopped freeze-dried chilli or a chilli paste or sauce.

TO SERVE

• For chilli-flavoured oil, heat 12 small fresh chillies in peanut oil until warm but not hot. Remove from heat and steep at room temperature for 2 hours. Drain the oil into hot, sterilised bottles (see Bottling, pages 240-242) and seal while the bottle is still hot. Store at room temperature for up to 6 months or refrigerate.

rosemary lamb skewers

8 sprigs fresh rosemary
600g (1¼ pounds) minced (ground) lamb
1 egg yolk
⅓ cup (25g) stale breadcrumbs
2 cloves garlic, crushed
1 tablespoon tomato paste
¼ cup (60ml) olive oil
1 large brown onion (200g), sliced thinly
1 tablespoon plain (all-purpose) flour
1 cup (250ml) beef stock
2 medium tomatoes (300g), chopped coarsely

1 Remove two-thirds of the leaves from the bottom part of each rosemary sprig to make skewers. Finely chop 2 teaspoons of the leaves and reserve.
2 Combine mince, egg yolk, breadcrumbs, garlic, paste and reserved rosemary in medium bowl. Shape lamb mixture into sausage shapes on rosemary skewers.
3 Heat 1 tablespoon of the oil in large frying pan; cook skewers until browned and cooked through. Remove from pan.
4 Heat remaining oil in same pan; cook onion until soft. Add flour; cook, stirring, until mixture bubbles and thickens. Gradually stir in stock until smooth. Add tomato; cook until gravy boils and thickens.
5 Serve rosemary lamb skewers with gravy.

prep & cook time 35 minutes **serves** 4
note Stale breadcrumbs are one- or two-day-old bread made into crumbs by blending or processing.

mussels with tomato and chilli

mussels with tomato and chilli

Pot-ready mussels come in 1kg (2 pound) bags. They have been scrubbed and bearded and are ready to cook.

1 tablespoon olive oil
4 shallots (100g), sliced thinly
4 cloves garlic, sliced thinly
3 fresh long red chillies, sliced thinly lengthways
1 cup (250ml) dry white wine
2 x 400g (12½ ounces) canned cherry tomatoes
2kg (4 pounds) pot-ready black mussels
½ cup coarsely chopped fresh flat-leaf parsley

1 Heat oil in large saucepan; cook shallot, garlic and chilli, stirring, until fragrant.
2 Stir in wine and undrained tomatoes; bring to the boil. Add mussels; cook, covered, 3 minutes or until mussels open (discard any that do not). Stir in parsley.

prep & cook time 25 minutes **serves** 4

stir-fried tofu with vegetables and lemon grass

2 teaspoons sesame oil
400g (12½ ounces) firm tofu, diced into
 1cm (½ inch) pieces
1 large red capsicum (bell pepper) (350g), sliced thinly
750g (1½ pounds) baby buk choy, chopped coarsely
2 x 10cm (4 inch) sticks fresh lemon grass (40g),
 chopped finely
2 cloves garlic, crushed
½ cup loosely packed fresh coriander leaves (cilantro)

1 Heat oil in wok; stir-fry tofu, capsicum, buk choy,
lemon grass and garlic until vegetables are just tender.
Stir in coriander. Serve with lemon wedges, if you like.

prep & cook time 15 minutes **serves** 4
note Tofu, also known as bean curd, is an off-white,
custard-like product made from the "milk" of crushed
soya beans. Firm tofu is made by compressing bean curd
to remove most of the water; it is often used in stir-fries
because it can be tossed without falling apart.

stir-fried tofu with vegetables and lemon grass

chilli coriander jam

8 large tomatoes (2kg), cored
⅓ cup (80ml) olive oil
10 cloves garlic, peeled
4cm (1½ inch) piece fresh ginger (20g), grated
10 fresh small red thai (serrano) chillies,
 stems removed
2 tablespoons cumin seeds
2 tablespoons black mustard seeds
¾ cup (180ml) red wine vinegar
¼ cup (60ml) fish sauce
1¼ cups (335g) grated palm sugar
1 tablespoon ground turmeric
½ cup finely chopped fresh coriander (cilantro)
 leaves and roots

1 Preheat oven to 180°C/350°F.
2 Rub tomatoes with oil, place in roasting pan; roast
about 30 minutes or until soft but not coloured.
3 Blend or process garlic, ginger, chillies and seeds
until chopped and well combined. Transfer mixture to
large heavy-based saucepan; add tomatoes, vinegar,
sauce, sugar and turmeric. Simmer about 2 hours or
until thick and jammy.
4 Blend mixture, in batches, until chopped coarsely; stir
in coriander. Spoon into hot sterilised jars (see Bottling
pages 240-242); seal while still hot.

prep & cook time 2 hours 45 minutes **makes** about 6 cups
notes Store in a cool dry place for up to 6 months.
Refrigerate jam once opened.
Fish sauce, also called nam pla or nuoc nam, is made from
pulverised salted fermented fish, most often anchovies.
It has a pungent smell and strong taste, so use sparingly.
Available from supermarkets and Asian food stores.
Ground cumin is also known as zeera or comino; it has a
spicy, nutty flavour and is available from supermarkets.

chilli coriander jam

winter

Winter garden diary

There are two schools of thought on winter.

There are those people who dread it, hide away and grizzle about the cold air, the clothing layers, the dampness that seems to cling to everything and the cost of heating. Then there are those who relish the battle that nature thrusts their way, the extra energy and 'go' that cool air engenders, the brilliance of sunlit days or the haze of cloudy ones, and long cook-ups in the kitchen.

THE MEDITERRANEAN WET SEASON WILL BE FLATTENING ALL IN ITS PATH, AND THE LONGED-FOR RAIN WILL BE SOAKING THROUGH THE SOIL LAYERS. THE SOUND OF ROOTS, STEMS AND LEAVES REFILLING IS ALMOST AUDIBLE AND PLANTS START TO STAND UP PROUD AGAIN UNTIL A POLAR BLAST MAKES THEM RECONSIDER. IN PROTECTED SITES WHERE WATER DOES NOT POOL, THERE WILL BE VEGETABLES AND HERBS APLENTY, AND MAINTENANCE TASKS TO MATCH.

IN CONTRAST, IN SUBTROPICAL AREAS, GARDENERS NEED TO BE WARY OF DRYING WINDS. THE SUN IS NOT AS HOT AS IN SUMMER, BUT IF THE SIGNS ARE IGNORED, PLANTS WILL DIE. THERE'LL BE SUPPLIES OF WINTER VEGETABLES AND HERBS, AND LITTLE INSECT DAMAGE.

In winter, gardeners everywhere busy themselves with what they consider to be the season's appropriate business.

pick now	plant now
cool continental, temperate and Mediterranean gardens with frequent frosts beetroot, broad beans, broccoli, brussels sprouts, cabbage, cauliflower, lettuce (with protection), mushrooms, spinach (with protection), swede, turnip	cold zones with frost, plant under glass on heated trays or in the house towards the end of winter capsicum, chillies, corn, cucumbers, eggplant, lettuce, melons, squash, tomatoes
temperate, Mediterranean and subtropical gardens with no frosts asian greens, carrots, endive, mizuna, peas, rocket, plus all the above with no protection	frost-free zones beetroot, broad beans, cabbage, lettuce and salad greens, peas, potatoes, silver beet, spinach, plus all the above
tropical gardens beans, capsicum, corn, cucumber, eggplant, tomatoes, zucchini, plus all the above except brussels sprouts	tropical gardens beans plus all of the above

For some in the tropics, winter is pure heaven with dry, balmy days and cool breezes at night. The subtropics see cool mornings and evenings, with wintry days interspersed with sunny ones. Cool weather is deemed an inconvenient disruption. Those in cold zones rug up to go outside, and those with inefficient heating rug up to stay inside.

So let's view the winter garden bounty.

In cold zones there'll be scurries out to harvest fresh offerings, and a prowl around to view the cold and wind-wracked berries and skeletonised flower tops, and to look for signs of spring. Indoors, there will be growers' lists and seed catalogues to peruse, and some early seedling trays to establish to get things started.

In the tropics, winter is perhaps the busiest season. Fast-growing crops need trimming and feeding, vines need controlling, and the soil cries out for revitalising in preparation for the series of replacement crops that warm conditions will allow.

The Brassicas

The brassicas, better known as the cabbage group of vegetables, are the stalwarts of winter. Rounded, florid, bulbous and possessed of wonderful foliage colours from silver, red, grey-green, yellow to bright green, these over-sized and baroque-looking vegetables make striking crops when the winter garden beds might otherwise be bare.

Brassicas prefer the cold conditions of winter and are not much pleased by hot temperatures and the baking sun. They make ideal home crops during that time of the year when the garden has withdrawn for winter and gardeners themselves prefer the great indoors.

The family is a large one, and includes cabbages, broccoli, cauliflower, brussels sprouts and kale. These are slow-growing and take between 3-5 months to be ready to pick. Also part of the brassica family are the quick-growing asian greens that have had such a culinary impact in the West over recent years. Buk choy (chinese chard), tatsoi (chinese flat cabbage) and choy sum (chinese flowering cabbage) are ready to harvest in 6-8 weeks. The salad feathers of mizuna are the speed champions with early leaves harvestable in 20 days.

Over the following pages we feature the most common brassicas grown in home gardens. Fast-growing asian greens are ideal for staggered planting and harvesting to ensure a steady supply for quick stir-fries and winter salads. Slow-growing brassicas are tantalising to watch as they solidly progress, their leaves unfurl and their large, tightly-packed hearts and flower buds form.

General cultivation

Brassicas do best in soil that has been well-manured a month prior to planting to make it light and full of organic matter. Two weeks before planting, dig in a generous supply of nitrogen-rich fertiliser and a sprinkling of lime so all required trace elements will be available from the soil. If you haven't room to spare for a month of growing nothing, brassicas can be planted as a follow-on to beans, and they'll make use of the nitrogen stored in bean roots. However, the seedlings will still need extra fertiliser and lime to boost them along.

The slow-growers are usually raised in seedling trays or shallow pots, or bought as seedlings and planted out when the soil is ready. This gives them a head start and allows their roots to become firmly established.

The fast-growing brassicas are usually planted from seed in-situ or in seed trays, and can be harvested and thinned as they develop.

If wanting to raise crops from seed, cover the seeds with 0.5cm (¼") of sand or seed-raising mixture. They'll emerge in 6-10 days with two almost heart-shaped leaves. Once they've developed their miniature, true leaves, thin them in the garden or plant out seedlings 50-75cm (20-30") apart for the slow-growers, 10-15cm (4-6") for the speedsters. Firm them in well. Brassicas must be planted in full sun with well-drained soil to reduce the risk of fungal problems. Raise the soil into mounds or furrows and plant seedlings on top. Always keep well watered. Irrigation by means of the furrows is preferable to overhead waterings.

PESTS AND DISEASES

The whole brassica family is the mainstay in the life cycle of the cabbage moth and the cabbage white butterfly, both of which deposit their eggs on the leaves. The leaves are then eaten by the developing caterpillars. The leaf surfaces are eaten first, then whole sections of leaf. The cabbage moth caterpillar will eat right into the heart of the cabbage. Pick the caterpillars off by hand as soon as you see them or spray with a bio-insecticide based on bacteria toxic only to caterpillars. See page 17 for home-made non-chemical sprays and organic alternatives.

Aphids can gather among the grey foliage, and weaken the plant as they suck out its nourishment. Keep alert for mass attacks and pick off, hose off or spray. Again, see page 17 for home-made non-chemical treatments.

Broccoli

A bouquet of broccoli is a fetching sight in an edible garden. And that's what broccoli is: a cluster of unopened flower buds harvested from the centre of rich blue-green leaves.

In the garden

For general soil preparation and cultivation notes, see page 184. Broccoli grows best when the weather is cool, and will develop strongly and be more resistant to insect attack if given liquid fertiliser every 2-3 weeks.

Its bouquet of tight buds is produced in 3-4 months at the top of the stem. Always cut broccoli early when the buds are still tightly furled and coloured either purplish or green, depending on the variety. If left too long before harvesting, the buds start to open and the flavour and texture change, and stems with yellow flowers form. After the initial harvest, each plant starts to produce small stem offshoots of useful broccoli for another month or two. These small broccoli shoots are harvestable and good to eat. However, if any of the florets are allowed to ripen to yellow and open, the plant is satisfied it has run its course and will start to fade. So, for the longest possible harvest, keep trimming the side shoots until they become too small.

Some broccoli varieties have been specially bred to grow during warm weather so plant these for an early autumn crop. 'Romanesco' is a recently developed variety that has a limey-green flower-head with tightly spiralled cones. It is sweetly flavoured and dramatic to serve whole but it behaves more like cauliflower in that it does not produce successive shoots.

For the table

TO PREPARE

• Aphids, bugs and caterpillars love to hide in the florets of broccoli, so soak for a short time in cold water and shake gently to release unwanted dinner guests.

• Broccoli can be boiled, steamed, stir-fried or microwaved. Cut the florets from the stalk and use separately. Covering broccoli while cooking will preserve a stronger flavour.

• The stems are edible, but need to have their tough outer skin removed before using raw in salads or tossing in a stir-fry (avoid over-cooking).

• Try saving the stems and cook all at once in an Asian-style oyster sauce.

TO SERVE

• Use broccoli florets to carry strong flavours such as garlic and lemon. Use only lemon rind, as the acid from the juice darkens and wrinkles the broccoli stems.

• Dotted with anchovy butter, steamed broccoli becomes a great accompaniment to a simple meal.

• Toss broccoli florets with brown butter and toasted almonds.

• Add finely chopped broccoli to a pasta sauce with Italian sausage and lots of garlic.

• Broccoli makes great soup. Cook in chicken stock with fresh herbs and garlic; puree and add a dash of cream for a very elegant starter.

preserving the crop

STORING	Store in a vegetable storage bag in the refrigerator for up to 3 days. It's also possible to store broccoli, with stems in a container of water, covered by a vegetable storage bag, for about 5 days.
FREEZING	Broccoli can be blanched and frozen for several months. Pack into rigid containers (see Freezing, page 240). Cook when needed in boiling water, unthawed. Cooked and pureed broccoli freezes very well for several months.

crêpes with creamy broccoli

wholemeal vegetable spaghetti with garlic crumbs

6 slices wholemeal bread (270g), discard crusts
375g (12 ounces) wholemeal spaghetti
200g (6½ ounces) broccoli, cut into small florets
150g (4½ ounces) sugar snap peas, trimmed
1 tablespoon olive oil
2 cloves garlic, crushed
1 medium zucchini (120g), sliced thinly
2 drained anchovy fillets, chopped finely
2 green onions (scallions), chopped finely
2 teaspoons finely grated lemon rind
¼ cup (60ml) lemon juice

1 Blend or process bread until fine.
2 Cook pasta in large saucepan of boiling water until tender. Add broccoli and peas to water for last 5 minutes of pasta cooking time. Drain; reserve ¼ cup cooking liquid.
3 Meanwhile, heat half the oil in large frying pan; cook breadcrumbs and garlic until browned and crisp. Remove from pan.
4 Heat remaining oil in same cleaned pan; cook zucchini, anchovy and onion until zucchini is tender.
5 Combine pasta mixture and zucchini mixture in large bowl with rind, juice and reserved cooking liquid.
6 Serve pasta sprinkled with garlic crumbs.

prep & cook time 40 minutes **serves** 4

crêpes with creamy broccoli

8 frozen french-style crêpes (400g), thawed
¼ cup (20g) coarsely grated parmesan cheese
broccoli filling
750g (1½ pounds) broccoli, trimmed, chopped coarsely
30g (1 ounce) butter
2 green onions (scallions), chopped coarsely
1 tablespoon wholemeal plain (all-purpose) flour
½ cup (125ml) milk
½ cup (125ml) pouring cream
pinch ground nutmeg

1 Preheat oven to 180°C/350°F.
2 Make broccoli filling. Divide filling between crêpes; fold crêpes into triangles.
3 Place crêpes in oiled ovenproof dish; sprinkle with cheese. Bake crêpes, in oven, about 10 minutes or until cheese has melted and crêpes and filling are heated through.
broccoli filling Boil, steam or microwave broccoli until tender; drain. Heat butter in medium saucepan; cook onion, stirring, over medium heat, 1 minute. Stir in flour; cook, stirring, 1 minute. Remove from heat; gradually stir in combined milk, cream and nutmeg; stir over high heat until mixture boils and thickens. Stir in broccoli.

prep & cook time 25 minutes **serves** 4

wholemeal vegetable spaghetti with garlic crumbs

Cauliflower

Here's another flower-bud head that is prized when it's densely packed and its 'curds', just like fresh cheese, are pure in colour and firm. As a gardening cook, you can assess the right moment to harvest. Straight from the garden, the cauliflower will break apart with a snap. Cauliflower is always less odorous when cooked fresh.

In the garden

For general soil preparation and cultivation notes, see page 184. Cauliflowers are the fussiest of the brassicas to grow. They are very sensitive to soil pH. Diseases (such as club root) and deformed growth (whiptail) are caused by soil that is too acidic. Always add a generous handful of garden lime to each square metre (square yard) of soil when preparing the garden beds 2 weeks before planting. Sprinkle another dusting of lime over the soil 1 week after the seedlings have been planted. Cauliflowers are generally ready to harvest in 4-6 months and need cool temperatures and full sun to grow well. Start to raise seeds in early or mid-summer so you can plant them before summer's end. Seedlings are also available from nurseries. Plant them out 60-80cm (24-32") apart. The young cauliflower plants need to be well established by the time winter begins as cool weather is essential for the cauliflower heads to develop. In the heat of summer the heads start to open and break up.

As the heads form, protect them from the sun by tying their large leaves into a teepee above or breaking them and folding over the white heads. The heads will yellow if exposed to the sun. The leaves of some varieties grow around the head and automatically shelter it. Peep regularly under their covers to watch for when the flowers become tight and solid. Harvest them straight away or they'll open out.

Unlike broccoli, cauliflowers put their all into one flower, so there is no repeat harvest. It is a good idea when planting the seedlings to hold a few back and plant 2-3 weeks later to stagger the crop. Several white cauliflower varieties are available and differ only in the length of time they take to form. 'Alverda' is a variety with greenish curds. Pink, green, purple and even orange varieties are available in Europe. Their flavours are as individual as their colourings. Mini cauliflowers are formed by planting seedlings only 25-30cm (10-12") apart and harvesting the small heads as soon as they reach 10cm (4") across, in about 4 months. Keep up follow-on plantings as the cauliflowers are harvested one by one.

For the table

TO PREPARE

• Soak the florets in cold water for a short period before cooking to flush out any bugs or caterpillars.

• If serving whole, use a sharp knife to cut off the heavy main stem and cut a cone-shaped core out of the base to allow heat to penetrate; make deep incisions in any other thick stems. Trim off large leaves, but leave young ones on.

• For miniature cauliflowers, cut off main stems and trim off coarse or damaged leaves, leaving the smaller ones on.

• Note that cauliflower should be cooked in non-reactive pans as aluminium pans can react with its chemicals and discolour it and create off-flavours.

TO SERVE

• Cook cauliflower and onions in chicken stock; blend, adding fresh dill sprigs. Reheat mixture, adding enough cream to make a thick but smooth soup.

• Top cooked cauliflower with crisped chopped bacon, breadcrumbs and a drizzle of butter; brown under a grill.

• Add to a salad of red and yellow capsicum, tomatoes and strips of crisped salami; toss with italian dressing.

• Cauliflower cheese is an age-old favourite; blend any leftovers until smooth, then thin with a little milk to make an instant soup.

preserving the crop

STORING	Cover the cauliflower with paper towel before storing in a vegetable storage bag in the refrigerator for up to a week.
FREEZING	Cauliflower can be blanched and frozen (see Freezing, page 240) for up to 4 months. Store in rigid containers so the florets do not break up.

cauliflower, lentil and pea curry

cooking-oil spray
1 medium brown onion (150g), sliced thickly
1 clove garlic, crushed
2cm (¾ inch) piece fresh ginger (10g), grated
1 fresh long red chilli, chopped finely
1 teaspoon ground cumin
½ teaspoon ground turmeric
¼ teaspoon ground cardamom
¼ teaspoon ground fennel
1 tablespoon tomato paste
1 small cauliflower (1kg), trimmed, chopped coarsely
2 cups (500ml) vegetable stock
400g (12½ ounces) canned crushed tomatoes
1 cup (250ml) canned light coconut cream
½ cup (100g) dried red lentils
1 cup (120g) frozen peas
½ cup firmly packed fresh coriander leaves (cilantro)

1 Lightly spray heated large saucepan with oil; cook onion, garlic, ginger and chilli, stirring, until onion softens. Add spices and paste; cook, stirring, about 2 minutes or until fragrant.
2 Add cauliflower, stock, undrained tomatoes, coconut cream and lentils; bring to the boil. Reduce heat; simmer, uncovered, about 10 minutes or until cauliflower and lentils are tender. Add peas; stir until hot. Season to taste.
3 Serve curry sprinkled with coriander.

prep & cook time 35 minutes serves 4
notes You can use a whole 270ml can of coconut cream in this recipe.
All spices are available from specialty spice shops and most major supermarkets. Cardamom is one of the world's most expensive spices; it has an aromatic, sweetly rich flavour. Cumin, also known as zeera or comino, has a spicy, nutty flavour. Turmeric is a member of the ginger family; the dried, ground root adds a rich yellow colour to dishes. It is pungent but not hot.

cauliflower gratin

1 small cauliflower (750g), trimmed,
   broken into large florets
50g (1½ ounces) butter
¼ cup (35g) plain (all-purpose) flour
1½ cups (375ml) hot milk
½ cup (60g) coarsely grated cheddar cheese
¼ cup (20g) finely grated parmesan cheese
1 tablespoon packaged breadcrumbs

1 Preheat oven to 220°C/425°F.
2 Boil, steam or microwave cauliflower until tender; drain. Place in medium shallow ovenproof dish.
3 Meanwhile, melt butter in medium saucepan, add flour; cook, stirring, until mixture bubbles and thickens. Gradually stir in milk until smooth; cook, stirring, until mixture boils and thickens. Remove from heat, stir in cheeses.
4 Pour cheese sauce over cauliflower; sprinkle with breadcrumbs. Bake, in oven, about 15 minutes or until browned lightly.

prep & cook time 30 minutes **serves** 6
note If you can find them, use six baby cauliflowers, (weighing a total of 750g), instead. There is no need to break them into florets, just cook them until tender, then bake them whole.

cauliflower gratin

piccalilli

1 tablespoon salt
1kg (2 pounds) mixed vegetables, coarsely
   chopped (see notes)
1 litre (4 cups) white vinegar
1 cup (220g) white sugar
1 tablespoon ground turmeric
1 tablespoon mustard powder
3 cloves garlic, sliced
4 fresh small red thai (serrano) chillies,
   halved lengthways
⅓ cup (75g) cornflour (cornstarch)

1 Sprinkle salt over vegetables; stand overnight. Rinse under cold water; drain well.
2 Combine vinegar, sugar, turmeric, mustard powder, garlic and chilli in large saucepan. Bring to the boil, add vegetables; simmer, covered, about 5 minutes or until vegetables are just tender.
3 Take ½ cup of liquid from pan and blend with cornflour; stir into pan. Return to the boil; boil about 3 minutes or until thickened. Pour into hot sterilised jars and seal while hot (see notes).
4 Store in a cool, dry place for 4 weeks before using. Once opened, store in the refrigerator.

prep & cook time 25 minutes (+ standing)
makes about 8 cups
notes Use a mixture of cauliflower, carrots, celery, green tomatoes, cucumber and pickling onions.
To sterilise jars, see Bottling, pages 240-242.
Drain away some of the liquid before bottling, if the mixture seems too wet.

piccalilli

Cabbage & Brussels Sprouts

Perhaps not the most glamorous duo in the brassica folio, cabbages and brussels sprouts are both stout winter growers and can be extremely attractive and a reason for pride in the garden. They are also just as attractive on the table.

In the garden

For general soil preparation and cultivation notes for both cabbage and brussels sprouts, see page 184.

CABBAGE

Of all the brassicas, cabbages are the most tolerant of warm conditions and, as long as you sow or plant varieties that are suitable for the warmer months, you can grow cabbages to provide a continuous harvest right through the year in most climates. Cabbages can be picked small or left to become full-sized, but their holding ability is better in cooler weather. They start to crack open, even rot, if left too long.

In cold climates, ensure autumn seedlings are solidly established before the frosts arrive and in the tropics, plant seedlings in time for them to mature in the dry rather than the wet.

There are an astounding number of varieties. There are those with conical heads such as 'sugarloaf' or 'durham early', which are quick maturing for speedy, warm-weather crops. Others develop tight, round heads and varieties include the fast-growing minis and 'earliball' and the larger, slower winter regulars like 'primo' and 'january king' (don't suppose this is a summer variety, though – the January is the European January). Colours vary from deep to light green, grey, purple-green and rich beet red. Leaf textures offer more variety with some tightly stretched and smooth around the head and others rumpled and creased as in the 'savoy' cabbages.

Then there are the kales, which are loose-leaf cabbages. The leaves fan out in the same manner as spinach and silver beet (swiss chard). Their young leaves, and also the older leaves though strongly flavoured, can be cooked. They are particularly suited to stir-frying. There are plain-leafed varieties that can stand nearly 1m (3') tall like 'cottages' and 'chou moellier'. Others are curly and fringed like the 'scotch', 'tall green curled' and 'ornamental'. 'Palm tree kale', or 'italian cabbage', has dark grey, crumpled leaves.

Experiment with cabbage varieties that you have never tried before. Certainly choose according to culinary desires, but also be adventurous and use cabbages as ornamental winter garden features for there are few vegetables as showy and dramatic. You'll be rewarded with a wintertime chorus of cabbage leaf shapes and colours, all with a sweet cabbage flavour.

Red cabbage is good raw in salads; otherwise, it repays slow, gentle cooking with a minimum of water plus an acid ingredient such as apple, vinegar or wine. The acid component is needed because plain water may be alkaline, which turns red cabbage a discouraging blue-green with flavour to match.

Savoy cabbage, crinkly-leafed and rich green shading into cream at the centre, is less compact and more flavoursome than white cabbage. It can be used in the same ways as white cabbage.

White cabbage, which is really a pale green shading to cream or white at the centre, comes in round or long (sugarloaf) varieties. It is good for coleslaw, stir-fries or steamed in a steamer or a covered saucepan with butter, just until it wilts.

Wombok (also known as chinese cabbage or peking or napa cabbage) is a long, rather loosely packed pale green cabbage with thin, crinkly, delicately flavoured leaves. It can be used in the same ways as white or savoy cabbage and is also used in stir-fries and other Asian cooking.

preserving the crop

STORING	Cabbages are best stored whole in the refrigerator. Once cut, they should be used within a few days. Brussels sprouts can be stored in a vegetable storage bag for several days in the refrigerator.
FREEZING	Cabbage can be shredded and blanched, then frozen for up to 6 months; cook from frozen. Brussels sprouts can be blanched and frozen for up to 6 months in rigid containers to keep their shape (see Freezing, page 240).
PICKLING	Pickled red cabbage is popular. Salt the cabbage and stand overnight; rinse well the following day. Pack the cabbage into hot sterilised jars (see Bottling, pages 240-242). Heat white vinegar with sugar and spices, such as cloves and cinnamon, until boiling and pour over cabbage in jars; seal while hot.

savoy cabbage

green cabbage

red cabbage

BRUSSELS SPROUTS

Brussels sprouts are like tiny cabbages. They grow along a thick centre stalk and are at their best in winter. If you can't provide a long, cold winter, it's best not to try to grow brussels sprouts – the sprouts will not form properly if the weather is not cold enough. They grow in the same manner as their brassica relatives but develop a tall, strong stem. Feed regularly with liquid fertiliser and hill up the soil around the stem base to support it. The more leaves that develop up the stem, the more sprouts you'll be able to gather from the leaf junctions.

As the sprouts start to form near the base, strip the lowers leaves from the stem with a sideways pull so the sprouts can develop round and firm. You'll be able to harvest in 4-5 months. Gather the sprouts as they develop, or cut the stem at the growing point when it's about 40cm (16") tall and they'll all mature at once. Discard those sprouts that start to burst open; the ideal sprout is tightly furled and about 5cm (2") in diameter. As soon as the buds start to form, remember to spread around a slug and snail deterrent as both of them relish such new morsels.

For the table

Because cabbage grows well in almost any soil and most climates, peasants have always been able to grow it as a staple of their diet. The result is a legacy of splendid, hearty dishes from generations of peasant cooks who built cabbage into generous soups and nourishing casseroles, pickled it to last through the winter, paired it with the poultry and pork they raised themselves, and turned leftover cabbage and potatoes into those delicious, homely Irish and British dishes, colcannon and bubble and squeak.

TO PREPARE

• The key to cooking any kind of cabbage is to make it brief. White cabbage, savoy cabbage or wombok should be cooked just until it wilts if it is to be served as a separate vegetable; overcooking releases rank aromas and flavours from sulphur compounds in the leaves.

• All these cabbages respond well to long, slow cooking with rich meats, herbs and other vegetables. However, don't forget to add an acid ingredient to red cabbage to keep its colour and flavour intact.

• Cabbage leaves briefly blanched (dropped into boiling water) to soften them can be wrapped round meat and rice stuffings and steamed or casseroled.

• Whole, halved or quartered brussels sprouts can be briefly boiled or steamed, pan-fried or stir-fried. They are cooked when a fine skewer can be pushed, against some resistance, into the centre.

kale

TO SERVE

• Sprinkle cabbage generously with crisp chopped pancetta or bacon, garlic and a little butter.

• Stir-fry shredded cabbage until crisp; drizzle with sesame oil and sprinkle with sesame seeds. This is great tossed through noodles.

• Finely shredded cabbage also shines, raw, as a salad. Shred or grate carrots and capsicums; toss with mung bean sprouts and a chilli-flavoured vinaigrette for a new-look coleslaw. A packet of fried noodles added just before serving adds crunch.

• Finely shred cabbage and add to a pan of boiling water with a spoonful of caraway seeds; return to the boil. Remove from the heat; drain and add a knob of butter before serving.

• The mild flavour of white cabbage is enhanced by cooking it with butter and a sprinkle of caraway seeds or with chopped streaky bacon that has been lightly fried before adding the cabbage.

• Sauerkraut is shredded white or red cabbage fermented in brine, which makes it pungently sour. It is served with cured and smoked meats.

• Brussels sprouts, steamed lightly, then tossed in a hot pan with olive oil and fresh chestnuts will accompany a grilled steak perfectly.

• Toss halved brussels sprouts in melted butter. Add some white wine and chicken stock and a handful of sultanas. Cook, covered, until sprouts are soft; remove lid and cook until liquid is almost absorbed. Serve with grilled or roasted meats.

brussels sprouts with cream and almonds

50g (1½ ounces) butter
⅓ cup (25g) flaked almonds
1kg (2 pounds) brussels sprouts, trimmed, halved
2 cloves garlic, crushed
1¼ cups (310ml) pouring cream (see note)

1 Melt 10g (½ ounce) of the butter in large frying pan; cook nuts, stirring, until browned lightly, remove from pan.
2 Melt remaining butter in same pan; cook sprouts and garlic, stirring, until sprouts are browned lightly. Add cream; bring to the boil. Simmer, uncovered, until sprouts are tender and sauce thickens slightly.
3 Serve sprout mixture sprinkled with nuts.

prep & cook time 10 minutes **serves** 4
note It's fine to use just 1 x 300ml carton of cream for this recipe.

roast beef and coleslaw on rye

roast beef and coleslaw on rye

1 cup (80g) finely shredded cabbage
1 small carrot (70g), grated coarsely
2 green onions (scallions), chopped finely
¼ cup (75g) mayonnaise
1 tablespoon lemon juice
4 slices rare roast beef (120g)
4 slices rye bread (180g)

1 Combine cabbage, carrot, onion, mayonnaise and juice in medium bowl.
2 Divide beef between two slices of bread; top with coleslaw, then remaining bread.

prep time 10 minutes **serves** 2
notes Use whatever cabbage you like; try wombok, it's easy to shred finely.
You can buy the roast beef, already cooked, from any deli.

mixed cabbage coleslaw

⅓ cup (80ml) olive oil
2 tablespoons cider vinegar
2 teaspoons dijon mustard
2 cups (160g) finely shredded green cabbage
2 cups (160g) finely shredded red cabbage
2 cups (160g) finely shredded wombok
1 medium carrot (120g), grated coarsely
4 green onions (scallions), sliced thinly

1 Whisk oil, vinegar and mustard in large bowl; mix in remaining ingredients.

prep time 20 minutes **serves** 4
notes Cider vinegar (apple cider vinegar) is made from fermented apples. It is available from supermarkets. Dijon mustard is a pale brown, distinctively flavoured, fairly mild french mustard.

mixed cabbage coleslaw

Asian Greens

Asian greens are the speedsters of the brassica family. They grow very quickly and are best cooked rapidly to preserve their brilliant green colouring, as it's their stems and leaves that we relish. They are the soft and juicy members of the brassica troupe and many have a deliciously sharp flavour.

In the garden

Asian greens grow fast and succulent only if hurried along. Start with rich soil and add weekly applications of liquid fertiliser so that their stems and leaves don't become stringy. Frequent watering keeps them bulky. Flood the root zone every 3-4 days if the weather is dry and test the soil with your finger after rain to make sure moisture has gone through to the roots. Often the large leaves deflect light showers. Asian greens don't tolerate frosts, but will grow year-round in frost-free areas and the tropics.

In very small gardens, grow varieties you can harvest leaf by leaf, and plant replacement crops every 2 weeks or so. Move the brassica site every 6 months to deter insects, prevent the build-up of soil diseases and to rest the soil.

A shallow, 30-40 cm (12-16") pot filled with very rich potting mix will support a selection of strongly flavoured greens and lettuce for a garden salad mix. It must be in full sun and well watered. Your 'salad bowl' will last a month or two, and so plant a second pot 3-4 weeks after the original.

Gai lan (chinese broccoli) has long, slender stems, large leaves and a small bud or white flower cluster. When the buds are closed, they are edible but should be removed if open. They can be picked in 8-10 weeks.

Buk choy (chinese chard, pak choi, baby buk choy, senposai) has heavy white stems the same length as its leaves. It takes 5-6 weeks to grow but the odd leaf can be used while it's developing.

Gai choy (mustard cabbage) is more leaf than stem and is ready in 6-8 weeks, odd leaves being available as they grow. When full size, cut off at the roots and cook whole.

Tatsoi (chinese flat cabbage, rosette buk choy, komatsuma) forms an open cluster of deep green leaves with brilliant white stems. It spreads out to 30cm (12") like a glorious green posy. Use leaf by leaf or cut off whole. It has a slightly strong flavour and is ready to harvest in 8 weeks.

Choy sum (chinese flowering cabbage) is very similar to gai lan with long stems, rounded leaves and a small bud or yellow flower cluster. Again, the closed buds are edible while the open buds are not. They can be picked in 8-10 weeks.

Wombok (chinese cabbage) is a tall, elongated cabbage, though lighter and less tightly packed, and develops its fully enwrapped form in 8-10 weeks. (See also page 196.)

Mizuna, also called mitsuba, is a leafy Japanese herb with a crisp, aromatic flavour, used in salads, sandwiches, soups and savoury custards, and also as a garnish. (See also page 79.)

PESTS AND DISEASES

Asian greens are prone to the same cabbage moth and butterfly caterpillar attacks as the slow-growing brassicas but their faster growth makes damage less likely. Slugs and snails love the lush, new growth, so protect seedlings as they emerge and keep renewing the baits as the plants develop. See page 17 for home-made alternatives.

preserving the crop

STORING	Store all asian greens in vegetable storage bags in the refrigerator for 1-2 days only. Wombok will last for longer if stored whole. Once cut though, use as quickly as possible.
FREEZING	These vegetables don't survive the freezing process well.

For the table

TO PREPARE

• Harvest all asian greens as close to preparation as possible. Pick whole, or pick only as much as you need. Only wash when ready to prepare.

• Harvest choy sum and gai lan as the flowers open and while many buds are still tightly furled.

TO SERVE

• Choy sum can be lightly boiled, steamed or microwaved and served with oyster sauce.

• Stir-fry some chilli, garlic and ginger for a minute in a hot oiled wok. Add some choy sum, trimmed into 5cm lengths, and stir-fry until almost tender. Add a couple of tablespoons of fish sauce and lime juice and stir-fry until hot. Serve sprinkled with cashew nuts.

• Buk choy and baby buk choy can be boiled, steamed, stir-fried or microwaved. Stir through pancetta or bacon, parmesan and garlic.

• Stir-fry buk choy with garlic and serve with sesame oil and a sprinkling of sesame seeds.

• Wombok can be used in the same way as green cabbage and is great raw in salads.

• Stuff wombok leaves with a pork mince and rice vermicelli filling and steam; drizzle with soy sauce mixed with rice wine just before serving hot.

• Cook sliced onion in a hot wok until soft. Add 2 cups of shredded wombok and stir-fry until just wilted, then stir through some soy sauce.

• Use tatsoi in the same way as buk choy or wombok. Add raw to salads but remember it has a stronger flavour than the buk choy we're used to.

• Remove the tough outer stem layer of gai lan before cooking the stems first and the chopped leaves towards the end. It's great with a little butter and seasoning. It's also good stir-fried with pork or chicken.

• Gai choy can be added whole to soups. It is also good served with rich meats such as duck and pork.

grilled asian vegetables

400g (12½ ounces) baby buk choy, trimmed, halved lengthways
2 tablespoons peanut oil
175g (5½ ounces) broccolini, halved
100g (3 ounces) snow peas, trimmed
200g (6½ ounces) baby corn, halved lengthways
2 tablespoons mirin
1 tablespoon vegetarian oyster sauce
1 tablespoon light soy sauce
1 clove garlic, crushed
1 teaspoon white sugar
½ teaspoon sesame oil

1 Boil, steam or microwave buk choy until wilted; drain. Brush with half the peanut oil; cook on heated oiled barbecue flat plate (or pan-fry) until tender.
2 Combine broccolini, peas and corn in large bowl with remaining peanut oil; mix well. Cook vegetables, in batches, on flat plate until tender.
3 Meanwhile, combine mirin, sauces, garlic, sugar and sesame oil in bowl; add vegetables, mix well.

prep & cook time 20 minutes **serves** 4
notes 'Vegetarian' oyster sauce is made from blended mushrooms and soy sauce; it is available from health-food stores and some supermarkets.
Mirin is a champagne-coloured cooking wine made of glutinous rice and alcohol; it is used in Japan expressly for cooking and should not be confused with sake. It is available from supermarkets and Asian food shops.

steamed gai lan in oyster sauce

buk choy steamed with chilli oil

steamed gai lan in oyster sauce

1kg (2 pounds) gai lan, halved
1 tablespoon peanut oil
2 tablespoons oyster sauce
1 tablespoon light soy sauce

1 Boil, steam or microwave gai lan until tender; drain.
2 Heat oil in wok, add gai lan and sauces; stir-fry about
2 minutes or until mixture is heated through.

prep & cook time 10 minutes
serves 6 (as an accompaniment)
notes Light soy sauce is the best type of soy sauce to use
in dishes where the natural colour of the ingredients is to
be maintained, such as stir-frying, braising, seasoning
soups and for dressing salads. It's fairly thin in consistency
and, while paler than the others, it is the saltiest tasting;
it is not a salt-reduced or low-sodium soy sauce.
Oyster sauce is a rich, brown sauce made from oysters
and their brine, cooked with salt and soy sauce, and then
thickened with starches. Both sauces are available from
major supermarkets and Asian food stores.

buk choy steamed with chilli oil

4 baby buk choy (600g)
1 tablespoon peanut oil
2 cloves garlic, crushed
2 tablespoons light soy sauce
1½ teaspoons hot chilli sauce
2 green onions (scallions), sliced
¼ cup fresh coriander leaves (cilantro)
1 fresh small red thai (serrano) chilli, sliced thinly

1 Halve buk choy lengthways; place, cut-side up,
in large bamboo steamer, drizzle with combined oil,
garlic and sauces.
2 Steam buk choy, covered, over large saucepan of
simmering water about 5 minutes or until just tender.
Serve sprinkled with onion, coriander and chilli.

prep & cook time 10 minutes **serves** 4

caramel fish and baby buk choy

⅔ cup (150g) caster (superfine) sugar
⅓ cup (80ml) fish sauce
4 shallots (100g), sliced thinly
1kg (2 pounds) baby buk choy, leaves separated
2 tablespoons peanut oil
500g (1 pound) white fish fillets,
   cut into 3cm (1 inch) pieces

1 Heat sugar in medium saucepan over medium heat until sugar melts and turns a light caramel colour. Remove pan from heat; add sauce. Return pan to heat; simmer caramel sauce, stirring, until sauce becomes syrupy. Stir in shallot.
2 Meanwhile, boil, steam or microwave buk choy until wilted; drain. Cover to keep warm.
3 Heat oil in wok. Stir-fry fish, in batches, until browned. Add caramel sauce; bring to the boil. Simmer, uncovered, until fish is cooked.
4 Divide buk choy between serving plates; top with fish, drizzle with sauce. Serve with some steamed jasmine rice.

prep & cook time 25 minutes **serves** 4
notes We used blue-eye fish fillets in this recipe, but you can use any white fish fillets.
Caramel sauce can be made in advance. Cover; refrigerate until required.

caramel fish and baby buk choy

stir-fried choy sum

1 tablespoon peanut oil
1 fresh long red chilli, sliced thinly
2 cloves garlic, crushed
2cm (¾ inch) piece fresh ginger (10g), grated
1kg (2 pounds) choy sum, trimmed, cut into
   5cm (2 inch) lengths
2 tablespoons fish sauce
2 tablespoons lime juice
1 cup (150g) roasted unsalted cashews

1 Heat oil in wok; stir-fry chilli, garlic and ginger 1 minute.
2 Add choy sum; stir-fry until almost tender. Add sauce and juice; stir-fry until hot.
3 Serve stir-fry sprinkled with nuts.

prep & cook time 15 minutes **serves** 4
note Serve this with rice or noodles. Buk choy and gai lan can also be cooked this way.

stir-fried choy sum

Mushrooms

With their softly furred white skins and brown-grey gills, mushrooms are invitingly tactile and very ornamental. Their aroma is clean and earthy and their flavour follows suit. In all honesty, however, we can't claim that mushrooms are a garden crop. The mushroom we recognise, harvest and appreciate is the fruiting body, the seed or (more accurately) the spore-releaser of the underground system – which is the real 'plant'. Harvesting wild mushrooms can be dangerous for the uninitiated as not all mushrooms are edible so, in a word, don't. It's much tamer, and safer, to raise mushrooms from a kit. Mushrooms are a fascinating form of life, and are very easy to grow once you've opened the box and watered the compost mix.

In the garden

Mushroom kits are readily available from nurseries and produce stores. They consist of two packages of compost material, one of which contains the thread-like vegetative part of mushrooms called the mycelium. This layer is dampened to activate its growth and, after a week, is combined with the second bag of mix.

The container is stored in a dark, cool position as the fungi won't 'fruit' if they're too hot or too light. Mushrooms like temperatures around 12-18°C (55-65°F), and storage in a cupboard, shady shed or cellar is ideal. Choose a spot with easy access for checking and harvesting.

The first pinheads will appear within 14-20 days. The mushrooms develop quickly, from small specks to recognisable button forms overnight and full-blown mushrooms the following day. Harvest them as soon as they reach a suitable size and thus avoid overcrowding. Use a knife to make clean cuts and to disturb the mass as little as possible.

Several flushes of mushrooms will continue for a month or two, but eventually the mycelium is exhausted. If no fresh mushrooms develop after 21 days, consider the season over. Add the compost to the garden where its final performance will be helping other plants to grow.

Wild mushrooms are a treasure, and there are avid bands of experts who know what to gather and where. You often see groups combing fields and forests after the rain. You may be lucky enough to be invited to join a group or go to classes. But it must be stressed that ill-informed wild mushroom gathering is nothing but dangerous.

For the table

WARNING

Never eat a mushroom unless you are certain that it is edible. It is advisable to get a field guide to mushrooms and take it with you if you go mushrooming. Most toxic mushrooms will only make you sick, but the deathcap is deadly and is known to be in Australia. Before you go mushrooming, go to *www.anbg.gov.au/fungi/deathcap.html*. It has large, clear colour pictures of the deathcap with detailed descriptions, pictures of safe mushrooms that could be confused with the deathcap, and the frightening information that a single mushroom can kill a man and less than that can kill a child. It also provides the emergency phone number for the Australian Poisons Information Centre.

preserving the crop

STORING	Never store mushrooms in a plastic bag. Paper bags are great; a plain cotton drawstring bag, used just for this purpose, is wonderful. Store in paper or cloth in the refrigerator.
FREEZING	Mushrooms can be frozen whole (for buttons) for about a month if raw, or sauté in butter and they can be frozen for about 3 months. Add these mushrooms whole to casseroles as they go a little soggy. Soup of pureed mushrooms can be frozen for up to 3 months (see Freezing, page 240).
DRYING	Mushrooms can be dried in paper bags in an airy position (see Drying, page 243).
PICKLING	If you've a glut of mushrooms, try pickling them whole and using as finger food or on antipasto platters.

button mushrooms

chestnut mushrooms

cup mushrooms

TO PREPARE

• Cultivated mushrooms are harvested and eaten at three different stages: buttons (still joined to the stems), cups (larger than buttons but with caps still closed), flat (fully open but still firm).

• Cultivated mushrooms need no washing. If they have a covering of compost, brush gently with a damp piece of paper towel.

TO SERVE

• For perfect breakfast mushrooms, sauté sliced cups in a little butter and oil until they have released their liquid; stir over high heat until the liquid evaporates. Sprinkle with a good quantity of lemon juice and chopped fresh parsley.

• Flat mushrooms beg to be filled. Stuff with minced pork, water chestnuts and Asian flavourings (chilli, lemon grass, coriander); pan-fry until the filling is cooked through.

• Button mushrooms are great when dipped in a thin batter and deep-fried; serve with a very lemony herb or garlic mayonnaise.

• For an easy pâté, cook chopped mushrooms with thyme, green onions and garlic; combine with cream cheese and a little cream. Press mixture into a loaf pan lined with plastic wrap; cover and refrigerate until firm. When firm, roll in chopped fresh parsley and serve with crackers.

chilli pickled mushrooms

3 cups (750ml) cider vinegar
½ cup (125ml) lemon juice
10 whole white peppercorns
2 fresh bay leaves
2 sprigs fresh thyme
2 cloves garlic, thinly sliced
3 fresh small red thai (serrano) chillies
1kg (2 pounds) button mushrooms

1 Combine all ingredients except mushrooms, in large saucepan. Bring to the boil; reduce heat and simmer, covered, 10 minutes.
2 Add mushrooms to pan; simmer uncovered 10 minutes.
3 Pour mushrooms and cooking liquid into hot sterilised jars and seal while hot (see Bottling, pages 240-242). Store in a cool, dry place for up to 6 months; refrigerate once opened.

prep & cook time 30 minutes
note These are great as an appetiser or served alongside strong cheese as in a ploughman's lunch. Cup mushrooms can also be used, but they may need to be quartered.

kecap manis fish and mushroom skewers

kecap manis fish and mushroom skewers

2 tablespoons salt-reduced soy sauce

¼ cup (60ml) kecap manis

2 cloves garlic, crushed

3 green onions (scallions), chopped finely

600g (1¼ pounds) skinless white fish fillet, cut into 2.5cm (1 inch) pieces

8 medium swiss brown mushrooms (180g), halved

600g (1¼ pounds) buk choy, chopped coarsely

2 tablespoons water

1 Combine sauces, garlic and onion in large bowl; add fish and mushrooms. Thread mushrooms and fish onto eight skewers. Reserve marinade.

2 Cook skewers, in batches, in heated oiled large frying pan. Remove from pan; cover to keep warm.

3 Add buk choy, reserved marinade and the water to pan; bring to the boil. Simmer until buk choy is wilted.

4 Serve buk choy mixture with skewers, and lime wedges.

prep & cook time 25 minutes **serves** 4

notes Soak bamboo skewers in water for at least 30 minutes to prevent scorching during cooking. We used ling fillets in this recipe.

marinated mixed mushrooms

2 cloves garlic, crushed

4cm (1¼ inch) piece fresh ginger (20g), grated

⅓ cup (80ml) light soy sauce

2 tablespoons mirin

2 tablespoons sake

2 tablespoons peanut oil

1 tablespoon white sugar

200g (6½ ounces) oyster mushrooms

200g (6½ ounces) shiitake mushrooms

200g (6½ ounces) button mushrooms

200g (6½ ounces) swiss brown mushrooms

200g (6½ ounces) enoki mushrooms

4 green onions (scallions), sliced diagonally

1 Combine garlic, ginger, sauce, mirin, sake, oil and sugar in large bowl; add mushrooms, mix gently. Cover; refrigerate 2 hours.

2 Drain mushrooms; reserve marinade in bowl.

3 Cook mushrooms, in batches, on heated oiled barbecue flat plate until tender.

4 Combine mushrooms and onion in bowl with reserved marinade.

prep & cook time 25 minutes (+ refrigeration) **serves** 4

marinated mixed mushrooms

shiitake mushrooms

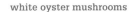
white oyster mushrooms

pink oyster mushrooms

mixed mushroom fettuccine boscaiola

10g (½ ounce) dried porcini mushrooms
¼ cup (60ml) boiling water
375g (12 ounces) fettuccine pasta
1 tablespoon olive oil
200g (6½ ounces) pancetta, chopped coarsely
100g (3 ounces) button mushrooms, sliced thinly
100g (3 ounces) swiss brown mushrooms, sliced thinly
1 flat mushroom (80g), sliced thinly
2 cloves garlic, crushed
¼ cup (60ml) dry white wine
1¼ cups (310ml) pouring cream (see notes)
1 tablespoon lemon juice
½ cup (40g) finely grated parmesan cheese
2 tablespoons coarsely chopped fresh chives
2 tablespoons finely grated parmesan cheese, extra

1 Combine porcini mushrooms and the water in small heatproof bowl; cover, stand 15 minutes or until mushrooms are tender. Drain; reserve soaking liquid, chop mushrooms coarsely.
2 Cook pasta in large saucepan of boiling water until tender; drain.
3 Meanwhile, heat oil in large frying pan; cook pancetta until crisp. Add all mushrooms and garlic; cook, stirring, until mushrooms are browned lightly. Add wine; bring to the boil. Boil, uncovered, until liquid has almost evaporated. Add cream, juice and reserved soaking liquid; simmer, uncovered, until sauce reduces by half and thickens slightly. Stir in cheese and chives.
4 Combine pasta and sauce in large bowl. Serve sprinkled with extra cheese.

prep & cook time 40 minutes (+ standing) **serves** 4
notes It is fine to use just 1 x 300ml carton of cream for this recipe.
Porcini, also known as cèpes, are the richest-flavoured mushrooms. Though expensive, they are so strongly-flavoured only a small amount is required for any particular dish. They are available from specialty food stores and some supermarkets.
Pancetta is an Italian salt-cured bacon. It is available from delicatessens and major supermarkets.

Silver Beet & Spinach

These two leafy greens are often confused. Silver beet (or swiss chard) is related to beetroot. It grows in a clump and its leaves are a thing of beauty: tall white stems with deep green, crinkly leaves that grow to 30-40cm (12-16"). Spinach, on the other hand, stands not quite so tall, has thin stems with clear, green leaves and a delicate, subtle taste. Spinach is one of the most nutritious vegetables, being an excellent source of fibre, vitamins A, C and E and the B vitamin folate (especially important for women planning pregnancies as it helps to guard against birth defects). It also has good levels of the antioxidant lutein, which has been linked with a lower risk of macular degeneration, a leading cause of blindness.

In the garden

Both spinach and silver beet require well-prepared soil and both also need mulch protection from frosts. Dig in plenty of chicken manure and well-matured compost, with a dressing of nitrogen-rich fertiliser 2-3 weeks before planting in a sunny or lightly shaded spot with morning sun.

Silver beet prefers full sun. It performs best in the garden as it develops a large root system, but if grown in pots, silver beet needs replacing often.

SILVER BEET

Silver beet or swiss chard seeds benefit from a soak in cold water for a few hours. Push the softened seeds down to the first finger joint, spacing them 30-40cm (12-16") apart. Stems and leaves will appear in 2 weeks. They may need thinning as several can emerge from each seed. Mulch and keep well watered. Give liquid feeds every 2 weeks in the cool of the day as fertiliser can burn in sunlight.

Harvest silver beet leaves by breaking off outside leaves with a downward and sideways pull. Always keep 4-5 leaves in the centre. Break off any flower stems that start to form, but when this happens prepare new seeds and garden beds as the end of the existing plants is nigh. Silver beet grows happily in most climates all year, though it displays a distinct preference for cool weather as it tends to run to seed in the heat and suffers rust spotting in humid conditions. In ideal conditions silver beet keeps producing new leaves for almost a year and the stem will end up looking like a trunk. It's the ideal cut-and-come-again vegetable.

There is a variety of silver beet known as 'perpetual spinach' that is beautifully leafy and fine-stemmed. It grows very well in a pot as well as in the garden. Don't be deluded by the name 'perpetual', however; it will need replacing in 3-6 months, especially if grown in a pot. Coloured 'rainbow' forms are available with yellow, red, orange and pink stem colours, and ruby chard with red stems alone. They are stunning in the garden and add drama to the dinner plate.

SPINACH

When planting spinach seeds, position them 1cm (½") deep and 15cm (6") apart if planning to harvest leaf by leaf, and 20-30cm (8-12") apart for whole-plant harvesting. Closely planted seedlings can be thinned out later. They'll sprout in 2-3 weeks. Mulch well to keep their roots moist and cool and to suppress weeds.

Keep regularly watered and give boosts of liquid fertiliser every month. You'll be able to pick the outside leaves in about 8 weeks. Spinach is an easy, cool-season crop and is

preserving the crop

STORING	Do not wash before storing. Place in a vegetable storage bag in the refrigerator for about 3 days.
FREEZING	Both silver beet and spinach can be blanched and frozen (see Freezing, page 240) for up to 6 months. On thawing you will need to squeeze out all the moisture and they will only be useful in cooked dishes such as pies, soups and casseroles.

happy planted in pots, in clusters or in regimental rows. It grows best during the short days of winter. Spinach can either be harvested leaf by leaf, or pulled out whole, roots and all. Another method is to cut it off above the soil and the remaining root will obligingly re-shoot to produce a second crop, making it doubly worthwhile. New Zealand spinach is a wild green that grows naturally along the coast in both Australia and New Zealand. It is also available as seed and will grow anywhere during the warm months; it is most lush when given adequate water. The leaves grow on lanky stems that are fleshy and mildly flavoured. Harvest a length of stem and strip off the leaves.

For the table

TO PREPARE

• Spinach and silver beet need thorough washing as dirt can hide in their crevices, but do so just before using. Holding the bunch upside down with both hands, plunge it into a sinkful of cold water and swish it vigorously several times, then lift it out. This works better than washing it under running water.

TO SERVE

• Silver beet and spinach can be used interchangeably but silver beet has a stronger flavour and carries stronger flavours well.

• Mix silver beet, fetta and pine nuts for seasoning a boned leg of lamb.

• Silver beet stems can be used as a dish on their own. Serve with a strong cheese sauce (with plenty of powdered mustard) and a gratin top.

• Add spinach by the handful to a risotto in the last moments of cooking.

• Combine spinach with ricotta to flavour gnocchi in a rich, cheesy sauce.

• Use both spinach and silver beet leaves to wrap a filling of minced chicken and almonds, before steaming.

• Deep-fry shredded silver beet and dress with a soy and rice wine dressing with lots of fried garlic, sesame seeds and a tiny sprinkle of sugar.

spinach and beetroot tart

1 sheet puff pastry
1kg (2 pounds) spinach, trimmed (see note)
1 cup (200g) fetta cheese, crumbled
425g (13½ ounces) canned drained baby beetroot (beets), sliced thinly

1 Preheat oven to 220°C/425°F.
2 Place pastry on an oiled oven tray. Fold edges of pastry over to make a 5mm (¼ inch) border all the way around pastry. Prick pastry base with fork. Place another oven tray on top of pastry (to stop it from puffing up during baking); bake 10 minutes, remove from oven. Remove top tray from pastry; reduce oven temperature to 200°C/400°F.
3 Meanwhile, blanch, steam or microwave spinach until just wilted; drain. When cool enough to handle, squeeze excess moisture from spinach.
4 Chop spinach thinly; combine with half the cheese in medium bowl.
5 Top tart with spinach mixture, beetroot and remaining cheese. Bake about 10 minutes.

prep & cook time 30 minutes serves 4
note You need 1kg untrimmed spinach to get enough trimmed spinach for this recipe. Drain the spinach thoroughly so the moisture does not seep into the tart base and make the pastry soggy.

rainbow silver beet with pine nuts, garlic & raisins

1 bunch rainbow silver beet (750g)
2 tablespoons olive oil
1 medium brown onion (150g), chopped finely
2 cloves garlic, crushed
½ cup (85g) raisins
⅓ cup (50g) roasted pine nuts
1 tablespoon lemon juice

1 Separate leaves and stems of silver beet; chop coarsely.
2 Heat half the oil in large saucepan; cook onion and garlic, stirring, until softened. Add silver beet stems; cook, stirring, until just tender. Add leaves; cook, stirring, until wilted.
3 Remove pan from heat; stir in raisins and half the nuts. Season to taste. Drizzle with lemon juice and remaining oil; sprinkle with remaining nuts.

prep & cook time 20 minutes **serves** 6

rainbow silver beet with pine nuts, garlic & raisins

spinach soup with fetta

40g (1½ ounces) butter
1 medium brown onion (150g), chopped coarsely
4 green onions (scallions), chopped coarsely
2 cloves garlic, quartered
1 tablespoon coarsely grated lemon rind
1.5kg (3 pounds) spinach, trimmed, chopped coarsely
3 large potatoes (900g), chopped coarsely
3 cups (750ml) vegetable stock
1.25 litres (5 cups) water
¾ cup (180ml) pouring cream
150g (4½ ounces) fetta cheese, crumbled

1 Melt butter in large saucepan; cook both onions and garlic, stirring, until onion softens. Add rind, spinach and potato; cook, stirring, until spinach is just wilted.
2 Stir in stock and the water. Bring to the boil; simmer, covered, about 15 minutes or until the potato softens.
3 Stand 10 minutes then blend or process soup mixture, in batches, until smooth.
4 Return soup with cream to same cleaned pan; stir over heat until hot. Divide soup into serving bowls; top each with cheese.

prep & cook time 40 minutes **serves** 8

spinach soup with fetta

Citrus Fruit

Delightful is the heavy drape of white blooms among lustrous, deep green foliage. Throughout spring that distinctive citrus perfume pervades the air and sends bees into overtime on nectar-gathering scurries. By autumn the branches arch gracefully and bow down laden with fruit. The fruits are filled with juice and bursting with flavour. They are decorative and long lasting, both on the tree and when chilled for storage. When not used for eating fresh or for their juice, the various fruits can be used in pickles or chutneys, salted as a condiment or sweetened for marmalades or desserts, and they're full of vitamins. Honestly, how have you managed without a citrus tree?

General cultivation

Citrus trees require free-draining soil. Where clay is the base layer or chief component of the soil, the water will drain away too slowly and the roots will rot. To plant a citrus tree in these soils, first apply gypsum to the surface, then follow with a mixture of sand and straw, then raise the soil 30cm (12") with a mixture of rotted manure, sand and compost. Let this rest for 2 weeks before planting.

To keep all citrus trees in top form, spread a special citrus-blend fertiliser or a combination of pelleted poultry manure and fish-food fertiliser in late winter or early spring and again in late summer. Water in well. The roots lie close to the surface, spreading out to the drip-line of each tree, so avoid disturbing the soil. Mulch with compost or lucerne hay to retain moisture but keep it well clear of the trunk. Apply fertiliser under the drip-line and water in well. Collar rot around the base, which shows up as cracked and split bark from which sap oozes, occurs from damp foliage and the build up of too much mulch around the stem. Always keep the area around the trunk clear.

Water regularly for good flower and fruit formation. Don't let the roots dry out during long, dry spells. Watering is especially important for trees in pots, and an automatic watering system is very effective.

Most purchased citrus trees are grafted onto hardy, disease-resistant rootstock. Never bury the tree's trunk more deeply in the ground than it was in the pot when planting, and don't pile up soil or mulch around the trunk. Keep a check that new stems don't shoot below the graft (a kink or lump in the trunk a few centimetres from its base) as this is the rootstock growing. The vigorous rootstock can rapidly overcome the grafted variety so always break off any stems that appear below the graft. If growing from seed, buy 'certified seed' to guarantee the variety you want.

Citrus don't like frosts or exposure to cold gales, and in cold climates they are grown in greenhouses. If grown in pots, they can be moved outdoors in warm weather, but specimens planted in the ground in a greenhouse needs wide open doorways during the warm weather for air circulation and bees. Protected by a sunny wall or within a courtyard, some citrus varieties cope with light frosts.

Citrus trees, unpruned, naturally assume a neat, compact shape. Lemon trees become open and wide-armed in full sun. Should their spread become too generous, they happily adapt to pruning back into their natural shape. Hard pruning can be used to re-invigorate an old tree. Cut back to a few short stubs of branches at the main trunk. Citrus trees can also be pruned as topiary balls at ground level or standardised on self-supporting trunks. Remember to leave the fruit on the tree until fully ripe and ready to fall as it doesn't ripen after picking.

preserving the crop

STORING	Citrus fruits should be stored in a cool, dry place for up to 3 weeks. Storing in the refrigerator will slightly lengthen their shelf life.
FREEZING	Both the rind and juice freeze well. Remove the rind before freezing and store in plastic containers ready to use. Juice can be frozen in small amounts, such as ice-cube trays, then transferred to freezer bags once frozen (see Freezing, page 240). Freeze juice and rind for up to 6 months. Cumquats and lemons can be frozen whole, packed into rigid freezer containers, for up to 6 months. You will not be able to grate the rind once it has defrosted, but the lemons can still be juiced and the cumquats used as desired. Frozen lemon slices can be added to summer drinks.
PICKLING	All citrus fruits make excellent jams, jellies and marmalades. Pour into hot, sterilised jars and seal while hot (see Bottling, pages 240-242).

PESTS AND DISEASES

Any discolouration or yellowing in the normally glossy evergreen foliage tells you that something in the soil is amiss, usually a lack of trace elements. The correct fertiliser regime is called for. Your nursery can diagnose the problem.

Holes bitten in the leaves are a minor problem caused by snails or caterpillars, which can be removed by hand. More disfiguring are leaf miners that make tracks just below the leaf surface and pucker the entire leaf. Damaged leaves can be clipped off or the problem prevented by spraying new growth flushes regularly and often with white oil starting mid-summer when leaf miners become active. They only attack fresh, new leaves.

Aphids will mass on new stems and leaves and disfigure or kill them. Crush by hand, hose off or spray with a non-toxic insecticidal soap. See page 17 for other safe spray alternatives. A black mould, called sooty mould, can appear on stems and leaves from the honeydew dropped by scale and aphids. Lightly sponge off with warm, soapy water and search for and remove the honeydew producers. Another visitor is the destructive bronze-orange bug that starts life in winter as a flat, paper-thin translucent green beetle. It grows and changes through green to orange with a black dot in the middle of its oval body. By the time it is able to breed, the bronze-orange or stink bug, has become a black, shield-shaped bug that sucks sap from the ends of new stems. The stems wilt and the bug squirts a burning liquid with an unpleasant aroma when disturbed. Use a proprietary spray or don rubber gloves and protective glasses and catch them one by one and crush or dip into a hot water bath to destroy.

Scales, with their white, pink or brown round waxy coatings or fine desiccated coconut appearance, also mass on the stems of citrus trees. They suck out vital fluids and are very weakening. Proprietary treatments are available. Alternatively, they can be removed with gentle scrubbing with a soft brush.

Fruit fall is another common problem and is usually related to irregular watering. Another reason may be spined citrus bugs, flattened green beetles with horns on either side of their flat heads. They suck from the immature fruits. Treatment is the same as for bronze-orange bugs.

In the garden

ORANGES

Oranges crop for 3-4 months over winter and into spring. The dwarf oranges, **Calamondin**, a sweet orange, and **chinotto,** a bitter one, look good in pots.

Blood oranges are startling when cut, but they taste like other oranges, differing only in having crimson flesh and pink juice and being especially sweet. The skin of some varieties is pink-flushed as well, but most look like any smallish orange from the outside.

Navel oranges are the most popular eating orange with no pips, lots of juice and are easy to peel. They ripen in winter and their bright, vitamin-packed flesh is a real energy booster. The 'washington navel' is richly coloured, with pebbly skin that is easy to remove. It is juicy, well flavoured and all-but seedless. The 'lane late navel', an Australian variety, is also seedless. It is lighter in colour than the washington, but just as flavoursome.

Seville oranges have thick skin, tough membranes, many seeds and a sour flesh with a strongly bitter edge, so their use is confined to cooking; it is excellent for marmalade and candying.

Tangelos are a cross between the tangerine, mandarin, and grapefruit (see pages 227-228), but resemble

oranges

mandarins

limes

oranges more than either of these. They look like an especially richly coloured, smallish orange with a slight neck at the stem end, and taste like a tangy orange. Their thick skin peels easily and they are easy to separate into segments.

Valencia oranges are an Australian variety. They don't have the bold good looks of navels: they are smaller, smooth-skinned and are often green-tinged because they ripen in warm weather, not the cold weather that gives the bright orange colour. They have seeds, but their flesh is sweet, richly coloured and very juicy.

LEMONS

Lemons provide two kitchen treasures: their acid juice, important as an ingredient in hundreds of dishes both sweet and savoury, and as an essential seasoning, and their rind, which provides an intense lemon fragrance and flavour with little acidity. Most cooks rank lemons second only to salt and pepper as a kitchen staple to always have on hand. Lemon season is winter, with a second, lesser crop in summer, but lemons are available all year round.

Lemon trees make ideal cook's companions as they are rarely without fruit. During winter the crop is most abundant, ready for marmalades, salting, juicing and freezing. Lemon is the tallest and most rambling member of the citrus troupe, but responds happily to pruning and shaping. 'Eureka' is productive all year in mild climates. 'Meyer' is suitable for areas of light frosts and adapts well to pots. 'Lisbon' only crops once a year. A newer cultivar named the 'lemonade tree' has a sweeter, less acidic juice.

LIMES

Limes are native to Asia and are the basic citrus fruit of tropical regions where they are used for cooling drinks and marinades, and as a sharp, refreshing seasoning for seafood, meats, vegetables and some tropical fruits whose flavour lacks acid and is much improved by a touch of lime juice.

Lime trees are more compact than lemons. Most varieties hold some fruit all year, but winter is their peak season. They are the most frost-sensitive of all citrus trees.

Kaffir limes are grown for their aromatic leaves and zest.

Native finger limes produce caviar-like balls of lime.

MANDARINS AND TANGERINES

Mandarins, a citrus fruit looking like smaller, flattened oranges, are nearly always eaten fresh, partly because they are so conveniently designed for it, having easy-to-peel skin and easily separated segments, and partly because their sweet flavour, lacking the acid edge of oranges, does not come through well in cooking, though it can be successful if the rind is used too.

These crop once a year from late autumn to winter. Don't leave the fruit too long before picking as they dry out on the tree. Leave some stem attached if you plan to store them. Easy-to-peel mandarin varieties include 'imperial'. Seedless varieties include 'emperor'. Cross-breeds of mandarin and orange have produced the tangor, and mandarin/grapefruit crosses have produced the tangy tangelo (see page 226).

ruby red grapefruit

yellow grapefruit

cumquat

GRAPEFRUIT

Grapefruit can be white (actually yellow-skinned with cream flesh) or ruby red (with red-blushed yellow skin and pink flesh) and seeded or seedless.

Grapefruit appear once a year, in either autumn ('wheeny') or winter ('marsh seedless'). In Britain, 'golden special' is prized, and pink and blood grapefruits are becoming a garden must. Grapefruit are prone to fruit-fly attack, so treat as advised (see page 17). Bag the fallen fruit, 'cook' it in the sun and dispose of carefully.

CUMQUATS

Pretty little cumquats look like miniature oranges although they are not really related. These ornamental trees have miniature fruit and leaves. The oval-fruited 'nagami' has fewer seeds and sour flesh concealed in a thin, bitter-sweet skin. 'Marumi' has round fruit and sharp-flavoured flesh. A variegated form is also available.

For the table

TO PREPARE

• To remove the rind and pith from thick-rind fruit: top and tail the fruit, then slit the skin from top to bottom. Gently work a spoon under the skin and around the fruit. You will end up with rind ready for making into sweet treats, and rind-free fruit ready to cook with or enjoy as they are.

TO SERVE

• There is, of course, their juice to enjoy.

• Slices and segments of blood orange look spectacular in salads, desserts and garnishes, and their juice makes sunset-coloured sorbets, jellies and other desserts. The rind is not as bitter as that of an ordinary orange: grated or thinly peeled, it can be strewn over salads, puddings or cakes.

• Remove the white pith from the rind of your chosen citrus fruit. Make sure the rind is dried thoroughly (see Drying, page 243), then place in jars of caster sugar. Limit yourself to one flavour per jar. After a month the sugar is wonderfully scented with the fruit and ready to add to sweet batters.

• Combine grapefruit segments, avocados and butter lettuce; toss with a dressing made with grapefruit juice.

• Grapefruit are usually eaten for breakfast, halved, with or without sugar, grilled or not. Its clean, sharp taste is a robust start to the day.

• Dust plenty of icing sugar onto a cake straight from the oven and squeeze over citrus juice: a good alternative to pouring over a sugar syrup.

blood orange

kaffir lime

lemon

• Cumquats are seldom eaten fresh as they are bitter and tart, but they are delicious as glacé (candied) fruit, pickled with spices or brandied, and they make wonderful marmalade.

• Serve butter, grated mandarin rind and a little chinese five-spice powder over steamed buk choy.

• North African recipes often call for preserved lemons. Quarter lemons lengthways and place in sterilised jars (see Bottling, pages 240-242) with salt and sugar; add flavourings such as cinnamon sticks, peppercorns, cumin seeds and bay leaves and cover the lemons with fresh lemon juice. Keep in the refrigerator for up to 6 months. To use, remove and discard the pulp. Slice the rind finely and serve over dishes. Note: the juice is not suitable to use as it's too salty.

• Preserved lemon is good sliced and served with seafood or roast lamb or chicken; added to lamb or chicken casseroles; mixed with couscous or rice; or used in dressings, salsas and salads, especially ones to go with seafood.

• To add extra zing to casseroles and slow-cooked meats, sprinkle with gremolata (a mixture of garlic, lemon rind and parsley). Excellent with veal, beef or grilled fish.

• Use lemon juice for its flavour and to prevent browning of apples, pears, peaches, bananas, potatoes, artichokes, celeriac, and avocados after they are peeled or cut.

• A squeeze of lemon juice will sour milk or cream as a substitute for buttermilk or sour cream in a recipe.

• A little lemon juice and sugar adds zing to any fruit salad, and adds flavour to a tasteless crop of fruit like peaches or strawberries; sprinkle sugar and juice over the cut fruit and stand at room temperature for an hour or more, gently mixing once or twice.

• Grated lemon rind may be added to cakes, biscuits and desserts, as well as meatballs, meat loaves and stuffings.

• Lemon rind matchsticks may be added to a vegetable, chicken, seafood or fruit salad. Add a strip to poaching liquid for fruit or a spiral into a cocktail. Lemon rind is also important in jam-making as its underlying white pith is rich in pectin, the substance that causes jam to set.

• Lemon slices may be dropped into fruit drinks or hot or iced tea, or may be slit from edge to centre to sit on the rim of the glass. Thin slices brushed with oil may be placed on chicken, pork or veal and cooked under a grill, or char-grilled or barbecued separately to place on the meat for serving.

• Lemon wedges are a standard garnish to hot or cold seafood and crumbed, fried foods such as lamb cutlets, veal schnitzel or chicken breast, and are frequently offered with grilled, char-grilled or barbecued lamb, pork or veal chops as well as curries, spicy rice and lentil dishes. For wedges to be served to diners, remove any seeds and cut off the strip of white core.

everlasting orange slices

lemon sour cream cake

250g (8 ounces) butter, softened
1 tablespoon finely grated lemon rind
2 cups (440g) caster (superfine) sugar
6 eggs
¾ cup (180g) sour cream
2 cups (300g) plain (all-purpose) flour
¼ cup (35g) self-raising flour
½ cup (80g) pine nuts
1 tablespoon demerara sugar
¼ cup (90g) honey, heated

1 Preheat oven to 160°C/325°F. Grease deep 23cm (9 inch) square cake pan; line base and two opposite sides with baking paper, extending paper 5cm (2 inches) over sides.
2 Beat butter, rind and caster sugar in bowl with electric mixer until light and fluffy. Add eggs, one at a time, beating until combined (mixture may separate at this stage, but will come together later). Stir in sour cream and sifted flours, in two batches. Spread mixture into pan; bake 15 minutes.
3 Combine nuts and demerara sugar in small bowl.
4 Remove cake from oven; sprinkle evenly with nut mixture, pressing gently into cake. Bake a further 45 minutes. Stand cake in pan 5 minutes before turning, top-side up, onto wire rack. Drizzle hot cake evenly with hot honey; cool before serving.

prep + cook time 1 hour 15 minutes (+ cooling) **serves** 16
note Demerara sugar is a rich, golden-coloured small-grained crystal sugar having a subtle molasses flavour. It is available from most supermarkets.

everlasting orange slices

These orange slices can be used in trifles, cake fillings, as cheesecake toppings or even squeezed into split croissants for a special breakfast. They will keep in the refrigerator for up to 6 months.

12 medium oranges (2kg)
2.5 litres (10 cups) water
8 cups (1.75kg) caster (superfine) sugar
¾ cup (180ml) orange-flavoured liqueur

1 Bring a very large saucepan of salted water to the boil; add whole oranges. Return to the boil; drain, rinse under cold water. Repeat twice more. Cut oranges into 5mm (¼") thick slices, remove seeds.
2 Combine the water and sugar in same pan. Stir over heat until sugar is dissolved; do not boil. Add orange slices; simmer about 2 hours or until orange slices are soft and very shiny. Stir in liqueur. Gently spoon slices into hot sterilised jars; seal while hot.

prep & cook time 3 hours
note If you have a lot of syrup left over, you can bottle some separately to spoon over cakes or flavour creams.

lemon sour cream cake

soba salad with rocket and mandarin

fennel and ruby red grapefruit salad

2 ruby red grapefruit (700g)
1 medium fennel bulb (300g), trimmed, sliced thinly
2 stalks celery (300g), trimmed, sliced thinly
1 cup loosely packed fresh flat-leaf parsley leaves
¼ cup (25g) roasted walnut halves
white balsamic vinaigrette
¼ cup (60ml) olive oil
1 tablespoon white balsamic vinegar

1 Segment grapefruit over small bowl; reserve
2 tablespoons juice for vinaigrette.
2 Make white balsamic vinaigrette.
3 Combine grapefruit, vinaigrette and remaining
ingredients in medium serving bowl.
white balsamic vinaigrette Combine oil, vinegar and
reserved juice in screw-top jar; shake well.

prep time 20 minutes **serves** 4
note White balsamic vinegar (also known as balsamic
white condiment) is a clear and lighter version of balsamic
vinegar; it has a fresh, sweet clean taste and is available
from major supermarkets and delicatessens.

soba salad with rocket and mandarin

180g (5½ ounces) soba noodles
2 medium mandarins (400g), segmented,
    chopped coarsely
2 green onions (scallions), sliced thinly
½ cup (80g) roasted pine nuts
40g (1½ ounces) baby rocket leaves (arugula)
mandarin vinaigrette
¼ cup (60ml) olive oil
¼ cup (60ml) mandarin juice
1 tablespoon rice wine vinegar

1 Cook noodles in medium saucepan of boiling water
until tender; drain. Rinse under cold water; drain.
2 Meanwhile, make mandarin vinaigrette.
3 Combine noodles and vinaigrette in large bowl with
remaining ingredients.
mandarin vinaigrette Combine ingredients in screw-top
jar; shake well.

prep & cook time 20 minutes **serves** 6
note Soba noodles are long, flat thin Japanese buckwheat
noodles from Asian food stores and major supermarkets.

fennel and ruby red grapefruit salad

Winter Herbs

The perennial herbs available to us in the winter enjoy an uncanny sympathy with the foods we crave when the nights turn cold and dark: roasts, soups, dishes that require long cooking which draws out flavours and fills the house with rich scents and fireside warmth. Summer seems a long way off, and winter herbs capture that absent sunshine.

In the garden

BAY

Bay is one of the few tree herbs. And what a tree. It's not choosy about soils or climate and it can reach 11m (35') and spread almost as wide. A bay tree is more suited to a large garden or park rather than a herb patch, but it adapts to topiary shaping, and is often standardised as feature points in the centre or corners of a formal garden. Bay also grows well in a pot, and can be espaliered as a hedge, fence or border.

The leathery evergreen leaves are used to flavour stocks, marinades, casseroles and milk sauces. Dry and store in an airtight container. They can be used fresh, but some people insist the flavour is stronger when dried.

Watch for brown scale on the leaves because en masse they can weaken a small tree. Lightly scrub them off with soapy water or use a proprietary spray.

THYME

This low-growing herb is excellent in the garden as a border, in clumps among rocks or in pots. It needs full sun and gritty, free-draining soil to thrive. It will rot in damp, shady sites. It grows to about 30cm (12") but it usually masses on itself and leans over and sets roots. Cut it back when it gets too unmanageable and use the new rooted plants as replacements every couple of years. There are many leaf forms and varieties which are used fresh and dried. There are two well-known varieties, the 'common' one with tiny, pointed grey-green leaves and the lemon one with larger green leaves.

MARJORAM

Marjoram is a relative of oregano; grows lower at about 30cm (12") and its spread is more of a mound. Their flavours are similar. Marjoram will sulk and disappear in shady spots and needs protection from cold winter winds. It is well suited to life in a pot. Prune back hard at the end of summer and collect the trimmings to dry.

SAGE

Sage comes in the well known silver-grey variety and in a smaller variety with purplish leaves. The family also includes pineapple sage, whose pineapple-scented leaves can be chopped for fruit salad.

There are handsome purple-flushed and yellow-variegated sages available as well as the usual grey. Sage grows about 30cm (12") high, doesn't grow in acidic soil and will collapse with too much rain. Add dolomite to the soil if you've had failures before, and confinement to a well-drained pot will reduce 'wet feet' syndrome. Watch for caterpillars as they'll strip the leaves in no time. Its deep blue salvia flowers appear in spring, but for profuse leaves, snip off the stems as the flowers form.

For the table

TO SERVE

• Bay leaves, alone or as part of a bouquet garni (bay, parsley, thyme and celery), are essential to the flavours of hundreds of soups, casseroles and stocks. Its pungent taste can be overwhelming, so one is usually enough unless you are making a large quantity. Dried leaves are better than fresh for cooking, but they should still be green, not yellow.

preserving the crop

STORING	Store fresh herbs in damp paper towel in vegetable storage bags in the refrigerator for up to 3 days.
FREEZING	Bay leaves, thyme, marjoram and sage all freeze well. Freeze in small containers for up to 6 months (see Freezing, page 240). They don't need to be chopped before freezing; freeze in a covered tray with their stems intact. Frozen, the leaves are easily removed to use.
DRYING	All the winter herbs can be dried and stored in airtight containers for several months (see Drying, page 243). Hang bunches decoratively around the kitchen.

sage

marjoram

thyme

bay leaves

- Lemon thyme goes particularly well with mushrooms and veal. Add thyme at the beginning of cooking so the flavours meld. Pull off the small leaves if you don't want to serve them with their stringy stems.

- The savoury warmth of thyme is good with most meats and many vegetables from roast potatoes to sautéed eggplant and grilled tomatoes. It goes into bread and onion stuffings for poultry and rabbit or bread and lemon ones for fish; it pairs wonderfully with red wine in marinades and sauces.

- Common thyme is the stronger and is better to use in cooking, while lemon thyme's fresh flavour works best if added at the end of cooking or scattered over the finished dish.

- Except when you want the charm of the fresh leaves, dried thyme is a better ingredient because it is stronger.

- Cook crumbed lamb cutlets in butter and oil; remove from the pan and add lemon juice, thyme and more butter. Serve the butter sauce over the lamb.

- Marjoram teams well with tomato-based dishes, and dried stems burned on the barbecue add a tang to food.

- Marjoram is one of the herbs whose flavour is stronger and more developed when dried. Fresh, it is mildly savoury and works well, usually with thyme, in stuffings, soups, sandwiches, dumplings, savoury breads and scones.

- Dried marjoram lends its warm flavour to tomato sauces, and is crumbled and rubbed on lamb chops to be grilled. It mixes well with other herbs.

- Squeeze lemon juice and sprinkle chopped fresh marjoram over potatoes before roasting. The smell and flavour are both delicious.

- Sage leaves fried in butter or oil just until crisp make an attractive garnish for veal and liver.

- Sage with its full, dry, balsamic scent and flavour, needs to be used sparingly as it can easily dominate. It is splendid with pork and, with onion, is the traditional stuffing for duck and goose.

- Italians pair sage with veal and prosciutto for saltimbocca.

- Place a sage leaf and a piece of mozzarella in the centre of a pork schnitzel; fold into parcels, secure with string then dust in flour and cook in butter and olive oil until golden and cooked through. Remove the string before serving.

classic herb blends These include *bouquet garni* and *herbes de Provence*, and are used to flavour stocks, soups, sauces, stews and casseroles. They are tied together in a small bundle using unwaxed kitchen string, or placed in a small muslin (cheesecloth) bag, which is removed before serving.

A bouquet garni usually consists of 2-3 springs of parsley, 1 sprig thyme, 1-2 bay leaves; other herbs may then be added according to local region. For additional flavour, try adding sage, rosemary, lemon peel and some whole black peppercorns.

Herbes de Provence includes thyme, marjoram and bay leaves, as well as rosemary, fennel, mint, oregano and tarragon. This blend can be used with either fresh or dried herbs, and orange zest and lavender are sometimes included. The dry blend is good mixed with olive oil to coat meat, chicken or fish; the fresh blend is used in soups, stews and tossed over vegetables before roasting.

FOR THE PANTRY

- Bay leaves are said to ward off weevils so scatter through your pantry. Even if this doesn't work, the leaves will add a wonderful scent to the shelves.

grilled eggplant with marjoram vinaigrette

1 large eggplant (500g), sliced into 5mm (¼ inch) rounds
¼ cup (60ml) olive oil
1 small red onion (100g), sliced thinly
¼ cup (60ml) sherry vinegar
2 teaspoons caster (superfine) sugar
2 tablespoons finely chopped fresh marjoram
½ cup (125ml) olive oil

1 Preheat oven to 200°C/400°F.
2 Brush both sides of eggplant slices with oil; place, in a single layer, on baking-paper (parchment) lined oven trays. Bake about 25 minutes, turning eggplant slices once, until browned lightly both sides.
3 Meanwhile, combine onion, vinegar, sugar, marjoram and oil in small bowl. Spoon onion mixture over eggplant.
4 Serve warm or at room temperature with crusty bread.

prep & cook time 50 minutes **serves** 6
note Sherry vinegar is made from a blend of wines and is aged in wood vats to mature where it develops a rich mellow flavour. It is available from delicatessens and some major supermarkets.

grilled eggplant with marjoram vinaigrette

pumpkin and sage ravioli

pumpkin and sage ravioli

¼ cup (40g) pine nuts
2 teaspoons olive oil
3 cloves garlic, crushed
600g (1¼ pound) piece pumpkin, cut into
   1cm (½ inch) cubes
625g (1¼ pounds) ricotta ravioli
1¼ cups (310ml) pouring cream (see note)
¼ cup (20g) finely grated parmesan cheese
2 tablespoons coarsely chopped fresh sage
2 tablespoons lemon juice

1 Cook nuts in large frying pan, stirring, until browned lightly; remove from pan.
2 Heat oil in same pan; cook garlic and pumpkin, covered, stirring occasionally, about 10 minutes or until pumpkin is almost tender.
3 Meanwhile, cook ravioli in large saucepan of boiling water, uncovered, until just tender; drain.
4 Add nuts, cream, cheese and sage to pumpkin mixture; bring to the boil. Reduce heat; simmer, uncovered, 5 minutes. Add ravioli and juice; stir until hot.

prep & cook time 25 minutes **serves** 4
note It is fine to use just 1 x 300ml carton of cream for this recipe.

roasted thyme potatoes with spicy sauce

roasted thyme potatoes with spicy sauce

500g (1 pound) baby new potatoes, halved
2 tablespoons olive oil
1 tablespoon finely chopped fresh thyme
spicy sauce
1 tablespoon olive oil
1 small brown onion (80g), chopped finely
2 cloves garlic, sliced thinly
1 fresh small red thai (serrano) chilli, chopped finely
410g (13 ounces) canned crushed tomatoes
2 teaspoons caster (superfine) sugar

1 Preheat oven to 220°C/425°F.
2 Combine potatoes, oil and thyme in large baking dish; roast about 30 minutes or until potato is tender.
3 Meanwhile, make spicy sauce.
4 Serve spicy sauce with hot roasted potatoes.
spicy sauce Heat oil in medium saucepan; cook onion, garlic and chilli, stirring occasionally, until onion is soft. Add undrained tomatoes and sugar; bring to the boil. Simmer, uncovered, stirring occasionally, about 10 minutes or until sauce thickens.

prep & cook time 45 minutes **serves** 8

braised pork with fresh sage

90g (3 ounces) butter
1.5kg (3 pound) rack of pork (6 cutlets), rind removed
2 medium carrots (240g), sliced thickly
6 baby onions (150g), peeled
4 cloves garlic, peeled
2 bay leaves
6 sprigs fresh thyme
1⅓ cups (330ml) white wine
⅓ cup (80ml) white wine, extra
⅓ cup (80ml) chicken stock
1 tablespoon sage leaves

1 Preheat oven to 180°C/350°F.
2 Melt butter in large, flameproof dish in stove top; cook pork until browned, remove from dish.
3 Add carrots, onions, garlic, bay leaves and thyme to dish. Stir over heat 5 minutes or until beginning to brown. Return pork to dish with wine. Transfer to oven; cook about 1¼ hours or until cooked as desired. Remove pork; cover keep warm.
4 Strain cooking liquid into small saucepan; discard vegetables. Add extra wine and stock to pan; bring to the boil. Reduce heat; simmer 5 minutes. Stir in sage. Serve pork with sage sauce, and roasted baby new potatoes and baby truss tomatoes, if you like.

prep & cook time 1 hour 45 minutes **serves** 6
note Ask your butcher to remove the rind and tie the pork well. Roast the salted rind on a rack in a hot oven until crisp. Serve with the pork.

braised pork with fresh sage

Preserving the Crop

One danger of successful gardening is sheer over-abundance. What do you do with kilos of zucchinis? Mint gone mad? Too many beans? One of the delights of too-successful gardening is preserving the crop, giving away what you don't need, storing for winter, making gifts, and enjoying last year's apricots, oranges and tomatoes as this year's jams, marmalades and preserves. Here we provide you with general guidelines on simple home preservation techniques. Always choose the best, the ripest and the least blemished of your fruit and vegetables. And don't leave preserving until the season's end or you will miss the best of your crop.

Freezing

Containers must be airtight. Shallow dishes allow food to freeze and thaw more quickly. Containers must be microwave-safe if you plan to microwave from the freezer. Always allow cooked food to cool completely before freezing. Food expands as it freezes so allow 2-5cm (1-2") extra space in containers.

Use labels to record the contents, freezing date and quantity, and use a waterproof pen.

Ice-cube trays are the perfect-sized containers for freezing small quantities of chopped herbs, citrus rind, juice, chopped chillies, chopped lemon grass, grated ginger and passionfruit pulp. Each compartment holds about 1 tablespoon. Some herbs may need a little water to cling together. Once frozen, transfer the cubes to a container or bag. Each time you need the flavouring, add a cube. Sprigs of herbs can be crumbled while still frozen. Basil, oregano, mint and coriander freeze well. Once frozen, herbs are only useful in cooked dishes or salad dressings, not as salad ingredients.

To blanch vegetables before freezing, drop them into a large pan of boiling water and allow the water to return to the boil. Drain immediately and plunge into a large bowl (or sink) of iced water until cold. Drain well before packing into freezer containers. If blanching large quantities, check the temperature of the iced water as it does warm up. Add more iced water, if necessary.

Frozen stone fruit, apples, pears and oranges make quick desserts. Poach in a light sugar syrup with spices and freeze in rigid containers to keep their shape. To serve, thaw and spoon over ice-cream or freshly baked plain cakes.

Bottling

Old-fashioned bottling requires a bottling kit, a set of instructions and years of experience. Some practitioners have turned bottling into an art (visit any country show), but the technique is complex and not for the beginner or those rushed for time. If you want to try bottling, seek the help of a friend or relative with experience in this method of preservation.

Making preserves (jam, pickles, chutneys, relishes) is a much simpler alternative to bottling. The added sugar and vinegar act as preservation agents, lessening the need for precise temperatures and heating times. Follow our instructions for sterilising and sealing bottles and preserving will be easy.

Successful preservation requires still-warm, sterilised bottles, warm preserves and rapid sealing.

You'll need plenty of glass jars or bottles. They must have no chips or cracks and be thoroughly scrubbed clean. Choose bottles with airtight, coated metal lids. Uncoated lids will corrode. Snap-on and screw-top plastic lids do not seal tightly enough.

STERILISING JARS

Remember, the lids also need to be sterilised along with the bottles. There are three main methods of home sterilisation. Once sterilised, remove each jar carefully and turn upside-down onto a clean tea towel on a wooden board. Turn upright only when ready to use.

By far, the easiest method is to put the jars and lids in the dishwasher on the hottest rinse cycle available. Don't use detergent.

The second method is boiling. Lay the jars and lids in a large pan, cover completely with cold water and bring gradually to the boil; boil for 20 minutes.

The last method is in the oven. Place the jars and lids, upright, but not touching, on a clean wooden board. Place the board in a cold oven and turn the oven temperature to very low (120°C/150°F) for 30 minutes.

SEALING JARS

Sealing the jars is as important as sterilising them. Once you've filled the jars, seal them immediately. The sooner the jars are sealed, the less likely their contents will spoil. Paper, cellophane and foil are not suitable sealants. Cellophane and paper are not airtight and foil corrodes with any acids in the preserves. Brown paper can be used as an extra sealant. When you have placed the lids on the jars, cut out a large circle of brown paper, coat with glue and place over the lids and wrap down the sides of the jar to form a tight seal.

If you don't have enough lids, use paraffin wax. It is available from larger supermarkets and chemists and creates an excellent seal. Melt the wax over very low heat. Pour a thin layer over the preserves and allow to set. Next, pour over another layer of wax, this time including a piece of string to help you pull out the wax to open. Don't overheat the wax or it will shrink when it sets and not form a complete seal.

LABELLING JARS

Don't kid yourself you'll remember that the apple and date chutney has the green lid and the tomato cumin relish is in the tall thin bottle. Label with contents and preserving date.

Store preserves in a cool, dark place and leave for a week or so before opening. All preserves taste better when left to rest. In hot, humid climates, the best place to store them is the refrigerator. Once opened, all preserves must be stored, covered, in the refrigerator.

Drying

SUN-DRYING

Tomatoes, apples, pears, apricots, peaches and chillies are all good to dry. You need 4-5 days of constant sun with little or no humidity. (Beware: in humid conditions a mould develops very quickly.) Don't be disappointed if the fruit changes colour as it dries; its taste is not affected. Commercially dried fruits have ascorbic acid and sulphur added to retain their colour. It's not necessary to peel fruit before drying, but as drying can make the skin leathery (apples and apricots in particular), you may wish to peel some fruits.

You will need wooden or non-corrosive racks with rungs close enough together to stop the food falling through (as it shrinks greatly), but not too close to disrupt the airflow. Thicker fruits, such as apples and pears, need to be sliced; most other fruits just need halving. Place the fruit, cut-side up, on the racks, place the racks over a tray and cover with fine wire mesh (not touching the fruit). Clean fly-screens are ideal. Position in the hottest, sunniest place you can find.

It's a good idea to bring the trays inside or into an airy shed at night so they're not disturbed by animals, and so dew won't rehydrate the fruit and make it go mouldy. The fruit is dry when no moisture oozes when it is cut. Store fruit in airtight containers in a cool place for 6 months. Of course, label as you go.

AIR-DRYING

Fresh herbs and chillies can be air-dried. Hang bunches in an airy place or on racks covered with absorbent paper, away from direct sunlight to retain as much flavour as possible.

MICROWAVE-DRYING

You can dry herbs in a microwave oven, if you like, between several sheets of absorbent paper on HIGH (100%) for about 1 minute. If not dry, repeat, checking every 30 seconds (sometimes the paper will need to be changed). Label and store in airtight containers.

OVEN-DRYING

All fruits that can be sun-dried can also be oven-dried – especially tomatoes. Prepare the fruit on racks as for sun-drying (without the fly-screen).

A good drying oven temperature is about 50°C (120°F). Tomatoes need a higher temperature to dry out their extra juice. Don't hurry the process or you will spoil the fruit. You may need more than a day, so place as much fruit in the oven as you can. You can dry different fruits together. Once the fruit is dried, let it cool before storing in airtight containers.

Herbs dry very well in the oven and take little space and time (about 20 minutes), so are ideal to do in batches along with other fruit. That excess of chillies can be oven-dried as well.

essential gardening equipment

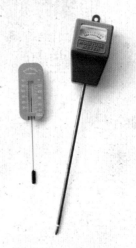

Pots are great to start off seedlings, and they're just what space-hungry city gardeners need – plenty of fruit and vegetables grow well in pots.

Connectors that don't split or drip are a blessing in the garden, as are sturdy hoses; they don't tangle and stop the water flow, and are easy to store.

Soil temperature and moisture gauges let you know when the soil is warm enough to transplant seedings and when it's time to water them.

Watering cans should be easy to fill, comfortable to hold and have a fine spray head for even watering. Use old cans as garden ornaments.

Plant identification is necessary to identify seedlings as they sprout. Write the date of planting, so you'll know when to plant a second crop.

Saving seeds is an easy and cheap way to ensure you have seeds next season. Dry, then store in an airtight container in a cool, dark, dry place.

A trowel and fork are necessary for all small planting and weeding jobs. You can dig without disturbing the roots of surrounding plants.

Small scissors are good to snip off herbs, and for cutting **twine** needed to tie plants to garden stakes to keep them trim, tidy and off the ground.

A hat, sunscreen and kneeling mat keeps sunstroke, sunburn and painful knees at bay. Sturdy boots also protect toes from dropped pots.

Wooden stakes will keep heavily-laden rambling plants off the ground. Tie string between two, and use as a guide for planting in a straight line.

Pruning shears come in long and short versions; use to remove dead stems and trim branches. A pruning saw is handy in hard-to-reach places.

Spades and pitchforks are used to lift, dig and turn the soil, or compost, over. Use pitchforks for 'pitching' hay and other loose material.

conversion chart

measures

One Australian metric measuring cup holds approximately 250ml; one Australian metric tablespoon holds 20ml; one Australian metric teaspoon holds 5ml.

The difference between one country's measuring cups and another's is within a two- or three-teaspoon variance, and will not affect your cooking results. North America, New Zealand and the United Kingdom use a 15ml tablespoon.

All cup and spoon measurements are level. The most accurate way of measuring dry ingredients is to weigh them. When measuring liquids, use a clear glass or plastic jug with metric or imperial markings.

The imperial measurements used in these recipes are approximate only. Measurements for cake pans are approximate only. Using same-shaped cake pans of a similar size should not affect the outcome of your baking. We measure the inside top of the cake pan to determine sizes. We use large eggs with an average weight of 60g.

dry measures

METRIC	IMPERIAL
15g	½oz
30g	1oz
60g	2oz
90g	3oz
125g	4oz (¼lb)
155g	5oz
185g	6oz
220g	7oz
250g	8oz (½lb)
280g	9oz
315g	10oz
345g	11oz
375g	12oz (¾lb)
410g	13oz
440g	14oz
470g	15oz
500g	16oz (1lb)
750g	24oz (1½lb)
1kg	32oz (2lb)

liquid measures

METRIC	IMPERIAL
30ml	1 fluid oz
60ml	2 fluid oz
100ml	3 fluid oz
125ml	4 fluid oz
150ml	5 fluid oz
190ml	6 fluid oz
250ml	8 fluid oz
300ml	10 fluid oz
500ml	16 fluid oz
600ml	20 fluid oz
1000ml (1 litre)	1¾ pints

length measures

METRIC	IMPERIAL
3mm	⅛in
6mm	¼in
1cm	½in
2cm	¾in
2.5cm	1in
5cm	2in
6cm	2½in
8cm	3in
10cm	4in
13cm	5in
15cm	6in
18cm	7in
20cm	8in
23cm	9in
25cm	10in
28cm	11in
30cm	12in (1ft)

oven temperatures

The oven temperatures in this book are for conventional ovens; if you have a fan-forced oven, decrease the temperature by 10-20 degrees.

	°C (CELSIUS)	°F (FAHRENHEIT)
Very slow	120	250
Slow	150	300
Moderately slow	160	325
Moderate	180	350
Moderately hot	200	400
Hot	220	425
Very hot	240	475

world climate zones

Use this map to locate areas of the world with a climate similar to your own.
Plants from those regions are most likely to be successful in your garden.

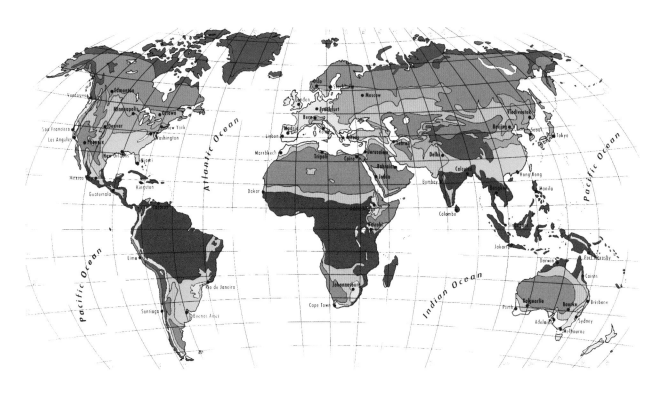

Tundra Average summer temperature 0-10°C (32-50°F). Very severe winters.

Sub-Arctic Severe winters. Average temperature above 10°C (50°F) for less than four months.

Cold continental Rain year-round or dry winters. Average summer temperatures below 22°C (72°F).

Cool continental Severe winters, but warm to hot summers. Average summer temperature 27°C (80°F). May be rainy year-round or dry in winter.

Temperate Cool winters, warm summers. Average summer temperature 16°C (60°F). May be rainy year-round or wet in winter.

Subtropical Cool to mild winters, warm to hot summers. Average summer temperature 27°C (80°F). May be rainy year-round or dry in winter.

Mediterranean Cool to mild winters, warm to hot summers. Average summer temperature 27°C (80°F). Summers are dry.

Semi-arid plains Seasonal or evenly spread low rainfall. Average summer temperature 32°C (90°F). Cold or mild winters.

Desert Very low rainfall. Average summer temperature 38°C (100°F). Winters may be cold or mild.

Tropical Year-round warmth. High humidity, high rainfall, heaviest in summer; winters may be dry or less wet. Average summer temperature 27°C (80°F).

glossary

anther The pollen bearing structure of a flower. *See also stamen.*

aphids Pinhead-sized, sap-sucking insects that cluster on new growth or flower buds. They cause wilting, distortion or death of affected plant parts. Aphids can be green, black, pink or yellow.

bolt The premature production of flower stems before an adequate harvest of leaves. In the wrong growing conditions lettuce and coriander can 'bolt' (that is, to flower and seed).

clods Big, solid clumps of soil that are brought to the surface by digging. Clods occur mostly in clay-based soils and should be broken down into smaller clumps when preparing soil for planting.

close planting The practice of growing vegetables at spacings less than those needed to allow the plant to attain its full spread. By doing so, less is produced by each plant but total yield is increased as a result of squeezing more plants into a given space.

coir peat *see peat beds.*

dak pots (dak·pots) A brand of open-ended containers that are hung in fruit trees to warn of the presence of fruit flies. When more than one fly is seen trapped in the pot it is time to begin your fruit-fly

control program. Dak Pots on their own will not control the pest.

dieback A disease that causes stems to die back from the tip usually to the point where the stem joins a major branch or another stem. Leaving stubs rather than pruning branches off cleanly often results in dieback.

dolomite A type of lime that also includes the plant food magnesium. Dolomite can be used instead of plain garden lime.

embryonic fruit A small, unpollinated fruit that is situated directly behind the female flower when that flower blooms. Female zucchini flowers have embryonic fruits attached to them.

fallow A patch of ground that is left unplanted for a full growing season in order to reduce the population of soil-borne pests and to restore soil fertility and structure.

furrow A trench made in the ground by a plough or other means (such as a hand tool or stick). Seeds are often sown in furrows.

foliar organic sprays A fertiliser or pesticide made from natural, non-chemical materials that is sprayed onto a plant's foliage (leaves).

fruiters A plant that forms fruits. In gardening, a 'fruit' is the seed-bearing organ, so tomatoes, peas, beans, zucchini, eggplant and capsicum are all fruits.

gypsum A naturally occurring mineral that, when applied to clay soils, causes the tiny clay particles to clump together into larger 'crumbs', thereby improving the aeration and drainage of the clay.

lucerne hay Long grass cut and dried for use as animal fodder. In gardening it's used as a mulch, or as an ingredient in a no-dig garden.

hilling Refers to the piling up of soil around the growing stems of certain plants. The soil is usually dug from the bare spaces between rows of plants. Potatoes are 'hilled' in order to both support the stems and to prevent the forming potatoes from being exposed to light.

lightly limed soils Describes the application of a small amount of garden lime to soil prior to planting or sowing. Lime reduces soil acidity and many vegetables respond well to light applications of lime dug into the soil once a year.

mealy Used to describe a powder-like coating or a powdery appearance on the leaves of plants.

midrib The central vein of a leaf that runs from stem-end to leaf tip.

nematode A type of worm of which there are numerous species, some of which attack the roots of plants causing stunting, wilting or death of the plant. They are hard to control and the best defence against them is to not plant the same crop in the same soil.

nitrogen nodules Small growths found on the roots of certain plants that have the ability to convert airborne nitrogen into the major plant food, nitrogen. The nitrogen is stored in the nodules and can be extracted by the roots of other plants. Plants with nitrogen nodules include peas and beans.

peat beds A layer of peat moss or coir peat often used in worm farms. Peat moss is partly decomposed vegetation found in swampy areas. It is not renewable. Coir peat is a substitute made from coconut fibre. It is renewable and is preferable to true peat moss. Both are sold in bags at nurseries.

perennials Plants that live for more than two years. While this can include trees and shrubs, in gardening, 'perennial' usually describes a non-woody plant that lives from year to year. Artichokes and asparagus are perennials.

pupate The transitional, non-feeding stage an insect passes through from grub or caterpillar to adult insect. In moths and butterflies, the pupa lives within a cocoon.

pyrethrum sprays Pyrethrum is an extract from a daisy, which works as an insecticide when sprayed onto the target insect. It has a very low toxicity and is considered one of the safest plant sprays.

ramble Describes a plant with an irregular, wandering habit of growth. A rambler may climb onto a support, grow through and over neighbouring plants, or may run along the ground to emerge some distance away.

rootstock The roots of a plant selected for superior performance (for example, disease resistance, speed of growth or size of growth) and onto which the above ground parts of another related plant will be grafted. The aim is to combine two plants into one with good roots and good upper, productive parts.

seed-raising mix A fine-textured potting mix made up of peat moss and sand designed to facilitate the germination of seeds sown in containers. It is sold in bags at nurseries and is sometimes labeled as propagation mix.

spore A dust-like, reproductive organism, more primitive than a seed. Spores are produced by ferns and fungi.

stamen The pollen-bearing or male part of a flower. The stamen consists of a stem or filament supporting an anther. *See also anther.*

stilt roots Also known as prop roots, these are roots that emerge above ground on the trunk to grow downwards and outwards. They act as supports, buttressing the trunk against wind movement.

tapering root A root that is widest at soil level and narrowest deeper down. Carrots and parsnips have tapering roots.

thrips Small, black, flying insects that disfigure flowers and cause leaf distortions by rasping (filing or scraping) the surface of foliage and petals. Thrips are attracted to light colours, and signs of an infestation can be their presence on white sheets hung out to dry.

topiary balls Topiary is the art of clipping suitable plants into tight, geometric or figurative shapes. A topiary ball is a sphere of foliage.

trace elements Those nutrients that are vital to plant health but which are needed only in tiny amounts.

tuber A swollen, food storage organ produced by the roots of certain plants. If left in the ground, it is from the tuber that the next season's plant will emerge. Potatoes and sweet potatoes are tubers.

weeping Describes plants with pendulous (hanging loosely so is able to swing or sway), rather than upright or horizontal branches.

index

GENERAL INDEX

A

apples
  cultivation 11, 161
  drying 160
  pickling 160
  preservation 160
  varieties 161-162
apricots
  cultivation 111
  drying 112
  preparation 112
  preservation 112
artichokes *see globe artichokes*
asian greens *see also brassicas*
  cultivation 184, 202
  pests and diseases 184, 202
  preparation 204
  preservation 203
  varieties 202
asparagus
  cultivation 40
  preparation 42
  preservation 41
  varieties 40
aubergine *see eggplant*
autumn
  fruit 156-171
  herbs 172-175
  planting and picking guide 124-125
avocado
  cultivation 132
  pollination 132
  preparation 134
  preservation 132
  varieties 132-134

B

baits *see pest control*
basil
  cultivation 7, 118
  drying 119
  preservation 119
bay
  cultivation 11, 234
  drying 235
  pests and diseases 234
  preservation 235
  weevils, to deter 236
beans *see also broad beans*
  companion planting 16
  cultivation 7, 68-70
  pests and diseases 70

  preparation 70
  preservation 69
  varieties 68, 70
beetroot
  cultivation 7, 48
  pickling 107
  preparation 50
  preservation 49
  varieties 48
berries
  cultivation 106-108
  preparation 108-109
  preservation 107
  varieties 106-108
bicarbonate of soda pest spray 17
blackberries 108 *see also berries*
blueberries 108 *see also berries*
bottling 157, 240-242 *see also preserving;*
  pickling
brassicas 184 *see also asian greens*
broad beans
  allergy to 44
  companion planting 16
  cultivation 44
  preparation 44
  preservation 45
  varieties 44
broccoli *see also asian greens; brassicas*
  companion planting 16
  cultivation 7, 11, 184, 186
  pests and diseases 184, 186
  preparation 186
  preservation 187
  varieties 186
brussels sprouts *see also brassicas*
  cultivation 184, 198
  pests and diseases 184, 198
  preparation 198
  preservation 197
buk choy *see asian greens; brassicas*

C

cabbage *see also brassicas*
  companion planting 16
  cultivation 184, 196
  pests and diseases 184
  pickling 197
  preparation 198
  preservation 197
  varieties 196
calendula 16, 80
cantaloupe 170 *see also melons*

capsicum
  cultivation 11, 84
  pests and diseases 84
  preparation 84
  preservation 85
  varieties 84
carrots
  cultivation 7, 144
  pickling 145
  preparation 144
  preservation 145
cauliflower *see also brassicas*
  companion planting 16
  cultivation 184, 190
  pests and diseases 184
  preparation 190
  preservation 191
  varieties 190
celery 16
chemical baits and sprays 16
cherries
  cultivation 11, 111
  preparation 114
  preservation 112
chervil
  cultivation 54
  drying 53
  preservation 53
chicory 76
chillies
  cultivation 7, 11, 175
  drying 173
  pest sprays 17
  preparation 175
  preservation 173
  varieties 174-175
chives
  cultivation 7, 52
  drying 53
  preservation 53
  varieties 52
chrysanthemum flowers 80
citrus fruit
  cultivation 11, 224
  pests and diseases 226
  pickling 225
  preparation 228
  preservation 225
  varieties 226-228
climate 8, 247
companion planting 16
compost 16

coriander
  cultivation 54
  drying 53
  preservation 53
corn *see sweet corn*
courgettes *see zucchini*
cress 78
crop rotation 15
cucumber
  companion planting 16
  cultivation 7, 11, 72
  pests and diseases 74
  pickling 73
  preparation 74
  preservation 73
  varieties 72
cultivation
  companion planting 16
  crop rotation 15
  fertilisers 13, 108-109
  pests see pests and diseases;
    pest control
  potted plants 11, 14
  seasonal 8
  soil 14
  worm farms 13
cumquats 228 *see also citrus fruit*
currants 108 *see also berries*

D
day lily 80
deathcap mushrooms 210 *see also*
  mushrooms
diseases *see pest and diseases*
drying
  air-drying 243
  apples 160
  apricots 112
  basil 119
  bay 235
  chillies 173
  edible flowers 77
  figs 158
  lemon grass 173
  marjoram 235
  methods 243
  microwave-drying 243
  mint 119
  mushrooms 211
  oven-drying 243
  pears 163
  rosemary 173
  sage 235

  sun-drying 243
  thyme 235
  tomatoes 65

E
edible flowers 79 *see also salad greens*
  cultivation 79
  drying 77
  preparation 81
  preservation 77
  varieties 80
eggplant
  cultivation 88
  pickling 89
  preparation 91
  preservation 89
  varieties 88
elderflower 80
endive 76, 79
equipment 244-24 5
eschalots 34

F
fertilisers 13, 108-109
figs
  cultivation 158
  drying 158
  pickling 158
  preparation 158
  preservation 158
fish emulsion 13
fruit
  apples 161-162
  apricots 111
  autumn 156-171
  avocado 132-134
  berries 106-109
  blackberries 108
  blueberries 108
  cherries 111
  citrus 224-229
  cumquats 228
  currants 108
  figs 158
  gooseberries 108
  grapefruit 228
  grapes 156-158
  kiwifruit 169
  lemons 227
  limes 227
  mandarins 227
  melons 170
  nectarines 111
  oranges 226-227

  passionfruit 109-110
  peaches 111
  pears 162-164
  plums 112
  quinces 165
  raspberries 106
  stone 110-114
  strawberries 106
  summer 106-114
  tangerines 227
  tomatoes 62-65
fruit blossoms 80
fruit-fly 17, 111
fungus 17

G
garden *see also cultivation; plants*
  equipment 244-245
  no-dig gardens 15
  pests *see pests and diseases; pest control*
  planning 7
  seasonal 8
  small spaces 7, 8
garden peas
  companion planting 16
  cultivation 7, 11, 22, 24
  pests and diseases 24
  preparation 24
  preservation 23
  varieties 22-24
garlic chives 52
garlic pest spray 17
geranium flowers 80
globe artichokes
  cultivation 7, 126
  pickling 127
  preparation 126
  preservation 127
gooseberries 108, 109 *see also berries*
grapefruit 228 *see also citrus fruit*
grapes
  bottling 157
  cultivation 7, 156
  pests and diseases 156
  pickling 157
  preservation 157
  varieties 156
green onions 34, 36
grevillea flowers 80

H
herb flowers 80
herbs
  autumn 172-175

basil 118, 119, 120
bay 234
blends 55, 236
chervil 54, 55
chilli 173, 174-175
chives 52, 55
coriander 54, 55
fertilisers 13
lemon grass 172, 173
marjoram 234
mint 118, 119, 120
parsley 52, 53, 55
pots, grown in 11
rosemary 172, 173
sage 234
spring 52-57
summer 118-120
tarragon 54, 55
thyme 234
vietnamese mint 54
winter 234-236
home-made pest sprays 17
honeydew melon 170 *see also melons*
honeysuckle 80
horseradish 16

J
jam melons 170 *see also melons*
jars, preparation of 242 *see also preserving*

K
kale *see cabbage; brassicas*
kiwifruit
  cultivation 169
  pickling 168
  pollination 169
  preservation 168
  varieties 169
kumatoes 62

L
laksa herb 118
lavender 80
lemon grass
  cultivation 7, 172
  drying 173
  preparation 172-174
  preservation 173
lemons 227 *see also citrus fruit*
  preserved 229
lettuce 7, 76, 78-79 *see also salad greens*
limes 227 *see also citrus fruit*

M
mandarins 227 *see also citrus fruit*
manure 13
marigolds 17, 80
marjoram
  cultivation 234
  drying 235

preservation 235
melons
  cultivation 170
  pickling 171
  preservation 171
  varieties 170
mildew 17
milk pest spray 17
mint
  cultivation 118
  drying 119
  preservation 119
  varieties 118
  vietnamese 54, 118
mizuna 76, 79, 202
mushrooms
  cultivation 210
  drying 211
  pickling 211
  preparation 213
  preservation 211
  toxic, consumption warning 210
  varieties 210

N
nasturtiums 7, 16, 80
nectarines 11, 111-112
no-dig gardens 15

O
olives
  cultivation 11, 150
  pickling 151
  salted 151
  preservation 151
  varieties 150
onions
  cultivation 34, 36
  pickling 35
  preparation 37
  preservation 35
  varieties 34
oranges 226-227 *see also citrus fruit*
organic fertilisers 13, 108-109

P
pansies 80
parsley
  cultivation 52
  drying 53
  preservation 53
  varieties 52
passionfruit
  cultivation 7, 109
  pests and diseases 110
  preservation 110
  varieties 109
peas *see garden peas*
pelargonium flowers 80

peaches
  cultivation 11, 111-112
  preparation 114
  preservation 112
  varieties 111
pears
  cultivation 162-164
  drying 163
  pickling 163
  preservation 163
  varieties 164
peppers *see capsicum*
pest control 16-17
  bicarbonate of soda spray 17
  chemical baits 16
  chemical sprays 16
  chilli spray 17
  garlic spray 17
  milk spray 17
  pyrethrum spray 16, 249
pest and diseases
  aphids 17, 248
  asian greens, in 184, 202
  bay trees, in 234
  beans, in 70
  beetles 17
  brassicas, in 184
  broccoli, in 184
  brussels sprouts, in 184
  cabbage, in 184
  capsicums, in 84
  caterpillars 16
  cauliflower, in 184
  citrus trees, in 226
  crop rotation, prevention through 15
  cucumbers, in 74
  fruit-fly 17, 111
  fungus 17
  garden peas, in 24
  grubs 17
  kale, in 184
  marigolds for 17
  mildew 17
  passionfruit, in 110
pest sprays *see pest control*
  rust 17
  scales 17
  snails and slugs 16
  squash, in 96
  stink bugs 17
  stone fruit, in 111
  sweet corn, in 102
  thrips 17, 249
  tomatoes, in 64
  weevils 236
  white fly 17
  zucchini, in 96

picking guide *see planting guide*
pickling
  apples 160
  berries 107
  cabbage 197
  carrots 145
  citrus fruit 225
  cucumbers 73
  eggplant 89
  figs 158
  globe artichokes 127
  grapes 157
  kiwifruit 168
  lemons 229
  mushrooms 211
  olives 151
  onions 35
  pears 163
  preserved lemon 229
  pumpkin 139
  quinces 165
  rhubarb 99
  sweet corn 103
  watermelon 171
planting guide
  autumn 124-125
  spring 20-21
  summer 60-61
  winter 182-183
plants *see also cultivation; garden*
  choosing 11
  identification 244
  pests see pests and diseases;
    pest control
  potted 11, 14, 15
plums 112
pollination
  avocado, of 132
  kiwifruit, of 169
potatoes
  companion planting 16
  cultivation 28
  preparation 29
  preservation 27
  varieties 26, 28-29
  potted plants 11, 14
  pot selection 11, 244
  re-potting 15
  watering 15
preserving *see also pickling*
  bottling 240-242
  drying 243
  freezing 240
  jars, preparation of 242
pyrethrum pest spray 16
pumpkin
  companion planting 16

cultivation 138
flowers 80
pickling 139
preparation 141
preservation 139
varieties 138

Q
quinces
  cultivation 165
  pickling 165
  preparation 165
  preservation 165
  varieties 165

R
radicchio 76, 79
raspberries 106 *see also berries*
rhubarb
  cultivation 98
  pickling 99
  preparation 98
  preservation 99
rocket 76, 79
rockmelon 170 *see also melons*
rosemary
  companion planting 16
  cultivation 172
  drying 173
  preservation 173
  varieties 172
roses 80
rust 17

S
sage
  companion planting 16
  cultivation 7, 234
  drying 235
  preservation 235
salad greens *see also edible flowers;*
  lettuce
  cultivation 78-79
  preservation 77
  varieties 76-78
seaweed emulsion 13
seeds
  raising 11
  saving 244
  shallots 34, 36
silver beet *see also spinach*
  cultivation 7, 218
  preparation 220
  preservation 219
  varieties 218
small spaces 7, 8
snow peas 22 *see also garden peas*
soil
  fungus 17

gauges 244
types 14
spring
  herbs 52-57
  planting and picking guide 20-21
spinach *see also silver beet*
  cultivation 218-220
  preparation 220
  preservation 219
  varieties 220
sprays *see pest control*
squash
  cultivation 94
  pests and diseases 96
  preparation 96
  preservation 95
  varieties 94
stone fruit 110-111
strawberries 106, 108 *see also berries*
sugar snap peas 22 *see also garden peas*
summer
  fruit 106-117
  herbs 118-120
  planting and picking guide 60-61
sweet corn
  companion planting 16
  cultivation 102
  pests and diseases 102
  pickling 103
  preparation 104
  preservation 103
swiss chard *see silver beet*

T
tangerines 227 *see also citrus fruit*
tarragon
  cultivation 54
  drying 53
  preservation 53
thyme
  cultivation 234
  drying 235
  preservation 235
tomatoes
  cultivation 7, 62-64
  drying 62, 63, 65
  pests and diseases 64
  preparation 65
  preservation 63
  varieties 62
toxic mushrooms 210 *see also mushrooms*
trees grown in pots 11

V
vegetable flowers 80
vietnamese mint 54
viola flowers 7, 80
violet flowers 80

W

watercress 78

watermelon 170 *see also melons*

wild garlic 52

wild mushrooms 210 *see also mushrooms*

winter

    fruit 224-229

    herbs 234-236

    planting and picking guide 182-183

witlof 76

wombok *see asian greens; brassicas*

worm farms 13

Z

zucchini

    cultivation 94

    flowers 80

    pests and diseases 96

    pickling 95

    preparation 96

    preservation 95

    varieties 94

RECIPE INDEX

A

almond cherry tarts, sweet 117

apples (serving ideas) 162

apricots (serving ideas) 114

artichokes

    anchovy and chilli pizza 129

    with lemon herb butter 130

    with lemon pepper hollandaise 130

asian greens (serving ideas) 204

asian vegetables, grilled 204

asparagus

    serving ideas 42

    and brie bruschetta 43

    with poached egg and hollandaise 43

avocado

    serving ideas 134

    guacamole 135

B

basil

    (serving ideas) 120

    pesto 120

bay leaves (serving ideas) 234

beans

    broad bean and ricotta pasta 46

    broad beans (serving ideas) 44

    bundles, prosciutto-wrapped 71

    serving ideas 70

beef, roast, and coleslaw on rye 200

beetroot

    and spinach tart 220

    pickled 50

berries (serving ideas) 109

blood oranges (serving ideas) 228

bouquet garni 234

broccoli

    crêpes with creamy 188

    serving ideas 186

bruschetta

    asparagus and brie 43

    tomato 66

brussels sprouts

    serving ideas 199

    with cream and almonds 199

buk choy

    serving ideas 204

    steamed with chilli oil 207

C

cabbage

    coleslaw, mixed 200

    serving ideas 199

cake(s)

    carrot, with cream cheese frosting 147

    lemon sour cream 230

caprese salad with figs 159

capsicum

    roasted, and goat's cheese terrine 86

    serving ideas 86

carrot

    and dhal soup 148

    cakes with cream cheese frosting 147

    orange and maple glazed baby,

      with hazelnuts 148

    serving ideas 147

cauliflower

    cauliflower gratin 194

    cauliflower, lentil and pea curry 193

    serving ideas 190

cherries

    and almond tarts, sweet 117

    serving ideas 114

chervil (serving ideas) 55

chicken

    and cucumber salad 74

    and sweet corn soup 105

    char-grilled, with broad beans and

      chive butter 46

chickpeas and pumpkin, spiced 142

chilli

    coriander jam 178

    serving ideas 175

chives (serving ideas) 55

choy sum

    serving ideas 204

    stir-fried 208

citrus fruit (serving ideas) 228

coleslaw, mixed cabbage 200

coriander

    crisps 56

    serving ideas 55

corn

    chicken and sweet corn soup 105

    fritters 105

crêpes with creamy broccoli 188

cucumber

    serving ideas 74

    yogurt and mint soup, chilled 75

cumquats (serving ideas) 229

curry, cauliflower, lentil and pea 193

D

dhal and carrot soup 148

dip, herb 56

E

edible flowers (serving ideas) 81

eggplant

    grilled, with marjoram vinaigrette 237

    moussaka timbales 92

    parmigiana 91

    serving ideas 91

    spread 92

everlasting orange slices 230

F

fennel and ruby red grapefruit salad 232

fettuccine boscaiola, mixed mushroom 217

fig(s)

    and quince paste 166

    serving ideas 158

    with mascarpone 159

fish and mushroom skewers,

    kecap manis 214

fish, caramel, and baby buk choy 208

flower salad 82

G

gai choy (serving ideas) 204

gai lan

    in oyster sauce, steamed 207

    serving ideas 204

    steamed, in oyster sauce 207

globe artichokes (serving ideas) 129

grapefruit

    ruby red, and fennel salad 232

    serving ideas 228

grapes (serving ideas) 156-158

green salad with fennel and herbs 82

guacamole 135

H

herb blends 55, 236

herb dip 56

herbes de provence 236

hollandaise 43

honeydew melon (serving ideas) 170

J

jam, chilli coriander 178

juice, peach, papaya and raspberry 115

K

kiwifruit
    lychee and lime salad 169
    serving ideas 169

L

lamb skewers, rosemary 177
lemon grass (serving ideas) 174
lemons (serving ideas) 229
lemon sour cream cake 230
lettuce (serving ideas) 81
lychee, kiwifruit and lime salad 169

M

mandarins (serving ideas) 229
marjoram (serving ideas) 236
melons (serving ideas) 170
mint (serving ideas) 120
mizuna (serving ideas) 81
moussaka timbales 92
mushroom(s)
    chilli pickled 213
    fettuccine boscaiola, mixed 217
    marinated mixed 214
    serving ideas 213
    skewers, kecap manis fish and 214
mussels with tomato and chilli 177

N

nachos 136
nectarines
    grilled, with passionfruit yogurt 117
    serving ideas 114

O

olives
    marinated 154
    pickled 154
    serving ideas 153
onion
    serving ideas 37
    tart 38
orange
    and maple glazed baby carrots
      with hazelnuts 148
    serving ideas 228
    slices, everlasting 230

P

pancakes, sour cream and chive potato 33
parmigiana, eggplant 91
parsley (serving ideas) 55
passionfruit (serving ideas) 110
pasta
    broad bean and ricotta 46
    mixed mushroom fettuccine boscaiola 217
    wholemeal vegetable spaghetti
      with garlic crumbs 188
peach
    papaya and raspberry juice 115
    serving ideas 114

pears (serving ideas) 164
peas
    serving ideas 24-25
    with mint butter 25
pesto
    basil 120
    spinach and walnut 86
piccalilli 194
pizza
    artichoke, anchovy and chilli 129
    tex-mex 135
plums (serving ideas) 114
pork with fresh sage, braised 238
potato(es)
    herbed baby 30
    pancakes, sour cream and chive 33
    portuguese 33
    roasted thyme, with spicy sauce 238
    serving ideas 29
    vichyssoise 30
preserved lemon (serving ideas) 229
pumpkin
    and chickpeas, spiced 142
    and sage ravioli 237
    flowers (serving ideas) 141
    soup with cinnamon cream, spiced 141
    roasted, and rosemary risotto 142
    serving ideas 141

Q

quince
    and fig paste 166
    and pistachio cake 166
    serving ideas 165

R

radicchio (serving ideas) 81
rhubarb
    apple and berry galette 100
    serving ideas 100
risotto, roasted pumpkin and rosemary 142
rockmelon (serving ideas) 170
rosemary (serving ideas) 172

S

sage (serving ideas) 236
salad(s)
    greens (serving ideas) 81
    salad niçoise 71
    caprese with figs 159
    chicken and cucumber 74
    fennel and ruby red grapefruit 232
    flower 82
    green, with fennel and herbs 82
    kiwifruit, lychee and lime 169
    soba with rocket and mandarin 232
    summer squash 97
shallots (serving ideas) 37

silver beet
    rainbow, with pine nuts, garlic
      and raisins 222
    serving ideas 220
soup
    chicken and sweet corn 105
    chilled yogurt, cucumber and mint 75
    dhal and carrot 148
    spiced pumpkin, with cinnamon cream 141
    spinach with fetta 222
    vichyssoise 30
spinach
    and beetroot tart 220
    and walnut pesto 86
    serving ideas 220
    soup with fetta 222
squash (serving ideas) 96
squash salad, summer 97
stone fruit (serving ideas) 114
strawberries
    balsamic, with mascarpone 115
    serving ideas 109
summer vegetables with herbed yogurt
    dressing, char-grilled 97
sweet corn (serving ideas) 104

T

tarragon (serving ideas) 55
tart(s)
    almond cherry, sweet 117
    onion 38
    spinach and beetroot 220
    tomato, pesto and olive 153
tatsoi (serving ideas) 204
terrine, roasted capsicum and
    goat's cheese 86
thyme (serving ideas) 236
tofu with vegetables and lemon grass,
    stir-fried 178
tomato
    bruschetta 66
    pesto and olive tart 153
    salsa 56
    sauce, simple 66

V

vegetables, char-grilled summer, with
    herbed yogurt dressing 97
vegetables, grilled asian 204
vichyssoise 30

W

watermelon (serving ideas) 170
witlof (serving ideas) 81
wombok (serving ideas) 204

Y

yogurt, cucumber and mint soup, chilled 75

Z

zucchini (serving ideas) 96

acp
books

Published in 2010 by
ACP Books, Sydney
ACP Books are published
by ACP Magazines,
a division of
PBL Media Pty Limited

PUBLISHED BY **ACP BOOKS, A DIVISION OF ACP MAGAZINES LTD.**
54 PARK ST, SYDNEY NSW AUSTRALIA 2000
GPO BOX 4088, SYDNEY, NSW 2001
PHONE +61 2 9282 8618 FAX +61 2 9267 9438
ACPBOOKS@ACPMAGAZINES.COM.AU WWW.ACPBOOKS.COM.AU
ADDITIONAL PHOTOGRAPHY **STUART SCOTT**
ADDITIONAL STYLING **GERLADINE MUNOZ**
ADDITIONAL FOOD PREPARATION **ANDREW de SOUSA**

Printed in China
through Phoenix Offset.

acp books

General manager **Christine Whiston**
Associate publisher **Seymour Cohen**
Editor-in-chief **Susan Tomnay**
Creative director **Hieu Chi Nguyen**
Art director & designer **Hannah Blackmore**
Senior editor **Wendy Bryant**
Junior editor **Abby Pfahl**
Food director **Pamela Clark**
Gardening writer **Caroline Gunter**
Additional text **Geoffrey Burnie**
Sales & rights director **Brian Cearnes**
Marketing manager **Bridget Cody**
Senior business analyst **Rebecca Varela**
Operations manager **David Scotto**
Production manager **Victoria Jefferys**

Australia Distributed by Network Services
Phone +61 2 9282 8777 Fax +61 2 9264 3278
networkweb@networkservicescompany.com.au

New Zealand Distributed by
Southern Publishers Group,
Phone +64 9 360 0692 Fax +64 9 360 0695
hub@spg.co.nz

South Africa Distributed by PSD Promotions,
Phone +27 11 392 6065/6/7 Fax +27 11 392 6079/80
orders@psdprom.co.za

THE EDIBLE GARDEN / FOOD DIRECTOR PAMELA CLARK.
ISBN: 978 1 74245 051 3 (PBK.)
NOTES: INCLUDES INDEX.
SUBJECTS: COOKERY. PLANTS, EDIBLE.
VEGETABLE GARDENING.
OTHER AUTHORS/CONTRIBUTORS: CLARK, PAMELA.
ALSO TITLED: AUSTRALIAN WOMEN'S WEEKLY.
DEWEY NUMBER: 641.5
COVER ILLUSTRATOR HANNAH BLACKMORE

To order books,
phone 136 116 (within Australia),
or order online at www.acpbooks.com.au
Send recipe enquiries to:
recipeenquiries@acpmagazines.com.au

The publishers would like to thank the following for
props used in photography: Newspaper Taxi, Ici et La,
Heaven In Earth, The Society Inc., Bunnings Warehouse,
Perfect Pieces, David Met Nicole, The Bronte Tram